Access 97 Further Skills

Sue Coles

Department of Business and Management Studies
Crewe and Alsager Faculty
Manchester Metropolitan University

Jenny Rowley

School of Management and Social Sciences
Edge Hill University College

CONTINUUM

London · New York

Acknowledgments

This book would not have been completed without the support that the authors received, during its production, from many of their colleagues and family. They are particularly grateful to husbands Martyn and Peter, children Helen, Shula, Lynsey and Zeta, who had to make do with even less of their time than usual.

Windows 95™ and Access™ © Microsoft Corporation, all rights reserved. Screen displays from Access 7 and Windows 95 reprinted with permission from Microsoft Corporation.

A CIP record for this book is available from the British Library.

ISBN 08264 5402 X

Continuum
The Tower Building, 11 York Road, London SE1 7NX
370 Lexington Avenue, New York, NY 10017-6550

Editorial and production services: Genesys Editorial Limited

Typeset by Kai, Nottingham

Printed in Great Britain by Ashford Colour Press, Gosport

Contents

About this book

About Access 97

Access is a powerful and exciting database management system for Windows 95. It provides standard data management features for data storage and retrieval but uses graphical tools made possible by the Windows environment to make these tasks easier to perform. Professional on-screen forms and report printouts are easily designed using a range of colours and fonts, and further sophistication can be added using macros to perform tasks such as non-standard data validation.

Access is produced by Microsoft and is one of a suite of Office 97 applications and as such can interface with the other applications, such as Word and Excel. Access will also import data in a variety of formats so existing databases may easily be upgraded.

Aims

Although this book is aimed at students on a wide variety of business studies and other courses, it is suitable for anyone who needs to learn about databases and their application through the use of Microsoft Access, one of the industry standard database packages. The book assumes no prior experience of other database packages.

Although the theme of this book is oriented towards business studies' students, it will be equally applicable to students on a variety of further and higher education courses as well as to the independent learner.

Structure

This book introduces the reader to the basics of databases and database design through a series of application oriented tasks. The basics are then developed further through basing the tasks on the operations of one organisation, Chelmer Leisure and Recreation Centre. A series of self contained but interrelated units takes the reader through the design of a database for Chelmer Leisure and Recreation Centre. Each unit comprises a series of tasks. As each new function is introduced, the book explains both why the function is useful and how to use it.

The approach does not assume any previous knowledge of databases or the Windows 95 environment. However, readers who are familiar with the Windows 95 environment and, in particular other Microsoft Office products such as Word, Excel, PowerPoint and previous versions of Access, will find their road into Access 97 to be much more intuitive than those who are not familiar with these related products. Equally, readers who have some familiarity with other database products may find the database concepts introduced in this book easier to grasp.

The approach is designed not only to introduce readers to Access but also to offer them a conceptual framework for the use and design of databases that will encourage the development of skills transferable to other applications.

The units will give readers the confidence to perform and understand the central tasks concerned with database design, creation and maintenance:

■ designing and defining a database

■ designing and using queries

■ designing and using screen forms

■ designing and using printed reports

■ using multiple tables

■ importing and exporting data

■ creating and using macros.

Getting started

Readers who have not used a Windows program before should first read through Quick Reference 1 **Basic Windows operations**, which summarises the key features of the Windows environment, and then turn to Unit 1 **An overview of Access.** Readers who are familiar with the Windows environment can move straight to **An overview of Access**.

Each unit commences with a summary of the objectives to be achieved and the skills to be gained and is divided into a number of activities. Each activity includes instructions on how to perform operations, and tasks that ask you to perform those operations. Series of related units conclude with integrative exercises that offer you the opportunity to practise your newly acquired skills further. These exercises have minimal instructions.

This book may be used as a basis for independent study or for class activities. In either instance it is important to:

■ work methodically through the exercises in the order in which they are presented; data entered in earlier exercises may be re-used in later exercises

■ take time for rest and reflection and break learning into manageable sessions

■ think about what you are doing

■ expect to make mistakes; think about the consequences of any mistakes and learn from them

■ use the integrative exercises at the end of unit series as a means of testing whether you have understood the earlier concepts and exercises.

Conventions

The following conventions have been adopted to distinguish between the various objects on the screen:

■ buttons and tabs are shown in bold in a tint box e.g. **Design**

■ dialog box names and menu items are shown in a tint e.g. **New Report**

- keys on the keyboard are shown in underlined italics e.g. *Ctrl*

- filenames,names of databases, fields, tables, forms, queries, reports and other items created by the user are shown in bold e.g. **Membership**

- typed text is shown in bold italics e.g. ***Aerobics***.

(d.) indicates text that gives a definition of a term. Note that all definitions are also included in the Glossary.

indicates a tip providing a helpful hint or short-cut method.

(!) indicates a cautionary note.

indicates a cross reference.

A note to lecturers and students

The learning material requires little, if any, input by lecturers, and can therefore be used in programmes based on independent learning. Students and independent learners learn by practising the commands and techniques.

The text is selective and does not deal with all of the features in detail. However, it does take students step-by-step to a level at which they can happily use the help provided by the Office Assistant to master further features.

Lecturers' disk

A $3\frac{1}{2}''$ disk is available (free of charge to lecturers recommending the book as a course text) containing files of data for completing the exercises, plus the reports and queries produced via the tasks in the text. It can be used as a shortcut to avoid lengthy keying in of data and as a means of checking the outcomes of the tasks. The disk, or selected files from it, can be made available to students to allow them to check their own work.

An overview of Access

All students, except those who have some experience of Access, should read this module. Quick reference 1 reviews the basic features of Windows for the benefit of inexperienced users or as a ready reference. It also introduces mouse techniques and acts as a summary of the terminology used throughout these units.

A tour of the Access window and the database window

It is worthwhile studying the two basic windows in Access – the Access window and the database window – for a few moments before trying to make use of the program. This section can be used as a ready reference and returned to later as necessary.

The Access window

When you first start Access, the Access window shown in FIGURE 1.1 is displayed.

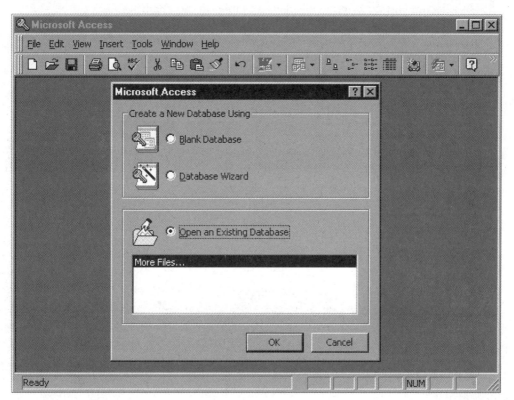

FIGURE 1.1

This window is used to open a database or to perform other tasks that are not possible once a database is open. The window has the following components:

Component	Description
Title bar	Shows that you are in Microsoft Access
Access control menu (in the very top left hand corner)	If you click on this box a menu with commands for sizing and moving the **Access** window, switching to other applications and closing Access is displayed
Access main menu	Shows the pull down menus
Toolbar	Shows the standard set of buttons
Status bar (at the bottom of the screen)	Shows the status of the system, and whether switches such as NUM for Number Lock are on or off

The database window

Once you have opened a database, a window like the one in FIGURE 1.2 is displayed. This window allows you to access any object (table, query, form, report, etc) in the database by clicking on one of the object 'tabs'. Initially the **Tables** tab is selected and the window displays all tables in the database.

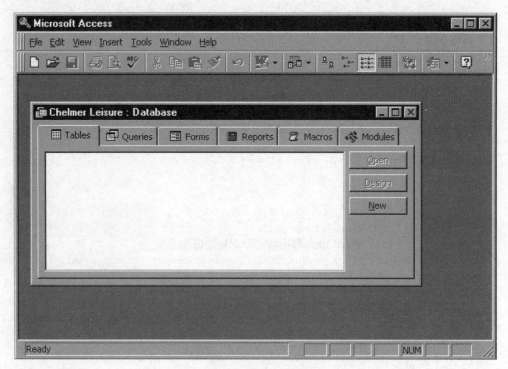

FIGURE 1.2

When the Database window is open, the Access window has the following components:

- **title bar**

- **Access control menu**

- **database window main menu**, which shows the pull-down menus, File, Edit, View, Insert, Tools, Window and Help

- **toolbar**, which shows the buttons for creating new objects. The buttons vary depending on the object that you are working on. For example, when working on a table there are toolbar options for choosing datasheet or design view. When designing a macro, there are buttons for single step mode, displaying conditions and macro names. All toolbar choices have equivalent menu selections.

- **status bar**: messages are displayed on the left of the status bar, for example, Ready.

Help and the Office Assistant

When you start using Access for the first time the Office Assistant will appear to guide you. This is an animated graphic that appears in a window of its own, and if your PC has a sound card, it also alerts your attention using various sounds.

Clicking on the Office Assistant button in the toolbar controls whether or not the Office Assistant is displayed. When you have a question about how to do something you can ask the Office Assistant, for example, 'How do I create a query?' To do this click on the Assistant window and key your question into the **What would you like to do** box and click on the Search button.

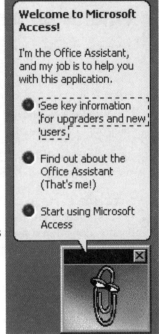

Welcome to Microsoft Access!

I'm the Office Assistant, and my job is to help you with this application.

- See key information for upgraders and new users

- Find out about the Office Assistant (That's me!)

- Start using Microsoft Access

The Assistant can, if you wish, provide help with tasks as you perform them without the need to ask questions.

You can choose an Assistant to match your personality, and as the Assistant is shared by the suite of Office programs, it will be a familiar guide when you are working with other applications. To select a different Assistant, click on the Assistant and choose one, but be prepared to install it from your Office 97 CD-ROM.

Help is also available through looking up an index of terms or by using the 'What's this' pointer. There are four main methods of getting into the help system.

- Pull down the **Help** menu and select **Microsoft Access Help**, press the function key *F1* or click on the **Office Assistant** button. The **Office Assistant** dialog box will pop-up with a choice of topics related to what you are currently doing as well as a request box into which you can type a question.

3

■ Pull down the **Help** menu and select **Contents and Index**. The **Help Topics** dialog box appears. In this box there are three tabs: **Contents** , **Index** , and **Find** . Under the Contents section you may select any of the topics to find information about that topic. Under the Index section you may type in a word that is matched by the index about which you can display information. The Find section enables you to search for specific words and phrases in help topics, instead of searching by category or index.

■ Pull down the **Help** menu and select **What's this** or press *Shift+F1*. The pointer changes to a pointer with a question mark after it and this can be used to point to anything. Clicking on that object will then bring up help. For instance, in this way you may get help on the meaning of all of the items in the status bar. To remove the question mark press *Esc*.

■ Most dialog boxes have a help button with a ? (question mark) on it, on the title bar. Click on this and then click on the part of the dialog box, about which you want more information.

What is an Access database?

Access is a database management system and provides a means of storing and managing data or information. Microsoft refers to Access as a relational database product since it allows you to relate data from several different sets or tables. The purist would recognise that Access does not meet all of the criteria of a true relational database, but it is a sufficiently close approximation to be considered as a relational database product for the purposes of this book.

An Access database comprises all of the tables of data and all associated objects, such as screen forms and report forms, macros and program modules and queries.

Note: The use of the term database in connection with Access is broader than that encountered in earlier database products, such as dBase IV, where only the data itself is considered to be part of the database. For example, you may have an employee database, a client database and a supplier database. Each database is a separate file and there will be additional files for reports and screen forms.

Tables

Access stores data in tables that are organised by rows and columns. The basic requirement of having a database is that you have at least one table.

Columns represent fields of information, or one particular piece of information that can be stored for each entity in the table.

Rows contain records. A record contains one of each field in the database.

Generally a table represents each major set of information in a database. There might, for instance, be a Supplier table, a Client table and an Employee table.

We will return later to the issue of how data might be organised in tables, and how relationships can be defined between tables so that they can be used together, so that, for instance, data from more than one table can be shown in a report.

Queries

Queries are used to select records from a database. Access has three different types: select, action and parameter.

(d.) Select queries are the standard type of query. They are questions that you may wish to ask about entries in fields. They choose records from a table and store them in a table called a dynaset. Queries are specified by completing entries in the Query-by-Example (QBE) window. It is possible to specify complex combinations of criteria in order to select a specific set of records.

(d.) Action queries update values in a database table. They can be used to change an entire group of records, as in, for example, the removal of all records for former employees.

(d.) Parameter queries allow you to change the criteria for a query each time you use it. Access prompts for criteria entries with the QBE grid. They are a useful way of creating an environment for end users where users complete dialog boxes instead of a QBE (Query by Example) grid (see Unit 10).

Reports

(d.) Reports are used to print information from a number of records. They can show the data from either a table or a query. In addition to records, they may show summary information relating to the records displayed. Graphs created using Microsoft Graph may be added to reports.

Screen forms

Screen forms can be used to customise the way in which records from tables or queries are presented on screen. They help provide a user-friendly interface for adding new records or editing existing ones. Subforms allow you to display related records from another table at the same time.

Controls are placed on a form to display fields or text. Text on the form acts as labels to controls and headings. Changing the font or adding bold or italic emphasis can change the appearance of text on a form. Text can also be shown as raised or sunken or displayed in a specific colour, and lines and rectangles can be added to give the form a pleasing appearance. Controls, attached labels, form sections and the form itself all have properties that can be changed.

Macros

(d.) Macros are a series of steps or keystrokes that you record; you use macros by pressing just one or two keys. Examples of potential uses of macros are:

■ to add a button to a form so that it will open a second form

■ to create custom menus and pop-up forms for data collection.

Modules

 Modules are programs or sets of instructions designed to perform a specific task or series of tasks. Modules are written in Visual Basic code, the programming language provided with Office 97.

Task 1: Questions

Answer the following questions.

1 What is the difference between a report and a screen form?

2 What types of queries may be used in Access?

3 What is a table? What is the relationship between a table and a database?

4 Give an example of when you might use a macro.

Defining a new database, creating tables

What you will learn in this unit

This unit focuses on the creation of an Access database file. This file is used to store all the components of an Access database, which you will be creating as you work through these units.

By the end of this unit you will:

■ appreciate the reasons for analysing data before creating a database

■ be able to define a new database

■ be able to retrieve this database

■ understand that data is kept in tables and there is usually more than one table in a database

■ understand that the tables in a database can be related or linked together.

Before a database can be created careful thought needs to be given to deciding on the data that should be held and in planning the way in which the data is to be organised. This is known as data analysis and you will be introduced to the basic concepts in this unit.

Data analysis

A database is used for storing data that can be used by a system. A system is not easily defined, though they abound in society and nature. Your body has many systems, of which the nervous system and digestive system are examples. In society there are legal systems, political systems, educational systems, tax systems, etc. Organisations may have order systems, management-information systems, product-information systems, personnel-data systems, sales-marketing systems, etc. Libraries have cataloguing systems and information retrieval systems. In general terms, systems can be viewed as being concerned with taking inputs or resources, executing some form of regulated change and achieving results or outputs. Systems often need access to data to act upon their inputs; if this data information is easily accessible, i.e. via a well designed database, then the system will perform well.

Data or systems analysts are highly trained individuals who design information systems of which databases usually form a major part. They use their skills to determine how to organise the data in the tables in the system's databases. It is not the intention of this book to impart analysis skills but it will give you a practical insight into the building of a database.

We shall be considering the database needs of a small leisure centre. Data is recorded about various aspects, such as membership details, court and course bookings and financial information. The information about these different things, or entities, may be kept in tables in the database. If data from more than one table needs to be retrieved then the tables can be linked or related together, as will be explained in a later unit.

A table generally holds data about one 'thing' or entity. There are usually several or many instances of this particular 'thing', for example, the members of the leisure centre. A members' table would hold details about each member.

Records and fields

For each member there is a separate record in the table. Each record is composed of data about the member, such as, name, address and so on. Each piece of data within the record is known as a field. In this first set of units we will see how each field in a record needs to be defined before data can be entered into the record. Fields are given names to describe the kind of data they will eventually hold. It is important to distinguish between the name of a field and the data that that field contains. For example, the field named **Lastname** will hold people's last names such as Harris. The field names can be considered to be the column headings in the table and each row in the table is a separate record. Therefore each record in the table will have fields with the same name but containing different data. We shall also see that fields need their size and the type of data that they will contain to be defined so that Access can store the data in the table correctly.

Defining a new database

A new database is used to store all the tables, queries, forms and reports that belong to the system. To begin with a database will hold the tables of data needed for the system. An Access file differs from traditional PC databases in that it can contain all of the tables, forms, reports, queries, macros etc that belong to a database. The one you have just created awaits the inclusion of these as you learn to create them.

Task 1: Defining the Chelmer Leisure database

1   Start Access by clicking on the **Start** button in the Task bar, selecting **Programs** and selecting **Microsoft Access**. If you have a shortcut icon on your desktop for Access then you may double-click on it to start the program.

2   Choose the Create a New Database Using blank database option and click on the **OK** button. If Access is already running then choose **File-New Database** and double-click on the **Blank Database** icon.

3   In the **Save in** dialog box select the drive and directory in which you wish to store your database.

If you do not change directory then your database is likely to be stored in the **My Documents** folder provided by Windows 95.

4   In the **File name** box give the data-base the filename **Chelmer Leisure**.

Access will give it the extension of .mdb. (You will not see this extension on screen)

5   Click on the **Create** button.

Access, as it is running in the Windows 95 environment, allows you to use long descriptive filenames. The complete path to the file including drive letter, folder path name and filename can contain up to 255 characters. Any characters may be used except the following: * ? ; \ / : " | < >. You cannot use a period (full stop) except to separate the filename from the extension. Note that Access stores all tables, forms, queries, reports, etc in this one file.

Closing and opening a database

When you have finished working with the database you can close the database using **File-Close**. If you have made changes that you have not saved then Access will prompt you to save them.

To open an existing database use **File-Open Database** or click on the **Open Database** icon on the toolbar. Select the drive and directory in which your database is stored and select the file name and click on the **Open** button.

When you have finished working with Access you can close the application using **File-Exit**. Next time you start Access you will see your database listed in the **Open an existing database** section of the **Microsoft Access** dialog box. Simply click on it to open the database.

Task 2: Closing and opening the Chelmer database

1   To close the database choose **File-Close**.

2   To open the database choose **File-Open Database**

In the **Look in** dialog box select the drive and directory in which your database is stored.

3   Select the file **Chelmer Leisure** from the list below the **Look in** box.

4   Click on the **Open** button.

5   To close Access choose **File-Exit**

6   To open Access and choose an existing database, start Access by clicking on its icon or using **Start-Programs-Microsoft Access**.

7   Select the file **Chelmer Leisure** from the list in the **Open an Existing Database** section and click on   **OK** .

Understanding relationships between tables

Having created the database, the next step is to create the tables that go into it. How do you decide what constitutes a table and the sort of data it should contain? First consider the nature of the Chelmer Leisure and Recreation Centre.

A leisure centre basically needs a building, staff and people that use it. Often it is cheaper to become a member of a leisure centre and some only allow you to use the facilities if you become a member. When someone joins the centre details about that person are obtained. Details about the staff that work at the centre will be needed so that they can be paid correctly. Details about the bookings of various rooms, halls and courts in the centre will be required so that the building is used efficiently. If the centre has a bar or café then details about food and drink kept in stock would need to be kept as well as, for example, sales records.

Let's look at the membership data in more detail. What sort of information will the centre be asking for on the membership form? Apart from name and address, date of birth is useful for targeting advertising to specific groups e.g. senior citizens. Also knowing something about the sporting interests of the member is useful. The information that Chelmer Leisure and Recreation Centre requires about each new member is shown in the table below.

Last Name	Occupation
First Name	Date of Birth
Title	Date of Joining
Street	Date of Last Renewal
Town	Sporting Interests
County	Smoker
Post Code	Sex
Telephone No	

The names in the table are the names of each piece or field of information. Before issuing a membership card the centre will allocate a membership number, which is different from any other member's number, and will charge a membership fee. The centre offers different categories of membership for which different fees are charged. Therefore it is necessary to have two additional fields, membership number and membership category.

The centre will need to hold data about the current fees charged for each category of membership. This forms another table in our system, the membership category table.

Category No
Category Type
Membership Fee

To discover the fee that a member has paid by matching his or her membership category with category number in the membership category table, the information in the two tables can be linked. This is known as relating the tables and, by creating links between them, they appear to be one table.

One advantage of using more than one table is that less storage space is required. Consider the situation where there wasn't a membership category table and the information about category type and membership fee was stored in the table containing the member's information. Say there are 500 members: 500 membership category descriptions and 500 membership fee details will need to be stored. If, on the other hand, there are two tables, then there will be 500 category identification numbers, which need only be one digit. If there are six categories, then the membership category table needs only hold six category identification numbers, six descriptions and six fee details. Another advantage is that the fees can be amended and the new data is available throughout the database simultaneously so that when a new member joins or membership is renewed the correct fee details are used.

Two other tables that form part of the Chelmer Leisure and Recreation Centre system we will be building are concerned with bookings of the rooms, halls and courts, and the classes that are held. The centre will need to keep track of room bookings to prevent double booking and to schedule classes. Rooms can be booked either by members or by a class so there is a link between a member and a room booking and there is a link between a class and a room booking. The bookings and classes tables are shown below.

Booking No
Room/Hall/Court
Member/Class
Member No
Class No
Date
Time

Class No
Class Day
Class Time
Class Tutor
Class Activity
Male/Female/Mixed

FIGURE 2.1 shows the relational database used by our system for Chelmer Leisure and Recreation Centre. It shows how the four tables: **Membership**, **Categories of membership**, **Classes** and **Bookings** are linked. Each table is composed of records and the fields in each table are listed in the boxes.

The fields in bold italics are known as primary key fields. You will be introduced to these in the next unit.

Note: This is just one database structure that could be used for part of the system at Chelmer Leisure and Recreation Centre. The total system would be more complex and a number of alternative database structures are also possible. The best database structure for a given application depends upon the way in which the database is to be used.

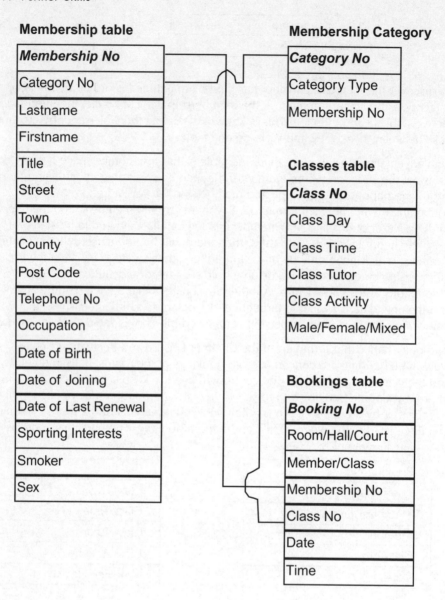

Membership table

Membership No
Category No
Lastname
Firstname
Title
Street
Town
County
Post Code
Telephone No
Occupation
Date of Birth
Date of Joining
Date of Last Renewal
Sporting Interests
Smoker
Sex

Membership Category

Category No
Category Type
Membership No

Classes table

Class No
Class Day
Class Time
Class Tutor
Class Activity
Male/Female/Mixed

Bookings table

Booking No
Room/Hall/Court
Member/Class
Membership No
Class No
Date
Time

FIGURE 2.1

Task 3: Creating and linking tables

The centre will need to have details of the class tutors that it employs. Design a tutors' table on paper by considering the fields that will comprise the records in this table. How could this table be linked in with the tables in FIGURE 2.1?

Choosing data types

The first stage in building the database is to define the tables, that is, to name them and define the names of the fields that will be contained in each table's records. The next stage is to define the type of data to be stored in each of the fields. No data has yet been entered but before it can be, Access needs to know what sort of data to expect. Take the member's last name. You need to tell Access the field name, i.e. **Lastname**, and whether the data is text, numeric, date/time, etc before you can actually start entering people's names!

Every field in your table will be of a particular data type, for example a name is alphanumeric text, a price would be currency and a date would have a date data type. The data type that you choose for your field determines the kind and range of values that can be entered into it and the amount of storage space available in the field. Select the appropriate data type for each field. For example, you will probably define most fields in a table of names and addresses as Text fields.

There are likely to be instances where a Text field should be used when the data is actually numbers. Fields such as telephone numbers or employee works numbers that contain only digits should be defined as Text fields. One reason is that there is no need to do calculations with such numbers. Also telephone area codes often start with a zero, and employee works numbers may also start with one or more zeros (known as leading zeros), which is not allowed in a true number. So, reserve the Number data type for fields on which you want to perform calculations.

The table below lists the data types available in Access and their uses.

Data type	Use for...
Text	Text and numbers. A Text field can contain up to 255 characters. Examples, names and addresses, class activity.
Memo	Lengthy text and numbers. A Memo field can contain up to 32,000 characters. For example, comments about a hotel in a travel company's database.
Number	Numerical data on which you intend to perform mathematical calculations, except calculations involving money. Set the FieldSize property to define the specific Number data type. Example, number of items in stock.
Date/Time	Dates and times. A variety of display formats are available, or you can create your own. Example, date of joining.
Currency	Money. Don't use the Number data type for currency values because numbers to the right of the decimal point may be rounded during calculations. The Currency data type maintains a fixed number of digits to the right of the decimal point. Example, membership fee.
AutoNumber	Sequential numbers automatically inserted by Microsoft Access. Numbering begins with one. Makes a good primary key field. The AutoNumber data type is compatible with the Number data type with the FieldSize property set to Long Integer. Example, membership number.
Yes/No	Yes/No, True/False, On/Off. Example, smoker/non-smoker.

13

Task 4: Choosing data types

Think about the following questions.

1   What would be the effect of rounding on currency (money) data?

2   What data type do you think you would choose for the following fields?
>   Category No
>   Lastname
>   Street
>   Telephone No
>   Date of Birth
>   Sporting Interests

3   Later we suggest that you use a Yes/No field for Sex. Explain this!

4   Why would you use a text field for a post code?

Defining a new table

What you will learn in this unit

This unit focuses on the creation of a database table. This requires the definition of the fields in the table. Each field requires a name to distinguish it from the other fields and the type of data which is to be stored in the field needs to be defined.

By the end of this unit you will be able to:

■ name the component parts of a table

■ create a table

■ define data types for fields.

Defining a new table

This activity takes the form of an exercise in which you will define the membership table. In the exercise you will set up the fields so that they correspond to the type of data that will be stored in those fields.

Task 1: Creating a new table

1 The database window should be active (indicated by a blue title bar if you are using the standard Windows colours).

2 The **Tables** tab should be selected as shown in the illustration. If it is not then click on it.

3 Click on the **New** button in the table window to display the New Table dialog box.

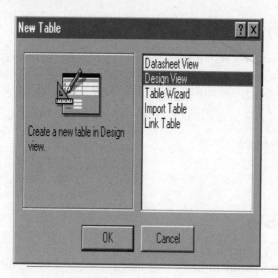

4 Select **Design View** and click on the **OK** button to display the Table window.

The Table window allows you to define the structure of your table. By filling in the Field Name, Data Type and Description cells and by setting Field Properties the structure of the table is defined. This is described in Task 2.

Task 2: Defining the fields in a table

In this task the fields for the membership table will be defined, the name, data type and description will be entered into the table design window. You should be able to complete this exercise by following the immediate instructions, but additional notes are also given in the activities described in the following few pages, which you may wish to consult. The membership table is defined as follows.

Field Name	Data Type	Description
Membership No	AutoNumber	Automatic membership numbering
Category No	Number	Categories are 1-Senior, 2-Senior Club, 3-Junior, 4-Junior Club, 5-Concessionary, 6-Youth Club
Lastname	Text	
Firstname	Text	
Title	Text	
Street	Text	
Town	Text	
County	Text	
Post Code	Text	
Telephone No	Text	
Occupation	Text	
Date of Birth	Date/Time	
Date of Joining	Date/Time	
Date of Last Renewal	Date/Time	
Sporting Interests	Memo	
Smoker	Yes/No	
Sex	Yes/No	

TABLE 3.1 Membership fields

1 Enter **Membership No** for the first field name.

Do not type a full stop after **No** as these are not allowed in field names. For more information on field names refer to the section on 'Naming Fields', below.

2 Press *Enter* to move to the Data Type
column and click on the drop down
list button which displays the
following list box.

▦ Table1 : Table	
Field Name	Data Type
▶ Membership No	Text ▼
	Text
	Memo
	Number
	Date/Time
	Currency
	AutoNumber
	Yes/No
	OLE Object
	Hyperlink
	Lookup Wizard...

3 Click on the data type AutoNumber. Press *Enter* and you will be in the description field. Key in the description as shown in the table above.

4 Press *Enter* to move to the next field   See below for details of moving around the table design window.

5 Continue to enter the definitions for   The table will be revisited later to set
the fields as detailed in the table.   individual field properties.
Where there is no description press
Enter to take you to the next field
name.

6 The next stage is to define the   Primary keys will be discussed in more
primary key. Click on the row   detail later.
selector (see below) for Membership
No and click on the **Primary Key**
button ▣ in the tool bar.

You will save this table definition in Task 4.

Moving around the table design window

Through the table design window you can enter the field name, the data type and a description of each field (the description is optional) into the grid in the upper part of the window. To move between cells you have a choice of pressing either *Enter,* *Tab* ➡ (right arrow key) or clicking in the required cell in the grid.

Row selector symbols

Along the left hand edge of the grid you will see the row selector symbols. By clicking in the row selector box you can select an entire row.

Row	Selector symbol
Current row	▶
Primary key field	🔑

Naming fields

Fields need names, lengths and data types to be defined. Many database products limit you to about 10 characters for a field name, which means that they often need to be abbreviated. Also the use of a space in a field name is not usually allowed. However, *Access allows field names to be up to 64 characters long with spaces.* Field names should be meaningful so that the data is easier to work with. Some characters are not allowed in field names: these are full stops (.), exclamation marks (!), and square brackets ([]) and you should note that you cannot start a field name with a space. You cannot give the same name to more than one field. Why not?

The length of a field (amount of storage space allocated to it) may be pre-determined according to the data type of that particular field. If the field is of a date type then it will have a standard length. Other data types such as text and number can have their lengths defined. If a text field is being used to hold the title of a song, for example, then you need to estimate the length of the longest song title and set the size of the field accordingly.

Adding a field description

You can add a description for any field in the description cell in the table's design view. The maximum length allowed is 255 characters. It is not necessary to enter a description but it can be useful to provide additional information about a particular field.

Correcting mistakes in field name or description

Point and click in the cell containing the mistake. Correct the mistake in a normal fashion by inserting or deleting text at the insertion point. Click back in the current cell to continue working.

Correcting mistakes in the data type

Click on the data type cell concerned. Open the list box and select the correct data type.

Creating a primary key

The primary key is a field or combination of fields that uniquely identifies each record in a table. As the main index for the table, it is used to associate data between tables. Though not required, a primary key is highly recommended. All the tables used in our system will have a primary key defined. It speeds data retrieval and enables you to define default relationships between tables. In FIGURE 2.1 in Unit 2 the primary field key is shown in bold italics. If the membership table is considered then the membership number is the primary key; each record has a different number as every member's number will be different.

 If the table does not include an obvious primary key field, you can have Microsoft Access set up a field that assigns a unique number to each record. This automatically numbers each record uniquely. See Unit 5 for more discussion of primary keys.

Task 3: Setting or changing the primary key

This is an optional task, which you may find useful to try on tables that you additionally create with Access.

To set or change the primary key

1   In the table's Design view, select the field or fields you want to define as the primary key.

To select one field, click the row selector. To select multiple fields, hold down the *Ctrl* key, and click the row selectors for each field.

---

2   Click on the **Primary Key** button ▯ on the tool bar, or choose **Edit - Primary Key**.

Microsoft Access places the primary key icon in the row selector column

---

To have Access define the primary key

1   With the table's Design view displayed, save the table without specifying a primary key.

Access asks if you want it to create a primary key field.

---

2   Choose Yes.

Access creates a field in your table called ID with the AutoNumber data type.

Saving the table definition

Once the structure of the table has been designed it needs to be saved. Access uses this information to set up templates through which you enter data into the table.

 The table is saved as part of the database file and its name distinguishes it from other tables in the database file. There may be more than one table in a database file and Access allows more freedom for naming tables. You will also find this true for naming queries, forms, reports and macros as all these are stored in one database file. Make use of this freedom to give meaningful names to tables as they will be used later in queries, forms and reports and it is important to be able to recognise the name of the table you require.

Task 4: Saving the table definition

Continuing from Task 2.

1   Choose **File-Save**.

2   In the **Save As** dialog box, type the   Note that the name that you choose may
    name ***Membership*** in the **Table Name**   be 255 characters long and contain any
    box and click on **OK**.   alphanumeric text.

3   Close the table using **File-Close** (shortcut key *Ctrl-w*).

Closing and opening the table

To close a table, either:

1   double-click on the table's control menu button, or

2   choose **File-Close**.

You can open an existing table in either Design view or Datasheet view. So far we
have only considered the Design view of a table.

To open a table in Design view:

1   in the Database window, click on the **Table** 'tab'

2   select the table you want to open, and then click on the **Design** button.

Defining field properties

What you will learn in this unit

Once a database table has been created, the fields named and the type of data which is to be stored in the field chosen, further refinements to fields may be made by setting field properties.

By the end of this unit you will be able to

■ define field properties.

Defining field properties

You may have noticed that once you start to enter the field definitions, field name, data type and description, then the Field Properties are displayed in the lower left hand section of the design window (FIGURE 4.1). You have defined the basic data type for each field and by setting the field properties you can specify the data type in more detail, for example, if the data type is text you can define the length of the field.

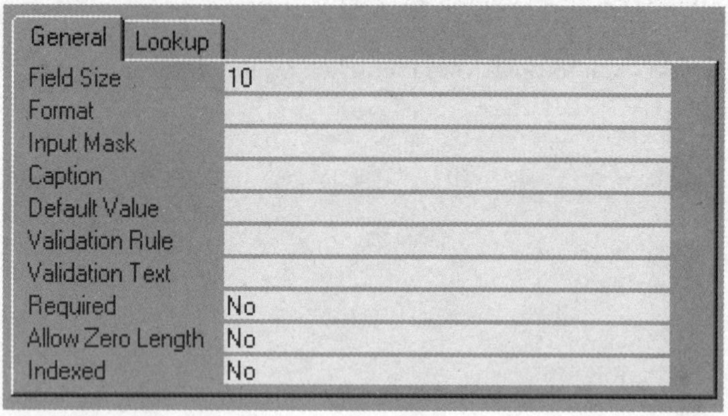

FIGURE 4.1

In the Field Properties section, you can set properties for individual fields. The available options depend on the data type you define for the field. In the lower right hand section of the window a description of the current column or field property is displayed.

Each field has a set of properties you use to specify how you want data stored, handled, and displayed. You set the properties in the bottom part of the table window's design view. The properties you can set for each field are determined by the data type you select for the field.

Setting a field property

To set a field's properties first select the field. Properties for the selected field are displayed in the bottom part of the window. Click on the property you wish to define and set the property, as explained in the following sections.

The table below lists all the field properties (remember those you actually see will depend on the field data type), and the following sections describe some of these in more detail.

Property	Description
Field Size	Maximum length of the text field or type of number
Format	How data is displayed; use predefined formats or customise your own
Input Mask	Data entry pattern
Caption	Default field label in a form or report
Default Value	Value entered in a field when records are created
Validation Rule	Expression that defines data entry rules
Validation Text	Text for invalid data
Required	Whether or not an entry must be made
Allow Zero Length	Allows you to store a zero length string ("") to indicate data that exists but is unknown
Indexed	Single-field indexes to speed searches

Field size

This property sets the maximum size of data that can be stored in a field. If the Data Type property is set to Text, enter a number less than 255. This number should be chosen by considering the length of the longest text data that is to be entered into the field. The default setting is 50.

If the Data Type property is set to Number, the Field Size property settings and their values are related in the following way.

Setting	Description
Byte	Stores whole numbers with values between 0 to 255. Occupies 1 byte.
Integer	Stores whole numbers with values between -32,768 and 32,767. Occupies 2 bytes.
Long Integer	Stores numbers from -2,147,483,648 to 2,147,483,647 (no fractions). Occupies 4 bytes.
Single	Stores numbers with six digits of precision, from -3.402823E38 to 3.402823E38. Occupies 4 bytes.

| Double | Stores numbers with ten digits of precision, from -1.79769313486232E308 to 1.79769313486232E308. Occupies 8 bytes. |

Defaults

Access will assign a default value to each of the fields in your table, which is automatically entered when a new record is created. These are values that are usually appropriate for the addition of new records to a table. The default value for Number, Currency and Yes/No fields is zero; in the case of Yes/No fields zero means No. Text, Memo and Date fields are empty by default. You can save time by specifying your own default values for fields.

You can specify a default using text or an expression. For example, in an address table you might set the default for the Town field to London, if the majority of records are London addresses. When users add records to the table, they can either accept this value or enter the name of a different town or city. If, for example, an Orders table contains the field **Order Date** then the expression *=Date()* can be used to put the current date into this field.

Validation

The data entered into tables must be accurate if the database is to be valuable to the person or organisation that it serves. However, even the most experienced data entry operators can make mistakes. To try to detect mistakes you can test the data entered by creating validation rules. These are simple tests, which are entered as short expressions into the Validation Rule text box.

If the data entered does not conform to your validation rule, a message box will be displayed to inform the operator that the data is incorrect. The message in the message box is defined by the text that you put in the Validation Text text box. The maximum length for both the Validation Rule and the Validation Text boxes is 255 characters. If data in a record is amended then the validation will still be performed. If a validation rule for a field hasn't been entered then no validation will be performed on that field.

Examples of expressions that can be used often relate to numeric fields, e.g. a credit limit that cannot be greater than a certain value. Fields with other data types may also be validated, for example a date may only be entered in a certain time period, or a department code can be checked.

Required entry

By setting the required property of a field to Yes, you will need to make an entry in that particular field for every record. Where it is not necessary to have an entry then this property can be left as its default value. In the **Membership** the **Category No** field has been defined as required, a member cannot be enrolled without being given a category of membership. As you create the **Membership** table in the following exercise, consider which fields in this table are required entry and set this property.

Task 1: Defining field properties

So far we have not changed any of the field properties. In this exercise the field properties of the **Membership** table will be defined. You should be able to complete this exercise by following the immediate instructions, but additional notes are also given in the activities described in the following few pages, which you may wish to consult. First open the **Membership** table in design view

1 From the Database window click on **Membership** and click on the **Design** button.

2 Select the field **Category No**

This field has a data type of Number and the Field Properties are preset as Field Size - Long Interger, Decimal Places - Auto, Default Value - 0, Required - No and Indexed - No. In this field the data that will be entered is a number between 1 and 6 inclusive, as there are 6 categories. Refer forward to the section entitled 'Field Size' to see a list of the different number properties that are available. The Byte number type allows whole numbers up to 255 so is a good choice for the number property of the Category No field.

3 Click in the **Field Size** box, open its associated list and select **Byte**.

There are only six categories so a validation rule can be created.

4 Click in the **Validation Rule** box and key in **<=6** and type the text *Please enter a category number between 1 and 6* into the **Validation Text** box.

5 To prevent a number less than 1 being entered, modify the validation rule to read *<=6 And >0*.

6 Open the **Required** list box and select Yes.

It is necessary for there to be an entry in this field.

7 Select the field **Lastname**.

8 Click in the **Field Size** box, delete the default size of 50 and replace it with *25*

9 Alter the sizes of the other text fields as follows:

Firstname	*30*
Title	*10*

Street	30
Town	25
County	20
Post Code	10
Telephone No	12

10 Select the **Town** field again and in the **Default Value** box type ***Chelmer***.

11 Select the **County** field and put ***Cheshire*** into its **Default Value** box. Why do you think these defaults are set? Refer to the section on defaults, above.

12 Select the **Date of Birth** field and in the **Format** box key the format ***d/m/yy*** (to suppress leading zeros on day and month) or ***dd/mm/yy*** (to display leading zeros). Repeat this for the two other date fields. Alternatively, select **Short date** from the drop down list of the **Format** box.

13 Select the **Smoker** field and in the **Format** box replace Yes/No with the format ***;"Smoker";"Non-Smoker"*** which will display Smoker for Yes and Non-Smoker for No.

Note it is important to put the first semi-colon.

14 Click on the **Lookup** tab and then click on the **Display Control** down arrow. Select **Text Box**. Click on the **General** tab.

This is so the defined formats will be displayed.

15 Select the **Sex** field and in the **Format** box replace Yes/No with the format ***;"Male";"Female"*** which will display Male for Yes and Female for No. Set the **Display Control** to **Text Box** as for the **Smoker** field.

16 Save the changes using **File-Save** and close the table using **File-Close**.

Creating custom display formats

Custom formats will display the data in the format that is specified regardless of the format in which it is entered. For example a display format can be created which will show all telephone numbers using a particular format e.g. (01777) 565656 or 01777-565656. A custom format is created from an image of the format. To design the image a special set of characters, known as *placeholders* are used. To illustrate the creation of a custom format some examples are shown in the following table.

Format	Description
Numeric format	The # indicates the place for a digit but if the place is not used then leading and trailing zeros are not shown. The **0** indicates a place for a digit and if the place is not used then a 0 is shown. The comma may be used as a thousands separator.
##,###.00	56.98 6.90 5,890.07 100.00
#0.000	12.456 0.020
Date	The days placeholder is **d. d** displays 1, **dd** 01, **ddd** Mon, dddd Monday. The months placeholder is **m. m** displays 1, **mm** 01, **mmm** Jan, **mmmm** January. The years placeholder is **y. yy** displays 98, **yyyy** 1998. The / or - separates the day, month and year.
Dddd d mmmm yyyy	Thursday 26 March 1998
dd/mm/yy	26/06/98
d-m-yy	2-5-98 (this format does not display leading zeros).
Time	The hours placeholder is **h. h** displays 3, **hh** 03. The minutes placeholder is **m. m** displays 6, **mm** 06. The seconds placeholder is **s. s** displays 7, **ss** 07. The colon separates hours, minutes and seconds. **AM/PM** or **am/pm** displays time in 12 instead of 24hr format.
h:mm AM/PM	6:34 PM
hh:mm:ss	11:09:57
Text	@ indicates that a character is required in the particular position.
>	Changes all text in the field to uppercase.
<	Changes all text in the field to lowercase.
(@@@@@) @@@@@@	(01777) 565656
Yes/No	;"Male";"Female" Displays Male for true and Female for false.

Task 2: Customising a field format

1 Open the **Chelmer** database (if not already open) and open the **Membership** table in design view.

2 Select the **Post Code** field and put **>** in the **Format** property.

3 Save and close the table using **File-Save** followed by **File-Close**.

Creating input masks

Data entry can be made simpler by creating an input mask, which is a particular format or pattern in which the data is entered. An input mask is only suitable where all the data for that particular field has the same pattern, for example, stock numbers like ABM-372-4590-C. To illustrate the creation of an input mask some examples are shown in the following table.

Input Mask	Sample Values
\ABM-000-0000->L	ABM-372-4590-C
0000-000000	0777-567890
>L<????????????????	Jackson

A mask is created using special mask symbols and these are described in the following table.

Mask character	indicates
0	a number (digit) must be entered
9	a digit may be entered
#	a digit, + or - sign or space may be entered
L	a letter must be entered
?	a letter may be entered
A	a letter or digit must be entered
a	a letter or digit may be entered
&	any character or space must be entered
C	any character or space may be entered
. , : ; - /	decimal point, thousands, date and time separators
<	characters to right are converted to lower case
>	characters to right are converted to upper case
\	the character following is *not* to be interpreted as a mask character
!	Causes the input mask to display from right to left, rather than from left to right. Characters typed into the mask always fill it from left to right. You can include the exclamation point anywhere in the input mask.

Task 3: Setting an input mask

Revisit the properties of the **Lastname** field and set the mask using the third example illustrated above. Check that you use the correct number of question marks, i.e. 24, one less than the field width of 25.

Creating table indexes

What you will learn in this unit

Fields in a database table may be indexed, which can speed up retrieval of records. This unit explains the function of indexes and indicates how to select indexes. It is important to maintain documentation concerning the fields and the properties chosen for them and a standard way to do this is by printing a table definition using Access' Documenter facility.

By the end of this unit you will be able to:

■ create table indexes

■ print a table definition.

Creating table indexes

What is an index? You are probably familiar with the index at the back of a book, which helps you to find a particular topic quickly. A table index works in a similar fashion enabling Access to locate a particular record without having to search through all the records from the first until it locates the one you want. When you enter data into a table the records are in chronological order according to when you entered them, in other words they are in no particular order.

A useful order for the table to be in would be that of the primary key because the primary key uniquely defines each record. If the records are not physically in primary key order then Access does not actually re-arrange them, instead it creates an index which it uses to locate the records in that particular order.

When a primary key is defined the indexed property is automatically set to Yes (No duplicates). 'No Duplicates' means that Access expects this field to be unique in each record, which it should be if it is a primary key field.

Indexes on other fields may be defined, as an index helps Access find specific records faster. For example an index on **Lastname** and **Firstname** together is useful if the Membership table is often searched using the member's name. Another index could be set on the **Date of Renewal** field, useful when the table is used to provide projected cash flow of membership fees. Do not index every field in your table as this slows record updating: each time a record is added the indexes need to be modified to account for the new record. The fields you should choose for indexing are those used repeatedly to search for data.

You can create indexes based on a single field or on multiple fields. For example, you can index just on a **Lastname** name field or on both the **Lastname** and the **Firstname** fields, if you think you'll often search or sort by these fields. An index on **Lastname** will not distinguish between Liam Locker and Alison Locker but an index on the multiple fields **Lastname** and **Firstname** will. Another example is a date and time in the **Booking table**. Multiple-field indexes enable you to distinguish records in which the first field may have the same value. Instead of finding nine booking records for Monday, you can find one record for Monday at 14:00 and Access will do this more quickly if an index on date and time has been set. Of course, the time saving will be most noticeable if there are thousands of records to be searched or sorted.

Creating a single-field index

In the table's design view, select the field you want to index. In the **Indexed** property box at the bottom of the window, choose **Yes (Duplicates OK)** or **Yes (No Duplicates)**.

Choose the **Yes (No Duplicates)** option to ensure that no two records have the same data in this field.

Creating a multiple-field index

In the design view of the table, choose **View-Indexes** or click on the **Indexes** icon in the toolbar. Access displays the **Indexes** dialog box. In the **Index Name** column enter the name of the index. In the **Field Name** column open the list box and select the field you require, set the sort order in the **Sort Order** column.

In the next row select the next field name of the multiple index and set its sort order. By leaving the **Index name** blank up to nine subsequent rows may be used to create a multiple field index, with each field having its own sort order defined. Note that fields should be listed in order of priority.

Task 1: Setting indexes

1   Open the **Membership** table in design view.

2   Select the **Category No** field and choose **Yes (Duplicates OK)** in the **Indexed** property.

3   Repeat for **Date of Birth** and **Date of Joining** choosing **Yes (Duplicates OK)** for the **Indexed** property. Why can't **Yes (No Duplicates)** be chosen?

4   Save these table design modifications using **File-Save**.

5   Display the **Indexes** dialog box. In the **Index Name** column enter the name *Member*. List the fields **Last Name** and **First Name** as illustrated below.

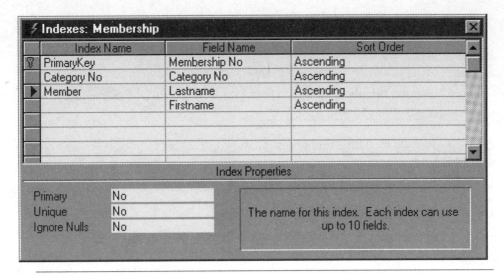

Index Name	Field Name	Sort Order
PrimaryKey	Membership No	Ascending
Category No	Category No	Ascending
Member	Lastname	Ascending
	Firstname	Ascending

Index Properties

Primary	No
Unique	No
Ignore Nulls	No

The name for this index. Each index can use up to 10 fields.

6　Close the **Indexes** dialog box and the table.

Making a printed copy of the table design

Access allows you to view and print the design characteristics (definition) of your tables, forms, queries and reports. To make a printed copy of the table design

1　Choose **Tools-Analyze**, and then click **Documenter**. Note: you may need to install Access' analysing tools.

2　Click on the tab corresponding to the type of database object you want to document and view or print. In this case choose the **Table** tab.

3　Click in the check box of each table for which definitions are required.

4　Click **Options** to specify which features of the selected object or objects you want to print, and then click on **OK**.

5　You might want to check the length of your definitions in the **Print Preview** window, because some definitions, particularly those for forms and reports, can be many pages long.

6　To print the definition, click on the **Print** button in the toolbar.

Before such tools were available, database designers created another table as a means of storing table definitions i.e. a data dictionary. This required more work but gave a more complete perspective and a chance to revise the work already done. Each data element in the database system had an entry in a dictionary table.

Task 2: Printing the Membership table definition

1 Display the database window, and follow steps 1 and 2 above.

2 Tick the **Membership** table check box and click on the **Options** button. Set the following options.

3 Include for Table: Properties

4 Include for Fields: Names, Data types, and Sizes

5 Include for Indexes: Names and Fields

6 Click on **OK** to exit the **Print Table Definition** window, then click on **OK** again, and be prepared that Access may take a little time to compile the definition.

7 Preview and print the table definition.

Entering and editing data

What you will learn in this unit

By the end of this unit you will be able to:

■ display a table's datasheet and use it to enter data

■ make a back up copy of your table.

Entering data

The next stage is to enter data into the tables. Up until now the table has only been opened in Design View. To enter data a table needs to be opened in the Datasheet View.

Opening a table in datasheet view

In the database window, click the **Table** tab. Double-click the table name or select the table and choose the **Open** button. The table will open in Datasheet View.

Once a table is open it is possible to switch from the Datasheet View to the design view and vice versa. If you make changes to the design you will be asked to save them if you switch back to the Datasheet View. There is a button on the tool bar for switching between the views.

When in Design View	*When in Datasheet View*

Datasheet **View** button   Design **View** button

In the Datasheet View the headings of the columns are the field names you previously designed. Each row in the datasheet is a record and as you complete each record it is automatically saved into the table.

Task 1: Membership data

1 Open the **Membership** table in Datasheet View.	Notice that there are some fields already filled in; these are the default values. A default value can be accepted or it can be overridden.

2   Do not enter a value into the **membership number** but press *Enter* to move to the next field.

This is an *AutoNumber* field and if you do try to enter data into it the entry will not be accepted. When you press *Enter* after entering data into the last field of the first record, Access saves the record. Notice what appears in the membership number field. Let Access number all the membership number fields.

3   Enter the data for the **Membership** table as shown in Quick Reference 2.

4   After entering the data for each field move to the next by pressing *Enter*, *Tab* or the right arrow key. When entering the data for the logical fields enter either **Yes** or **No** and the appropriate word as defined by the format appears, e.g. **Male** or **Female**. If you see a check box for a logical field, then refer back to Unit 4 and check the display property for the field. You may continue and enter data, a tick indicates Yes, a blank No.

5   While entering the data test the validation rules, those that Access applies and those that have been defined. Try entering text into a date-type field, Access expects the correct data type, and the Office Assistant will display a message informing you of your mistake.

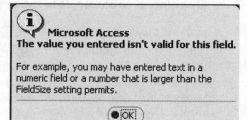

6   Entering a **Category No** greater than 6 will test the validation rule set up in the field properties for **Category No**. To prevent a number less than 1 being entered then the validation rule could be modified to read **<=6 And >0**.

7   Skip fields that are blank. Validation, skipping fields and using Undo are described below.

8   Save the table.

Validation

Data is validated as it is entered, if it does not conform to the data type set for that field an error message will be generated. If the data entered breaks the validation rule that has been set as a property for that field, if there is validation text, this appears as the error message.

Skipping fields, null values

Sometimes not all the data for a record is available, for example, the telephone number may be missing. To skip a field, simply press *Enter* or *Tabr* to take you to the next field. It is acceptable to skip fields where the data is not vital, but for data such as the Membership No it is not acceptable. Access automatically enters a membership number, as the field was defined with an AutoNumber data type.

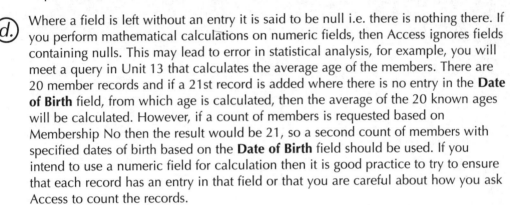

Where a field is left without an entry it is said to be null i.e. there is nothing there. If you perform mathematical calculations on numeric fields, then Access ignores fields containing nulls. This may lead to error in statistical analysis, for example, you will meet a query in Unit 13 that calculates the average age of the members. There are 20 member records and if a 21st record is added where there is no entry in the **Date of Birth** field, from which age is calculated, then the average of the 20 known ages will be calculated. However, if a count of members is requested based on Membership No then the result would be 21, so a second count of members with specified dates of birth based on the **Date of Birth** field should be used. If you intend to use a numeric field for calculation then it is good practice to try to ensure that each record has an entry in that field or that you are careful about how you ask Access to count the records.

Zero length strings

Nulls indicate that data may exist but is not known. To enter a null leave a field's **Required property** as No and leave the field blank. A zero length string can be used to indicate that there is no data for the field in that record, for example, a company without a fax machine doesn't have a fax number. To enter a zero length string check that the **Zero length string** property is set to **Yes**. In the datasheet, type two double quotation marks without a space between i.e. *""*. Nulls and zero length strings may be distinguished when searching the data table.

Using undo

Should you do anything wrong or if something unexpected happens always try **Edit-Undo** ↶ or click on the **Undo** button before doing anything else.

Editing data

Once the records have been entered into a table, this data is available to be used, as is evident in the following sessions. However, the data in the datasheet can be viewed, and if mistakes are spotted these can be rectified.

Moving between records

By using either **Edit-Go To**, the *Up Arrow*, *Down Arrow*, *Page Up* and *Page Down* keys, or the vertical scroll bar you can move between records in the datasheet. However, the most efficient way to move between records in large databases is with the navigation buttons in the lower-left corner of the window.

FIGURE 6.1

Access record indicators

In the status bar of the datasheet window are the Access record indicators (FIGURE 6.1). These are record movement buttons and the record number of the currently selected record.

To move to	Click
First record	◄
Last record	►◄
Previous record	◄
Next record	►
New record	►✱
Specific record	click in record counter box [6]

(or press *F5*), type the record number you want, and then press *Enter*.

Selecting data

Various parts of the datasheet can be selected. When an area is selected it appears in inverse colour, so if text is normally black on white, then selected text is white on black.

To select	Do This
A single field	move the pointer to the left hand side of a cell, so that it changes shape into a white cross and click.
A word in a field	double-click on the word
A record	click in the record selector at the left edge of the record, or click on any field of the desired record and choose **Edit-Select Record**
More than one record	click and drag in the record selector edge for the required number of records.
A field column	click on the column heading (the field name at the top of the column).
Several field columns	click on the first column heading required for the selection and drag to the last.

Moving and copying fields

A field may be moved, by selecting it, using **Edit-Cut**, clicking in the cell where the field is to be moved to and using **Edit-Paste**.

A field may be copied, by selecting it, using **Edit-Copy**, clicking in the cell where the copy is required and using **Edit-Paste**. Buttons are available i.e. **Cut** , **Copy** and **Paste** .

Hiding and showing columns

If there are a lot of fields in a table, as is the case with the **Membership** table then columns may be hidden. By using the **Unhide** command the columns may be re-displayed.

To hide a column in a datasheet

1   Click on the column selector at the top of the column. More than one column may be selected for hiding.

2   Choose **Format-Hide Columns**.

To re-display the columns

1   Choose **Format-Unhide Columns**.

2   In the dialog box select the column(s) to be unhidden and click on **Close** .

Freezing and unfreezing columns

You can freeze one or more of the columns on a datasheet so that they become the leftmost columns and are visible at all times no matter where you scroll.

To freeze a column or columns

1   Select the columns you want to freeze.

2   Choose **Format-Freeze Columns**.

To unfreeze all columns

1   Choose **Format-Unfreeze All Columns**.

Moving and copying records

You can copy a complete table or some records of a table to the clipboard. Records may be moved and copied using Edit-Cut/Copy and Edit-Paste. Generally moving isn't an operation you would need to carry out within the same table as the records can be displayed in any order chosen. Moving and also copying can be carried out between databases providing the table structures are similar. Importing and exporting data is considered in more detail in Units 35 to 38.

 One instance where copying is useful is for making a backup of a table. Should you decide to revise the data types of fields in a table then it is advisable to make a backup of the table first in case mistakes are made which could result in the loss of data.

Task 2: Backing up a table

In this task a backup of the **Membership** table will be made.

1   Click on the **Table** tab in the **database window**.

2   Select the table **Membership** and choose **Edit-Copy**.

3   Next create a database to hold the backup by choosing **File-New Database**, selecting the folder in which the backup file is to be stored, typing *Chelmer backup* in the **File name** box and clicking on **Create**. This database is now active.

4   Choose **Edit-Paste** and in the **Table Name** box of the **Paste Table As** dialog box type *Membership backup*.

5   Check that the default option **Structure and Data** is selected before clicking on **OK**.

6   Use **File-Close** to close the backup database.

If this backup is needed to restore a damaged file then open the backup database, select and copy the table, open the normal database (use **File-Open Database**) and paste as described above. Alternatively, you may back-up the entire database by first closing it, switching to Explorer and copying the file to another directory or to floppy disk or other back-up medium.

Managing data

What you will learn in this unit

By the end of this unit you will be able to:

■ use the spell checker

■ delete data

■ use find and replace to edit data

■ print the data in your table.

Managing records

It is very difficult to store a set of data that is perfect. Mistakes of transcription or keying occur despite data validation techniques and the data itself changes, for example members may move. Simple changes can be made using the Find technique described below and old records can be deleted. Where text fields are used to store descriptions such as occupation or sporting interests then it is useful to be able to spell check the entries.

Deleting records

 You can delete a record from a table using a datasheet or a form. (You will meet forms in Unit 14.)

To delete records using a datasheet:

1   Display the datasheet.

2   Select the record or records you wish to delete. Press the *Delete* key (or choose **Edit-Delete** from the menu).

3   Access prompts you to confirm the deletion. Choose **Yes** to delete the record or **No** to restore it.

Using the spell checker

With the data displayed in the datasheet, you may spell check a single entry or column(s) selection by clicking on the **Spelling** button. ᴬᴮC The spell checker will prompt you to correct words that it does not recognise.

Finding and replacing

To find data in a particular field:

1 Make that field current by clicking in that column.

2 Choose either **Edit-Find**or click on the ▐ **Find** ▌ button in the toolbar that displays the **Find in Field** dialog box.

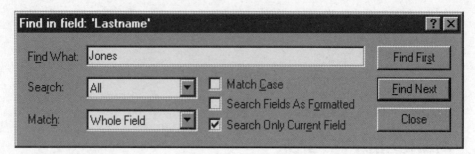

3 Key the string (set of characters) you wish to find into the **Find What** text box, such as the last name 'Jones'.

4 In the **Search** box choose between **Up, Down** or **All**.

5 In the **Match** box select whether your string should match the whole field, any part of the field or the start of the field.

6 In the **Match Case** option group you may choose between making your search case sensitive or not.

7 In the **Search Fields As Formatted** to choose between finding a field as say, a number 28/3/97 or as it is formatted 28-Mar-97.

8 In the **Search Only Current Field** you may choose between limiting your search to the current field or including all fields.

9 To start the search click on either ▐ **Find Next** ▌, which will search from your current position in the direction you have chosen, or ▐ **Find First** ▌ which will find the first occurrence in the field or table.

10 Each time a match is found it is highlighted. If either the top or the bottom of the table is reached Access displays a message asking whether you would like to continue the search from the bottom or the top of the table. When you have found the desired field click on ▐ **Close** ▌.

To replace a particular field entry, select **Edit-Replace**. The steps are the same as for finding a field, except that there is an additional text box, **Replace With**, in the dialog box in which you type the replacement string. Strings can be replaced according to which button is clicked.

Button	Description
Find Next	Finds and highlights but does not replace. Use when you don't want to replace.
Replace	Replaces the highlighted string and finds the next occurrence of the **Find What** string.
Replace All	Replaces all occurrences of the string without stopping.
Close	Closes the dialog box

Task 1: Editing data

In this task we experiment with finding and replacing data.

1   Open the **Membership** table. Move to the end of the table.

2   Add another record, **Category 3**. Move to record 9, select the **Lastname** field and use **Edit-Copy** to copy it.

3   Move back to the **Lastname** field of the new record and use **Edit-Paste**. Finish the record as shown below.

Firstname	Title	Street	Town	County	Post Code
Frances	Miss	70 Meir View	Chelmer	Cheshire	CH2 7BZ

Date of Birth	Date of Joining	Date of Last Renewal	Sporting interests	Smoker	Sex
5/5/82	1/3/96	1/3/97	Swimming, Judo	No	No

4   Go to the first record. Click in the **Telephone No** field.

5   Choose **Edit-Find** or click on the **Find** button in the toolbar.

6   Key *01778* into the **Find What** box and select **Start of Field** in the **Match** box.

7   Click on the **Find First** button. This should highlight the first occurrence. If the **Find in field** dialog box is in the way drag it out of the way.

8   Click on the **Find Next** button to find other matches. Close the **Find in field** dialog box.

9   Move to the top of the table again and click in the **Telephone No** field. Choose **Edit-Replace** and key *01777* into the **Find What** box and *01779* into the **Replace With** box. The current field should be selected to search in and the **Match Whole Field** check box should not be checked as shown below.

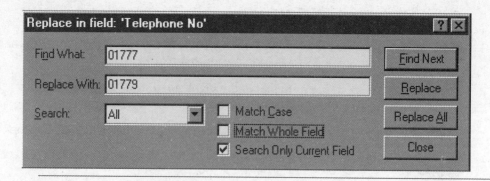

10 Click on the **Replace All** button.

11 Answer **Yes** to continue but note that at this point you could abandon the operation.

12 Now replace all 01779 codes with 01777.

13 Close the **Replace in Field** dialog box.

14 Select the last record, which you have just created, and delete it.

15 Select the **Sporting Interests** column and spell check it by clicking on the **Spelling** button.

Customising the datasheet layout

Adjusting column widths

To improve the datasheet display, you can alter the widths of the columns. Usually columns are made smaller, as field widths often err on the large side, and this is easily achieved, especially if you are familiar with Windows applications.

To alter a column width:

1 Move the pointer to the field name row (at the top of the table).

2 Move the pointer to the dividing line between the column you wish to change and the column to the right, it should change shape to a ✛ .

3 Click and drag the column to the desired width.

Adjusting row heights

Another way in which more fields can be displayed across the screen is by increasing the row height, which will make the data in the field wrap. To alter a row height:

1   Move the pointer to the row selector (at the left edge of table)

2   Move the pointer to the dividing line between the row you wish to change and the row below, it should change shape to a ✛

3   Click and drag the row to the desired height. Note all rows take on the new height.

Changing the font used in the datasheet

Choose **Format-Font** and select the required font and size from the **Font** dialog box.

Changing and re-organising fields

You may find it necessary to change a field data type as the design of your database develops or if you import data. Units 35 and 36 deal with importing data. Before you make any changes to field data types make a backup copy of the table in case you accidentally lose data because your changes were too great.

Before you make changes consider the following.

Numeric fields

Changing from one data type to another that can hold a larger number is generally safe, for example from Byte to Integer (refer back to Unit 4 for definitions of field size). If on the other hand you change to a data type that holds a smaller number, for example from Double to Integer, then your data will be truncated, in this case by losing the decimal part of the number. Truncation means reducing the number of digits in a number to fit the new field size property that you choose.

Note: You cannot convert any type of field into an AutoNumber type field as Access provides automatic numbering in this field type.

Text fields

The field size of text fields may be altered but if you reduce the field size text may be truncated. Text fields may be converted to Memo fields, but if a Memo field is converted to a text field it will be truncated to 255 characters

Conversion between data types

It is possible to convert a field from one data type to another.

Primary key or fields used in relationships

You cannot change the data type or field size property of these fields.

To change a field data type, make a backup copy of your table, display the design view of your table and make the necessary alterations.

Reorganising fields

If you consider that the order in which the fields are shown in the datasheet needs rearranging, then this can easily be achieved using a drag and drop method. First select the field column you wish to move, move the pointer over the selection so that it changes shape to a left-pointing arrow, click (pointer changes shape to drag and drop) and drag the column to a new position. A darker column dividing line will indicate where the field will go when the mouse button is released.

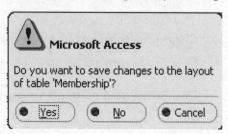

When you close the table you can choose whether or not to make the rearrangement permanent by selecting **Yes** or **No** in the save changes message box.

Displaying data in sorted order

The data displayed in a datasheet will be displayed in 'natural order', that is in the order in which the records were entered. This may not be the order in which you would like to see them. You can control the order using the **Sort Ascending** and **Sort Descending** buttons on the toolbar.

To change the displayed order of the records using one field:

1   Select a column by which you wish to sort (click on the field name at the top of the column).

2   Click on either the **Sort Ascending** or **Sort Descending** button. ![A↓Z↓ Z↓A↑]

To change the displayed order of the records using more than one field:

1   Select the columns by which you wish to sort (click on the field name at the top of the first column and drag to the last column). Sorting columns must be next to one another with the highest priority being assigned to the leftmost column. If necessary rearrange the columns in the datasheet.

2   Click on either the **Sort Ascending** or **Sort Descending** button.

Task 2: Customising the membership datasheet

The aim of this task is to see how columns of data may be re-arranged and also how to adjust their width.

1   Display the **Membership** datasheet.

2   Adjust the widths of the columns to accommodate the data displayed.

3   Select the **Sporting Interests** column and drag it to between the **Occupation** and the **Date of Birth** columns.

4   Close the table without making the rearrangement permanent by choosing **No** in the save changes message box when closing the table.

Task 3: Displaying records in sorted order

In this task the records in the **Membership** table will be viewed in different orders.

1   Open the **Membership** table in Datasheet View.

2   Select the **Lastname** column and click on the **Sort Ascending** button. Click on the **Sort Descending** button.

3   Try this for other fields in the table.

4   Select the **Category No** and **Lastname** columns together and click on the **Sort Ascending** button. Note the effect.

5   Drag the **Town** column so it is to the right of the **Category No** column, select these two columns, and click on the **Sort Ascending** button.

6   Drag the **Town** column so it is to the left of the **Category No** column, select these two columns, and click on the **Sort Ascending** button. Note the difference between these last two sorts.

7 Close the **Membership** table without saving the layout changes.

Printing a table

You can print a table from its datasheet. Access prints a datasheet as it appears on the screen. For large datasheets, Microsoft Access prints from left to right and then from top to bottom. For example, if your datasheet is three pages wide and two pages long, Microsoft Access prints the top three pages first, then the bottom three pages. You should preview your datasheet before printing by choosing **File-Print Preview** or clicking on the **Print Preview** button in the toolbar.

If you need to set up your printer, choose the **Setup** button in the **Print** dialog box.

To print a table datasheet:

1   Display the table datasheet.

2   If you intend to print selected records, select those records. To print all the records, select nothing.

3   Choose **File-Print Preview**, and if the preview is satisfactory choose **File-Print** to display the **Print** dialog box.

4   Under **Print Range**, choose one of the following:

   ■ **All**, to print all of the records in the table.

   ■ **Pages**, to print specific pages from your table.

   ■ **Selected Records**, to print a previously selected set of records.

   If you select **Pages**, specify the page numbers of the first and last pages you want to print.

5   Set other **Print** dialog box options if necessary.

6   Choose **OK**.

Task 4: Printing the membership table

1   Display the **Membership** table datasheet.

2   Choose **File-Print Preview**, and then select **File-Print** to display the **Print** dialog box.

3   Under **Print Range** select **All** and click on **OK**.

4   Close the table.

Relationships between tables

What you will learn in this unit

If you wish to use only one table in your database you may omit this unit. You will find that you can complete most of Units 10 to 31 as many tasks are based on the **Membership** table. You should then return to this activity before moving on to Unit 32.

In this unit you will be introduced to the concept of the relationship between tables.

By the end of the unit you will be able to:

■ define and create relationships between tables

■ apply referential integrity.

Defining relationships between tables

The relationships between the tables are shown in FIGURE 8.1. Relationships are made between a field in one table and a field in another table. Relationships fall into three types:

■ one-to-one

■ one-to-many

■ many-to-many.

A one-to-one relationship between two tables means that for a particular field in one table there is only one matching record in the other table and vice versa. A one-to-many relationship means that for one field in one table there are several matching records in the other table. A many-to-many relationship means that for one field in one table there are many matching records in the other table and vice versa.

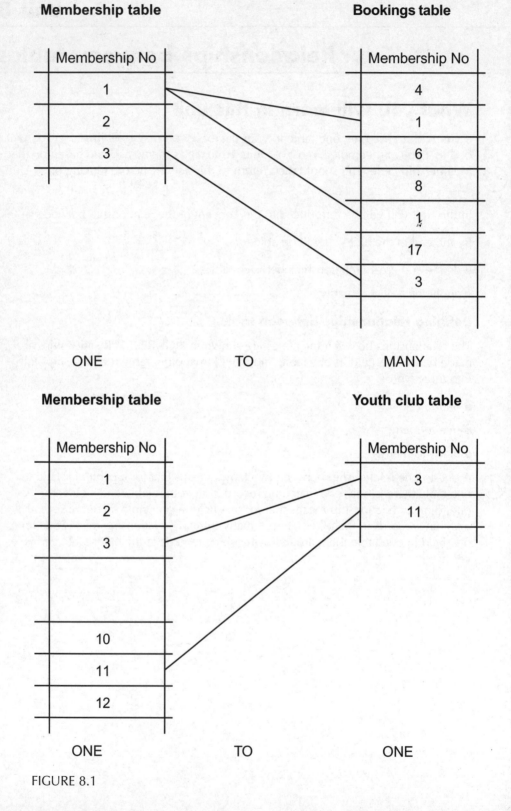

FIGURE 8.1

The most common type of relationship is one-to-many, and it is the only one used in our system. Consider the relationship between a member and that member's booking. A member may make no bookings, one booking or several bookings. So one member can make several bookings, a one-to-many relationship, i.e. there is only one record with that person's membership number in the membership table, yet there can be several records with that person's membership number in the bookings table.

However, in our database these relationships do not yet exist because they have not been defined. You need to set them up. The relationships can be set up before data is entered into any of the tables. Before any relationships between tables can be defined the tables must be closed. It is important that when a link is made between a field in one table and a field in another table, the two fields have the same data type.

Referential integrity

When a relationship is created between two tables Access allows the choice of whether or not to enforce referential integrity. If the relationship between the **Membership** and **Bookings** tables is considered then what is to stop a membership number being entered into the **Bookings** table that does not exist in the **Membership** table? By enforcing referential integrity Access will check the membership number entered into the **Bookings** table against those in the **Membership** table and will prevent non-existent membership numbers being entered.

Task 1: Creating relationships

As yet only one table has been created in the **Chelmer** database. Before relationships can be defined the other tables in the database need to be defined. For this task you will need to define the **Bookings** table.

 1 To create a **Bookings** table, click on the New button in the database window to open the table design window (you may wish to refer back to Units 3 and 4). Define the field types as shown below.

Field Name	Data Type	Description
Booking No	Auto Number	
Room/Hall/Court	Text	
Member/Class	Yes/No	
Membership No	Number	
Class No	Number	
Date	Date/Time	
Time	Date/Time	

2 Define **Booking No** as the primary key. Save the table as ***Bookings***

Amend the field properties as shown below. Save and close the table.

Field	Property	Setting
Room/Hall/Court	Field Size	20
	Required	Yes
Member/Class	Format	;"Member";"Class"
	Required	Yes
Membership No	Field Size	Long Integer
	Default value	=Null
Class No	Field Size	Long Integer
	Default value	=Null
Date	Format	d/m/yy
	Required	Yes
Time	Format	Short time
	Required	Yes

3 Make sure that both the tables are closed, i.e. just the database Window is left open. Now you can create the relationship between **Membership No** in the **Membership** table and **Membership No** in the **Bookings** table. The data type of the **Membership No** (**Bookings**) is a long integer number, which is compatible with the data type counter of **Membership No** (**Membership**). In one-to-many relationships the primary table in the relationship is the 'one' table, in this case the **Membership** table, and the related table is the 'many' table, i.e. the **Bookings** table.

To define a relationship between tables:

4 Choose **Tools-Relationships** and the **Relationships** dialog box appears with the **Show Table** dialog box within it. (If the **Show Table** dialog box does not appear click on the **Show Table** icon on the toolbar.

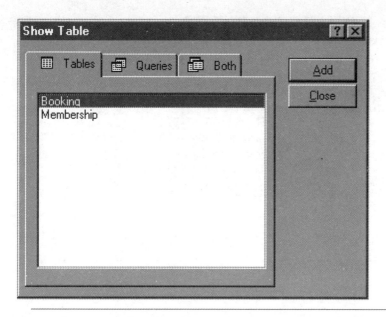

5 Select **Membership** and click on Add . Select **Bookings** and click on Add .
Click on Close . The two table windows should be displayed and you may re-
size them if you wish.

6 To create the relationship click on the **Membership No** field in the **Membership**
table and drag to the **Membership No** in the **Bookings** table. This displays a
Relationships dialog box.

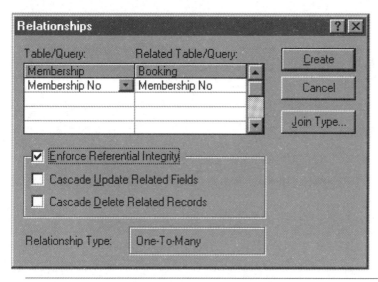

7 Click in the **Enforce Referential Integrity** check box and click on **Create** and the relationship between the tables will be shown.

8 Use **File-Save** to save changes to the layout and close the **Relationships** dialog box.

Defining the other tables in the database

What you will learn in this unit

If you wish to use only one table in your database you may omit this unit. You will find that you can complete most of Units 10 to 31 as many tasks are based on the **Membership** table. You should then return to this unit before moving on to Unit 32. This unit revisits techniques used in Units 2 to 8 so you may wish to refer back to these.

The aim of this unit, through a series of tasks, is to

■ reinforce techniques already introduced.

Task 1: Defining the other tables in the database

Create the tables **Membership Category** and **Classes**.

1 Click on the New button in the database window to open the table design window.

2 Define the field types as shown.

Membership Category

Field Name	Data Type	Description
Category No	Number	A one digit identification number
Category Type	Text	Categories are Senior, Senior Club, Junior, Junior Club, Concessionary, Youth Club
Membership Fee	Currency	

3 Define **Category No** as the primary key. Save the table as **Membership Category** and close the table.

Classes

Field Name	Data Type	Description
Class No	Auto Number	
Class Day	Text	
Class Time	Date/Time	
Class Tutor	Text	

Class Activity	Text	
Male/Female/Mixed	Text	

4   Define **Class No** as the primary key. Save the table as *Classes* and close the table. **Class Day** has been chosen to be numeric with 1 representing Sunday through to 7 representing Saturday. This is so that the classes can be listed in day and time order.

In your database window you should see four tables listed.

Task 2: Defining field properties for the other tables

1   Open each table in turn, in design view.

2   Amend the field properties as shown below.

3   Save and close the tables.

Membership Category table

Field	Property	Setting
Category No	Field Size	Byte
	Required	Yes
Category Type	Field Size	15
	Required	Yes
Membership Fee	Required	Yes

Classes table

Field	Property	Setting
Class Day	Field Size	10
	Required	Yes
Class Time	Format	Short time (equivalent to hh:mm)
	Required	Yes
Class Tutor	Field Size	30
Class Activity	Field Size	20
	Required	Yes
Male/Female/Mixed	Field Size	10
	Validation Rule	"Male" or "Female" or "Mixed"
	Validation Text	Please enter Male, Female or Mixed

Task 3: Creating indexes

In this task, indexes for the **Classes** and **Bookings** tables are created.

1   Open the **Classes** table in design view.

2   Select the **Class Tutor** field and choose **Yes (Duplicates OK)** for the indexed property.

3   Repeat for **Class Activity** choosing **Yes (Duplicates OK)** for the indexed property. Close and save changes.

4   Open the **Bookings** table in design view.

5   Select the **Room/Hall/Court** field and choose **Yes (Duplicates OK)**.

 6   Set a multiple field index (refer back to Unit 5) using the fields **Date** and **Time**. You may name this index **Date time**. Close and save changes.

Task 4: Defining the other relationships

 There are two other relationships in the database, (see Figure 1 in Unit 2). These are

■ between the **Classes** table and the **Bookings** table

■ between the **Membership Category** table and the **Membership** table.

Both these relationships are one-to-many relationships. Using the **Relationships** dialog box set these relationships up as follows.

1   Choose **Tools-Relationships**.

2   Add the tables **Classes** and **Membership Category** using the **Show Table** dialog box. Display this dialog box by clicking on the **Show Table** button on the toolbar.

3   To create the relationship click on the **Class No** field in the **Classes** table and drag to the **Class No** in the **Bookings** table. Note the direction of dragging is one to many.

4   Click in the **Enforce Referential Integrity** check box and click on **Create**. The relationship between the tables will be shown.

5   If you try to create the relationship between **Category No** in the **Membership Category** table and **Category No** in the **Membership** table you will find that if you check the **Enforce Referential Integrity** check box, Access will not create the relationship because there is no data in the **Membership Category** table. When the data is added in Unit 17 the relationship can be created. Close the **Relationships** dialog box.

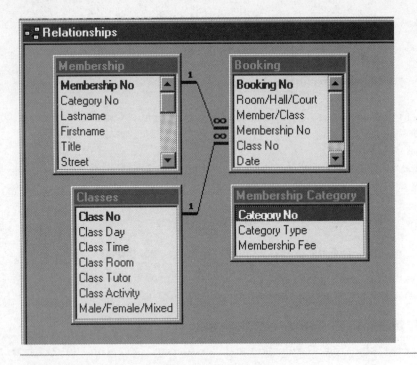

Task 5: Documenting the table definitions

Use **Tools-Analyze Documenter** to print the documentation for these two newly created tables, in the same manner as for the **Membership** table (Unit 5).

Designing a basic query

What you will learn in this unit

This unit introduces the ability of databases to answer questions asked of them. The information stored in a database is of no use unless it can be retrieved, and only if it can be retrieved in a useful way. Data stored in a telephone directory can be retrieved, for example, by knowing the name and address of someone in the directory and using the database to find out the telephone number.

By the end of this unit you will be able to:

■ question the database by creating a query

■ view the result of the query

■ save a query so that it can be retrieved for later use

■ print out your query.

There are many reasons for using queries; they have a very important role in database systems. Queries are used:

■ for on-line search and retrieval of specific records. For example, to look at a particular set of members for editing, to view the bookings for a given room on a certain day, or to find the class tutors who have a particular qualification.

■ for creating forms and printing reports. Queries retrieve a particular set of records and fields; reports are used to print this information. A form based on a query can be used to restrict data entry to certain fields. Units 14 to 20 introduce forms and reports.

Queries may be based on more than one table but in this session all the queries will be based on the **Membership** table. You will see in Unit 32 how to create queries based on more than one table.

The Simple Query Wizard and query design window

Creating a query involves two aspects, these are:

■ selecting the fields that are to be shown in the query. It is not usually necessary to retrieve all fields, for example, the name and the telephone number of a member may be all that is needed for a telephone survey of a particular group of members.

■ selecting the records that are to be shown in the query. For this Access provides a method of querying by which you can describe the characteristics of the data that you are looking for. This is know as Query By Example (QBE) and is achieved by allowing you to give examples of the data that you are searching for in the form of criteria.

Simple Query Wizard

The Simple Query Wizard helps you design a simple select query. A select query will select fields from a table. The Wizard will ask you to select the table you wish to query and which fields you want in your query. It will create the query, which you can then modify later using the query design window.

Query design window

The query design window (FIGURE 10.1) allows a query to be designed that will select the required fields and records that you ask for. This window is in two sections, the upper section is where the table windows of the tables used in the query are displayed. In the lower section is a grid for the query design. The two most important rows in the grid are **Field** and **Criteria**. Each column needs a field name and you can choose all or some of the fields in the table. In the criteria row an example of the data may be given. As you work your way through this session you will be introduced to the function of the other rows in the grid.

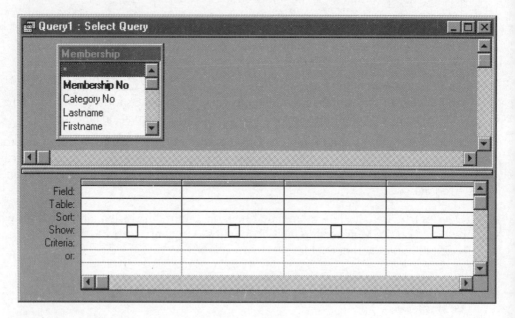

FIGURE 10.1

 Before asking questions of a database you must first decide which tables in the database are required to answer them. The following activities will describe how to ask questions of just one table, the **Membership** table. You will see later, in Unit 32 how to include more than one table in a query.

Displaying the query design window

■ Click on the   Queries   tab in the database window and click on the New button to create a new query. If you have not created any queries yet then the **Open** and **Design** buttons are not available.

■ Select **Design View** in the **New Query** dialog box and click on **OK**.

■ The **Show Table** dialog box appears in front of the query design window. This box allows you to select all the tables needed for the query.

■ Select a table and choose **Add** to add it to the query. When the selection of table(s) is complete click on the **Close** button.

Using the Simple Query Wizard to add fields to a query

After choosing Simple Query Wizard from the **New Query** dialog box the **Simple Query Wizard** dialog box will be displayed (FIGURE 10.2).

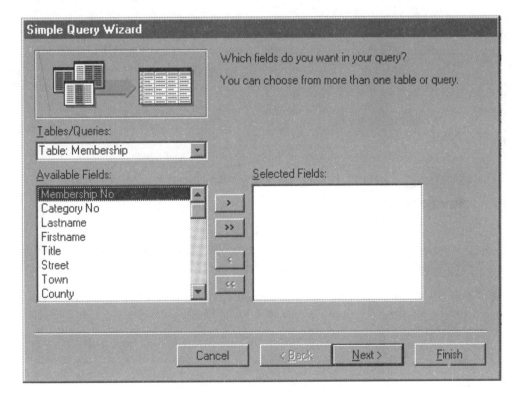

FIGURE 10.2

From the **Table/Queries** drop down list box select the table that the query is to be based on.

If you wish to add all the fields to the query, click on the **>>** button. If you want to add a selected set of fields, highlight each field and click on the **>** button. You may change your mind and use the **<<** button to remove all fields (so you

59

may start again) or use the < button to remove a selected field.

When the required fields have been chosen click on Next> . Select a Detail query and click on Next> . Give the query a title and click on Finish . The result of your query will be shown in Datasheet view.

Task 1: Selecting fields for a query using Simple Query Wizard

1 From the Database window click on the Queries tab and click on the New button. Choose the Simple Query Wizard from the New Query dialog box.

2 From the Table/Queries drop down list box in the Simple Query Wizard dialog box select the Membership table.

3 Add the fields Membership Female, Lastname, Sex, and Date of Joining to the query by highlighting each field in turn and clicking on the > button.

4 Click on Next> . Select a Detail query and click on Next> . Give the query the title *Dates of Joining* and click on Finish . The result of your query will be shown in datasheet view.

5 View and close the query window; the name of the query is listed in the database window.

Adding fields to a query without using the wizard

By choosing design view from the New Query dialog box the Show Table box will be displayed in front of the query design window. After choosing the table for the query it will be displayed in the upper section of the query design window as seen in FIGURE 10.1. The next step is to decide which fields in that table you wish to include in the query. Later we will explore query criteria which allow us to select specific records. The query is designed in the lower section of the query design window.

Adding all the fields in the table to the query

The simplest case is where we want to include all the fields in the table.

1 Double click on the title bar of the field list box of the table in the upper section of the window. This selects all the fields.

2 Click on any of the selected fields (not the *) and drag to the field cell in the lower section of the query window. The pointer should look like a set of record cards.

3   When you release the mouse button all the field names will have been added to the query. Use the horizontal scroll bar to move to the right as all the columns will not fit on the screen.

Adding individual fields in the table to the query

There are three alternative ways of adding the fields one by one to a query.

The first method is by double-clicking, thus:

1   Double-click on the name of the field required in the field list box in the upper section of the window. It will appear in the next available column in the grid below.

The second is to use the drop down list associated with each field cell, thus:

1   Click in the field cell in the lower section of the window. A **list box** button appears at the end of the cell.

2   Click on the **list box** button and a drop down list of field names will appear.

3   Select the name of the field required (if necessary scroll through the list), click on it and it will appear in the **Field** cell (FIGURE10.3).

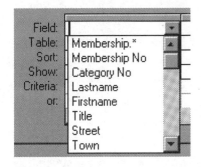

FIGURE 10.3

The third way is to use the *drag-and-drop* method, thus:

1   Click on the name of the field required in the field list box in the upper section of the window.

2   Drag and drop this field into the required field cell in the lower part of the Query window. While doing this the pointer should look like one record card.

3   If you drop the field onto a column containing a field, then a column will be inserted to contain the new field.

Removing fields from the query

Fields may be removed singly or in blocks from the query. To remove the all of the fields from the query:

1   Select the first column by clicking on the bar at the top of the column, (the pointer will change shape to a down arrow) drag to select all the columns.

2 Press the *Delete* key or choose **Edit-Delete**.

To remove an individual field from the query, just select the required column for deleting and use **Edit-Delete**.

Viewing or running a query

To see the result of a query, either click on the **Datasheet** button or the **Run Query** button in the toolbar. To return to the query design click on the **Design** button next to the **Datasheet** button in the toolbar.

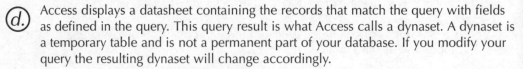

Design button   Datasheet button   Run Query button

(d.) Access displays a datasheet containing the records that match the query with fields as defined in the query. This query result is what Access calls a dynaset. A dynaset is a temporary table and is not a permanent part of your database. If you modify your query the resulting dynaset will change accordingly.

Task 2: Selecting fields for a query

In this task you will query the **Membership** table; data from all records will be shown in the dynasets. Initially all fields will be shown and then you will see how to select only certain fields.

1 Starting from the database window, click on the **Queries** tab.

2 Click on **New** to open a new query and choose **Design View** .

3 Select the table **Membership** from the **Show Table** dialog box and close the dialog box.

4 Add all the fields to the query, following the method described above.

5 Click on the **Datasheet** button in the toolbar; you should see the whole of the table forming the dynaset.

6 Click on the **Design** button in the toolbar to return to the query design window.

7 Remove all the fields from the query, following the method for removing fields from the query described above.

8 Add fields individually to the query, experimenting with the different methods described above. Add the fields **Membership No**, **Lastname**, **Sex**, **Date of Joining**.

9 Click on the **Datasheet** or **Run Query** button in the toolbar; you should see only these fields from all the records of the table forming the dynaset.

10 Click on the **Design** button in the toolbar to return to the Query design window.

11 By adding and removing fields alter the fields in your query so that they are **Lastname**, **Sex**, **Category No**, **Sporting Interests**.

12 Click on the **Datasheet** button in the toolbar, or the **Run Query** button and you should see only these fields from all the records of the table forming the dynaset.

Saving a query

Sometimes you may wish to ask the same question of a database over and over again, for example, is a membership subscription due? As time passes members need to renew their membership and it is useful to be able to send reminders. A query designed to do this would be saved so that it can be used repeatedly.

To save a query:

1 Choose **File-Save**

2 In the **Query Name** box of the **Save As** dialog box enter a name that will remind you what the query is about. The name can be up to 255 characters. Click on **OK** .

3 If you close the query window, you will see the name of your query in the Queries list of the database window, from where it can be opened for use on another occasion.

Closing and opening a query

To close a query, either

1 Double-click on the query's control menu button. or

2 Choose **File-Close**.

You can open an existing query in either Design View or Datasheet View.

To open a query in Design View:

1 In the database window, click on the **Queries** tab.

2 Select the query you want to open, and then click on the **Design** button.

To open a query in Datasheet View

1 In the database window, click on the **Queries** tab.

2 Select the query you want to open, and then click on the **Open** button.

Task 3: Saving a query

In this task you will save the query created at the end of the previous task.

1 Choose **File-Save**.

2 Give the name *Members' Sporting Interests* to this query and click on **OK**.

3 Close the query and you should see the name of the query in the database window.

Printing a query

Before printing the dynaset produced by your query it is advisable to preview it first. To preview a **Queries** table:

1 Open the query.

2 In the datasheet view, click on the **Print Preview** button on the toolbar. You will be shown a preview that displays a miniature version of what is to be printed.

3 The pointer becomes a magnifying glass and can be use to zoom-in to the page. If you use other Windows applications you will be familiar with this. Clicking will toggle between zoom-in and zoom-out modes. When zoomed-in the vertical and horizontal scroll bars can be used to scroll around your previewed page.

4 Clicking the right mouse button will give a shortcut menu of preview and printing commands.

 5 To adjust the column widths you need to return to the Datasheet View. To do this click on the **View** button. The column widths are adjusted in the same way as for table datasheets as described in Unit 7.

Once you are satisfied that the preview is correct, then from the Print Preview mode:

1 Choose **File-Print**. The **Print** dialog box appears. If you want to print without changing anything then *skip the following three steps*. Note, to print directly without displaying the **Print** dialog box then click on the **Print** button in the toolbar.

2 Click on the **Setup** button and the **Page Setup** dialog box appears.

3 To change the margins click in the appropriate box and edit the default setting. You can select the orientation of the page, the printer and the paper size. The **Print Headings** check box, if not checked, will suppress the printing of the field names as headings. Click on **OK** to return to the **Print** dialog box.

4 Click on **OK** . Click on the **Close** button to return to the query datasheet.

Task 4: Printing

In this task the dynaset produced by the query created in Task 3 will be printed.

1 From the database window open the query in Datasheet View.

2 Click on the **Print Preview** button on the toolbar.

3 Some columns may need widening. Change to Datasheet View and widen the columns (see *Customising the datasheet layout*, Unit 7).

4 Preview again, zoom in to check that the columns are wide enough, click on the **Print** button.

5 Click on **OK** in the **Print** dialog box and the following dynaset should be printed.

Surname	Sex	Category No	Sporting Interests
Walker	Male	2	Tennis, squash
Cartwright	Female	1	Aerobics, swimming, running, squash
Perry	Male	6	Judo, Karate
Forsythe	Female	2	
Jameson	Female	1	Aerobics, squash
Robinson	Female	3	Swimming, Judo
Harris	Male	5	Badminton, cricket
Shangali	Male	2	Weight training, squash
Barrett	Female	1	Keep fit, swimming
Weiner	Male	1	Weight training, squash
Ali	Male	6	Judo, swimming, football
Young	Female	2	Keep fit, Aerobics, squash
Gray	Male	5	
Swift	Female	5	
Davies	Female	1	Aerobics, squash, swimming
Robinson	Female	1	Tennis, Aerobics
Everett	Male	2	Squash, Fitness training, football
Locker	Male	4	
Locker	Female	4	
Jones	Male	1	Weight training

6 Click on the **Close** button to return to the Datasheet View.

Deleting a query

Some queries may only be used once, in which case it is not really worth saving them. Queries that will be used more than once should be saved but a query may have a limited usefulness or be superseded. Therefore, from time to time some queries will need to be removed.

However, care needs to be taken when removing a query. Later, we will see that reports and forms can be based upon queries so it is important to assign these to alternative queries or to delete them as well. At present there is nothing based on the queries we have created and they may be deleted safely.

To delete a query, from the database window, click on the **Queries** tab to display the queries. Highlight the query that is to be deleted and press *Delete*.

Task 5: Deleting a query

In this task you will delete the query created using the Simple Query Wizard.

1   Display the queries in the database window.

2   Select the query, **Dates of Joining** and press *Delete*.

3   Reply **Yes** to confirm the delete operation.

Sorting the dynaset

What you will learn in this unit

The dynaset or result of a query can be displayed in different orders. If no sorting order is specified then the records in the datasheet will be shown in their natural order, i.e. the order in which they were entered. Sorting is particularly useful. For example if the records are shown in date of birth order then it is easier to see an age profile; if records are shown in town order, geographical information becomes apparent. If a report is to be created from the query (see Unit 19) then the order of the records can be defined by the query.

By the end of this unit you will be able to:

■ sort the information shown in the answer to your query.

Sorting the dynaset

You may wish to see your result in a particular order, for example, by last name or according to postal area. The grid in the lower section of the query design window includes a sort row. To define the type of sorting:

1   Click in the sort cell for the field in which you are interested. A list box button appears at the end of the cell.

2   Clicking on the list box button will reveal the sorting choices.

| Ascending |
| Descending |
| (not sorted) |

Ascending will sort from low to high, descending from high to low and not sorted will not apply any sorting.

Note: There is an order of priority when more than one field is being sorted. This is determined by the order of the fields in the query; leftmost fields being of higher priority.

Task 1: Sorting

This task investigates the different orders in which the query created in Task 2 of Unit 10 can be displayed.

1   From the design view of this query, click in the sort cell for the **Lastname** field.

2   Open the list box and choose **Ascending**.

3 Display the dynaset by clicking on the [**Run Query**] button. Return to the Design View.

4 Change the sort order of the **Lastname** field to (**not sorted**).

5 Choose Ascending as the order for the **Sex** field.

6 Display the dynaset. Return to the Design View.

7 Choose Ascending order for the **Lastname** and Descending order for the **Sex** fields, respectively. What order do you expect the data for the twins to be shown? View the dynaset.

8 Close the query without saving it.

Task 2: Sort order priority

For this task you will create a simple query to illustrate the effect that the order of the fields in the query has upon the priority of sort order. By choosing different priorities and viewing the resulting dynaset, the effect can be appreciated.

1 Create a new query using the **Membership** table.

2 Add the fields **Category No**, **Town** and **Lastname** to this query.

3 Choose Ascending as the order for both the **Category No** and **Town** fields.

4 Run the query to view the resulting dynaset.

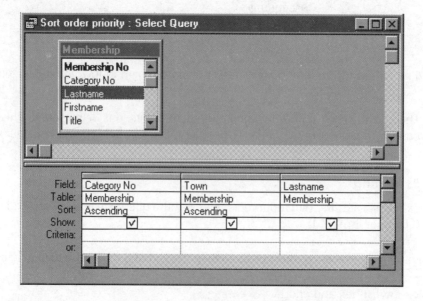

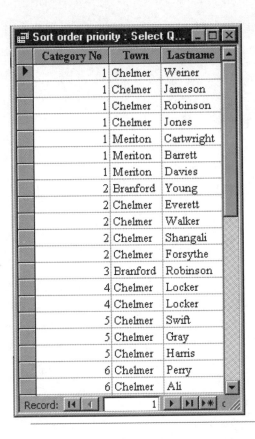

5   Return to the query design window and select the **Category No** field by clicking
    at the top of the column (while the pointer looks like a down pointing arrow).
    With the column selected point to the field header (pointer should be left
    pointing arrow shape) click and drag to reposition it *after* the **Town** field. Leave
    the sort order of **Category No** as ascending.

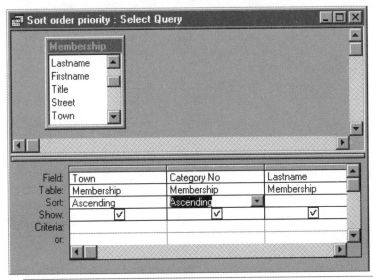

6 View the resulting dynaset, which should be in a different order from the previous one.

7 Close this query without saving it.

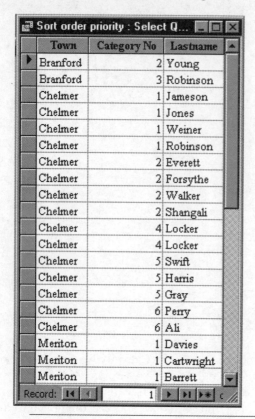

Town	Category No	Lastname
Branford	2	Young
Branford	3	Robinson
Chelmer	1	Jameson
Chelmer	1	Jones
Chelmer	1	Weiner
Chelmer	1	Robinson
Chelmer	2	Everett
Chelmer	2	Forsythe
Chelmer	2	Walker
Chelmer	2	Shangali
Chelmer	4	Locker
Chelmer	4	Locker
Chelmer	5	Swift
Chelmer	5	Harris
Chelmer	5	Gray
Chelmer	6	Perry
Chelmer	6	Ali
Meriton	1	Davies
Meriton	1	Cartwright
Meriton	1	Barrett

Sort order priority : Select Q...

Record: 1

Using query criteria

What you will learn in this unit

There are many reasons for asking questions. In business, questions are important in decision making, and to be able to question data relating to, for example, marketing or management, can be very effective using a database management system. In the case of Chelmer Leisure and Recreation Centre the answers to such questions can help with decisions regarding:

- where members come from and the effect of local competition

- no-smoking areas being introduced

- activities and facilities for older members

- discount scheme for loyal members

- fees charged for various categories.

To ask questions, criteria need to be set and entered into the criteria cells of the **Query** design grid. Querying is done by example, so an example of the answer to the question is entered into the criteria cell.

By the end of this unit you will be able to:

- enter query criteria

- rename and hide fields in a query

- use logic in queries.

Entering query criteria

Query criteria basically allow the enquirer to frame questions that enable specific records to be retrieved from the database. We might want to find out various things using the data stored in a table. For example, some questions that might be asked about the **Membership** table are:

- Which members live in Chelmer?

- Which members smoke?

- Which members are over 60?

- Which members joined before 1/1/92?

- Which members are in categories 1 and 2?

Task 1: Query criteria for the membership table

In this task the questions mentioned above will be formulated as queries for the

Membership table. The queries use the datatypes Text, Number, Date and Yes/No. Each question will be dealt with in turn.

1 Create a new query using the **Membership** table.

2 Add all the fields to the query.

Which members live in Chelmer?

1 In the **Criteria** cell of the **Town** field type *Chelmer*

2 Click on the **Datasheet** or **Run Query** button and the resulting dynaset should only contain records for which the Town field is equal to Chelmer.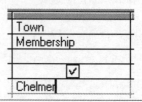

3 Return to the design view. Notice that Access puts double quotes around your criterion if it thinks it is text. Delete the criterion "Chelmer". Select the cell by double-clicking and press *Delete* to clear the cell. Alternatively click in the cell and use the backspace key to delete the criterion.

Which members smoke?

1 In the **Criteria** cell of the **Smoker** field type *Yes*. You may need to scroll to the right to display this cell on the screen.

2 Click on the **Datasheet** or **Run Query** button and view the resulting dynaset.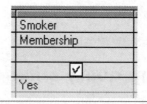

3 Return to the Design View. Delete the last criterion.

Which members are over 60?

1 In the **Criteria** cell of the **Date of Birth** field type *<1/1/37*.

2 Click on the **Datasheet** or **Run Query** button and view the resulting dynaset. Return to the Design View. Notice that Access has recognised your query example as a date and converted it to <#01/01/37#.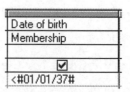

3   Delete this criterion.

Which members joined before 1/1/92?

1   In the **Criteria** cell of the **Date of joining** field type *<1/1/92.*

2   Click on the **Datasheet** or **Run Query** button and view the resulting dynaset.

3   Return to the Design View. Delete this criterion.

Which members are in categories 1 and 2?

1   In the **Criteria** cell of the **Category No** field type *<=2.*

2   Click on the **Datasheet** or **Run Query** button and view the resulting dynaset.

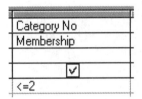

3   Return to the Design View.

4   Close the query without saving it.

Renaming and hiding fields in a query

When queries are printed it is sometimes necessary to widen the column so that the field name at the top of the column can be seen. This in turn can lead to unnecessarily wide columns, so it is useful to be able to rename the field. The field header can be renamed in a query with an alternative name, for example, **Last Renewed** instead of **Date of Last Renewal.**

Note: Renaming the field header does not affect the name of the field in the underlying table.

To change field header names:

1   Switch to query design mode by clicking on the **Query Design** button. Move the insertion point to the column containing the field header name you wish to change.

2 Point to the beginning of the field header and click. The aim is to put the flashing insertion point at the beginning of the header name. If you accidentally select the header, press *F2* to de-select it. If the insertion point is not at the beginning, then press the *Home* key to move it to the first character position.

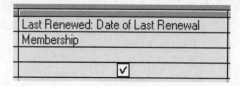

FIGURE 12.1

3 Type in the new name for the field, followed by a colon (FIGURE 12.1). Do not put a space between the name and the colon. The colon separates the name you type from the existing field name, which moves to the right to make room for your addition.

4 Click on the **Datasheet** or **Run Query** button and the query result with amended field header will be displayed.

In the previous two units you have seen how to select the fields you want in the result of a query and how to impose criteria. These can be combined so that the dynaset is only the records that match the criteria and contains only the fields specified in the query. To be able to impose a criterion on a field, that field needs to be in the query grid, which means that it will form part of the dynaset. This may not always be desirable so Access offers the choice of whether or not the field forms part of the dynaset. By default all fields in the query show in the dynaset as the 'Show' cell is on; to hide a field click in the box in the **Show** cell. The tick disappears and the field will not form part of the dynaset.

Task 2: Renaming and hiding fields in a query

Query 1

The following query lists the names and addresses of all the male members who are smokers.

1 Create a new query using the **Membership** table.

2 Add the following fields: **Membership No**, **Title**, **Lastname**, **Street**, **Town**, **County**, **Post Code**, **Smoker**, **Sex**.

3 In the criteria fields of **Smoker** and **Sex** put *Yes*. Hide these fields.

4 Sort the **Lastname field** in ascending order.

5 Rename **Membership No** as *Member No* and display the dynaset.

Member No	Title	Lastname	Street	Town	County	Post Code
13	Mr	Gray	4 The Parade	Chelmer	Cheshire	CH17ER
7	Mr	Harris	55 Coven Road	Chelmer	Cheshire	CH3 8PS
20	Mr	Jones	17 Mayfield Avenue	Chelmer	Cheshire	CH2 9OL
1	Mr	Walker	16 Dovecot Close	Chelmer	Cheshire	CH2 6TR

6 Save the query as **Addresses of Male Smokers**. Close the query.

Query 2

In this task you create a query which looks at the occupations of the female members of the centre. The result of this query will be selected fields from selected records.

1 Create a new query using the **Membership** table.

2 Add the following fields to the query: **Category No, Firstname, Lastname, Occupation, Sex.**

3 In the criteria cell of the **Sex** field type *No*.

4 Click on the check box in the **Show** cell of the **Sex** field to hide it.

5 Click at the beginning of the **Category No** Header and type *Cat:* (do not type a space before the colon).

6 Click on the **Datasheet** or **Run Query** button to view the result of the query. The **Category No** field should have the header **Cat** and the **Sex** field should be hidden.

7 Save the query as *Occupations of Female Members.*

Exploring types of query criteria

The queries that have been created so far in this session have only used criteria in one field. Criteria may be applied to all the fields included in a query. Each field may be sorted or hidden. By combining these, more complex queries can be produced.

We have already used some of the operators used in criteria. The table following summarises them.

Operator	Meaning
Mathematical operators	
<	less than
>	greater than

Operator	Meaning
<>	not equal to
>=	greater than or equal to
<=	less than or equal to
+	addition
-	subtraction
*	multiplication
/	division

Text operators

"J*"	text strings beginning with J
"*ton"	text strings ending with ton
"*k*"	text strings containing the letter k

Using logic in queries

You can ask questions in queries which relate to more than one field, for example, male smokers (Query 1 in Task 2). The question is 'Is the member male AND does he smoke?' There is a logical AND between the two criteria; both criteria must be true for the record to be retrieved.

What if a logical AND is required on the same field, for example, members whose date of joining was after 1/1/92 AND before the 1/1/93 (Query 2 in Task 3 below)? In the criteria cell the word 'and' is used between the two criteria, for example, **>=1/1/92 and <1/1/93**. More than two criteria may be specified but remember to put the word AND between them.

The other form of logic that is used in queries is OR. There is a row entitled or: in the query design grid. An example of this would be a query which requires as its answer the names and addresses of members that live in Chelmer OR Meriton. The way in which this query is set up is to enter **Chelmer** into the criteria row of the Town field and underneath in the or: row to enter **Meriton**. The example query below (Query 3 in Task 3) lists the names of the members who are likely to use the fitness suite as their sporting interests are Aerobics, Fitness training or Weight training.

Task 3: Using different types of query criteria

Query 1 - querying text fields

This query picks out people with particular sporting interests

1   Create a new query using the **Membership** table.

2   Add the following fields: **Membership No, Lastname, Category No, Sporting Interests**.

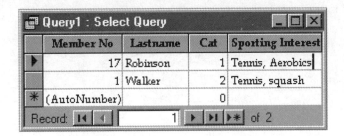

3   In the criteria field of **Sporting Interests** type **Tennis**. Note that Access will convert this to read **Like *Tennis***.

4   Sort the **Lastname** field in Ascending order.

5   Rename **Membership No** as *Member No* and **Category No** as *Cat*.

6   Display the dynaset.

7   Print the dynaset.

8   Save the query giving it the name *Sporting Interest* and close the query.

Query 2 - logic, using AND

This query picks out members who joined in 1992.

1   Create a new query using the **Membership** table.

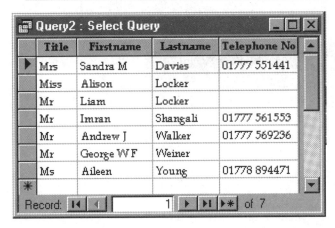

2   Add the following fields: **Title**, **Firstname**, **Lastname**, **Telephone No**, **Date of Joining**.

3   In the criteria fields of **Date of Joining** type *>=1/1/92 and <1/1/93*. Note that Access will convert this to read >=#01/01/92# And <#01/01/93#.

4   Hide the **Date of Joining** field.

5   Sort the **Lastname** field in ascending order.

6   Display the dynaset.

7   Print the dynaset.

8   Save the query giving it the name **_When joined_** and close the query.

Query 3 - logic using OR

This query picks out members whose sporting interests are either aerobics, fitness training or weight training and shows their home town so that local interest can be assessed.

1   Create a new query using the **Membership** table.

2   Add the following fields: **Membership No**, **Category No**, **Lastname**, **Town**, **Sporting Interests**

3   In the criteria field of Sporting Interests type **_*aerobics*_**. Note that Access will add the word **_Like_**, whether you type **_*aerobics*_**, **_'*aerobics*'_** or **_"*aerobics*"_**.

Member No	Cat	Lastname	Town
2	1	Cartwright	Meriton
15	1	Davies	Meriton
17	2	Everett	Chelmer
5	1	Jameson	Chelmer
20	1	Jones	Chelmer
16	1	Robinson	Chelmer
8	2	Shangali	Chelmer
10	1	Weiner	Chelmer
12	2	Young	Branford
(AutoNumber)	0		Chelmer

Record: 1 of 9

5 In the **or:** field of **Sporting Interests** type *fitness training*

6 In the row below type *weight training*

7 Hide the **Sporting Interests** field.

8 Sort the **Lastname** field in ascending order.

9 Display the dynaset. Notice that when querying text Access is not case sensitive, *aerobics* will find aerobics, AEROBICS or Aerobics.

10 Print the dynaset.

11 Close the query without saving.

More complex queries

What you will learn in this unit

By the end of this unit you will be able to:

- edit and rename a query

- create new fields by calculation

- count and average fields, and group and average fields

- use criteria in a summary query.

Queries can perform calculations on the data in the table. Calculations may count the number of records, add up or take the average of certain fields or create new fields by calculation. In the following task a new field **Age** is created and the average age of the members calculated. A new field can be created from a calculation using existing fields in the table, for example, if there is a price field which doesn't include sales tax then a **Sales Tax** field can be calculated by multiplying the price by the rate of the tax.

There is a wide range of different applications where it might be appropriate to perform calculations as part of a query. Here we briefly explain some of the basic concepts and give a few examples.

To create a calculated field, in the next empty field cell enter an expression to calculate the new field. The expression takes the form **Name of calculated field:Expression**. The expression is the formula for creating the value of this field. An expression involves other fields and these are written enclosed in square brackets, for example, **Taxable pay:[Gross Pay]-[Free Pay] or VAT:[Cost]*0.175**.

Expressions may be used with date data types and there are several date functions available, the two that are used in the task following are :

- Year() which returns the year of the date/time value enclosed in brackets as an integer number, for example Year([Date of Joining]) might result in 1992

- Now() which returns the date and time of the computer's system clock.

Sometimes it is useful to produce some summary statistics as a result of your query, for example the number of fields, the total of values in those fields or the average of the fields. These statistics may be for all the records in the table or just for the ones selected by the query. Click on the **Totals** or **Sigma** button on the toolbar to gain access to the statistics functions, which can be entered into the Total row Σ which appears when the **Totals** button is depressed (FIGURE 13.1).

FIGURE 13.1

Each cell in the **Total:** row has its own drop down list. Various statistical functions are available.

Function	Purpose
Count	will give the number of records
Sum	will give a total of all values in that particular field
Min, Max	will give the maximum or minimum value of that particular field
Avg, StDev, Var	the average, standard deviation, variance of a particular field
Group by	groups records according to this field producing summary statistics for each group
Where	allows criteria to be specified

Editing and renaming a query

Once a query has been saved it can be used again and again. More records may be added to the table; each time a query is used it uses the data currently held in the table. However, as a database develops then a query may be changed to accommodate changing requirements. If the query is modified it may be advisable to change its name so that it remains as meaningful as possible.

Task 1: Creating a new field by calculation

1   Create a new query using the **Membership** table.

2   Add the fields **Date of Birth** and **Lastname**.

3 Click in the next field cell and create
a calculated field by typing
**Age:Year(Now())-Year([Date of
Birth])**

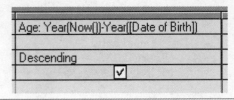

4 Sort the **Age** field in descending order.

5 Display the dynaset.

6 Print the dynaset.

7 Save the query with the name **Member ages**.

Task 2: Counting and averaging fields

Continue with the query created in Task 1.

1 Click on the **Totals** button to display the **Total**: row.

2 In the **Total** cell for the **Lastname** and **Date of Birth** fields select **Count**.

3 In the total cell for the **Age** field put **Avg**.

Field:	Lastname	Date of birth	Age: [Year(Now())-Year([Date of Birth])]
Table:	Membership	Membership	
Total:	Count	Count	Avg
Sort:			Descending
Show:	☑	☑	☑
Criteria:			
or:			

4 Run the query.

The result of this query is different from the normal dynaset display. One row is displayed which contains summary information according to the specification in the **Total** row. Returning to the design view and clicking on the **Totals** button will cause the **Total** row to disappear and the query reverts to that in Task 1.

CountOfLastname	CountOfDate of birth	Age
20	19	35.94736842

If you save the summary form of this query, and close it, when you open it again, notice that Access will have changed the calculated field to **Age: Avg(Year(Now())-Year([Date of Birth]))** and put **Expression** in the **Total** row.

Why is **Count of Lastname** different from **Count of Date of Birth?** Refer back to the section on null values in Unit 6.

Task 3: Grouping and averaging fields

Continue with the query in Task 2, by returning to the query design.

1 Add the **Category No** field to the query.

2 In the **Total** cell for the **Category No** field select **Group by** and choose **Ascending** as the sort order for this field.

3 Remove the sort order from **Age** and arrange your query as illustrated below:

Field:	Category No	Lastname	Date of birth	Age: [Year[Now[]]-Year[[Date of Birth]
Table:	Membership	Membership	Membership	
Total:	Group By	Count	Count	Avg
Sort:	Ascending			
Show:	☑	☑	☑	☑
Criteria:				
or:				

4 Run the query.

Category	CountOfLastname	CountOfDate of birth	Age
1	7	7	34.28571429
2	5	5	39.4
3	1	1	13
4	2	2	14
5	3	3	63
6	2	1	16

This time a row for each category is displayed, containing in the **Age** field the average age of members in each membership category.

Task 4: Using criteria in a summary query

Continue with the previous query by returning to the query design.

1 In the **Total** cell for the **Category No** field select **Where**.

2 In the **Criteria** row put 1 or 2 (this is equivalent to putting 1 in the **Criteria** row and 2 in the **Or** row).

3 Remove the sort order from **Category No**.

83

4   Hide the **Category No** field.

Field:	Lastname ▾	Date of birth	Age: Avg([Year(Now())-Year([Date of Birth])])	Category No
Table:	Membership	Membership		Membership
Total:	Count	Count	Expression	Where
Sort:				
Show:	☑	☑	☑	☐
Criteria:				1 Or 2
or:				

5   Run the query. The result should be the total number of members in categories 1 and 2 and their average age.

CountOfLastname	CountOfDate of birth	Age
12	12	36.41666667

6   Try this for categories 3 and 4.

7   Save the query.

8   Rename this query as **Average Ages** (see below).

9   With **Member Ages** selected in the database window, choose **Edit-Rename** and change the name to **Average Ages**.

Task 5: Additional queries

This task takes the form of a series of questions plus the rationale for the questions. All queries are created using the **Membership** table.

1   *What is the occupation of women members with sporting interests of aerobics?*

If a large majority of women members whose sporting interests include aerobics have stated that they are housewives then a ladies aerobics class could be scheduled in the day rather than the evening. The fields that might be appropriate for this query, in addition to **Sporting Interests** and **Sex**, are **Membership No**, **Category No**, **Title**, **Initials**, **Lastname** and **Occupation**. Try sorting on **Category No**.

2   *What is the home town of male members with sporting interests of weight training?*

Does the centre offer better weight training facilities than the local competition and so attract members from a wide area? The fields that might be appropriate for this query, in addition to **Sporting Interests** and **Sex**, are **Initials**, **Lastname**, **Category No** and **Town**. Sort on the **Town** field in Ascending order.

3 *Which members joined the centre between 1/1/93 and 1/1/94?*

This query can easily be created by referring to the second query in Task 3 in Unit 12. Such queries can be used to assess the success of the centre.

4 *Which members are aged between 18 and 25?*

Should the bar consider holding social events targeted at this age group? Are there enough members locally in this age group to make this worthwhile? The fields that might be appropriate for this query, are **Name**, all address fields and **Sporting Interests**. Sort the query in **Post Code** order in Ascending order.

5 *Which members are either housewives or unemployed or retired?*

Technically this query ought to include househusbands, although there are none listed in the data given for members! The centre may consider a range of day-time activities which would appeal to this group. The fields that might be appropriate for this query, are **Membership No**, **Category No**, **Date of Birth** and **Sex**. Sort the query in **Date of Birth** order.

6 *Which members have sporting interests of Keep fit and Aerobics?*

The fields that might be appropriate for this query, are **Membership No**, **Lastname**, **Category No** and **Date of Birth**. Sort in Ascending order both the **Category No** and **Date of Birth**, with **Category No** having the higher priority.

Designing and using screen forms

What you will learn in this unit

In this unit you will learn how to create a screen form. A screen form provides a more user friendly way with which to work with your data. Entering data can be made easier and less prone to error.

By the end of this unit you will be able to:

■ create a form using the Form Wizard

■ save a form

■ use a form

■ print a form.

In Units 2 to 9 the tables for the Chelmer Leisure and Recreation Centre were defined. Data was entered into the **Membership** table but as yet data has not been entered into the other tables. In this and the following two units you will enter the data into these tables. This could be done as it was for the Membership data, using the datasheet view of the table. The disadvantage of using the datasheet view is that the fields in a record often do not all fit on the screen. Also viewing and entering data in the datasheet grid can be somewhat tiresome.

When data is collected manually it is often by means of filling out a form. In a form there are boxes to fill in with, for example, name, address, etc, and there may be some that are ticked, for example Yes/No boxes. Access offers the facility to create a form on the screen so that data can be entered into a table by simply filling in the form. This should be more user-friendly than filling in the cells in a datasheet provided that the form has been designed carefully.

A form can be based upon a table or a view created from a query. A query can use more than one table so the form created from such a query can be used to enter data into several different tables. This will be explored in later sessions. In this session we will concentrate on designing forms to enter data into the tables in the database. It is usual to have a form for each table of data for the purpose of entering and editing data in that table.

Forms can be used to enter, edit, display and print data contained in your tables. They offer the advantage of presenting data, on screen, in an organised and attractive manner.

Standard forms are created for most applications or jobs, for example, a form for entering the details of a new member, as shown in FIGURE 14.1.

Access allows you to create forms to your own design, for which it provides a wide range of tools. If you are a new Access user or simply for convenience the Form Wizard provides a quick and easy way to create a basic form. This basic form can be customised later. To enable us to get started quickly on form design we will make use of the Form Wizard.

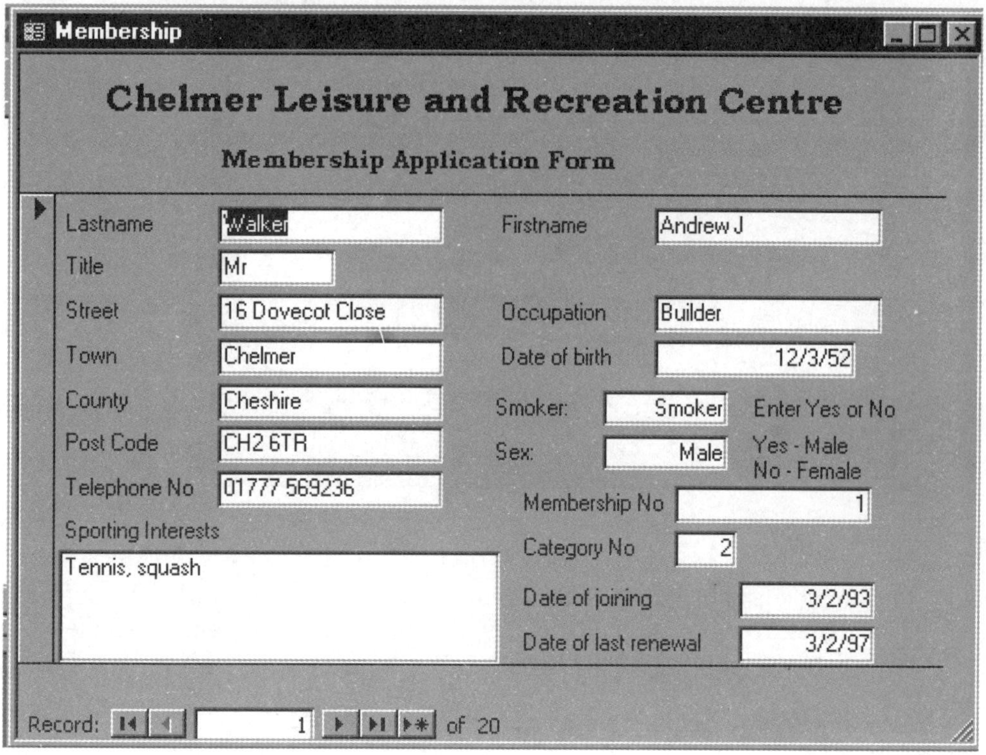

FIGURE 14.1

Creating a form with AutoForm

There are three types of form that can be created using AutoForm: columnar, tabular, and datasheet. A columnar form will display data from one record at a time, allowing the user to input one record at a time. The form shown in FIGURE 14.1 started as a columnar form but has been modified slightly. A columnar form has boxes to fill in, for the fields of information required for that record, and these are arranged in a column.

Tabular and Datasheet forms are very similar in that they display more than one record at once. Due to the tabular format, if there are a lot of fields in the records then an entire record will not fit on the screen.

AutoForm will create a form instantly using all fields in the records of the underlying table that you choose to base your form upon. To create a form using AutoForm, starting from the Database window, either:

■ click on the **Forms** tab and then click on the **New** button, or

■ click on the New Object button in the toolbar, select **Form** and a **New Form** dialog box appears (FIGURE 14.2).

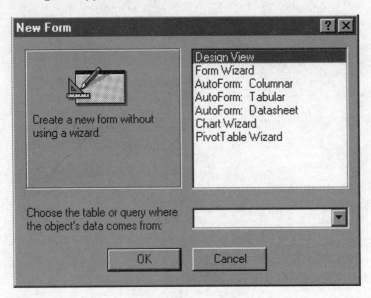

FIGURE 14.2

Click on the list box button of the **Choose the table or query where the object's data comes from** box, to produce a list of tables and queries, and select the table for which you wish to create a form.

Select one of the **AutoForm** options and click on OK .

Creating a form using Form Wizard

Form wizard allows a further type of form to be created called a justified form. This displays one record at a time in a row format.

To create a Form Wizard form, perform the two steps as above, then select **Form Wizard**, and click on OK . Check that the correct table is listed in the **Tables/Queries** box (if it isn't select the right one).

The next stage is to choose which fields are to be on the form. The fields that you can have in the form are shown in the **Available Fields** box.

These can be transferred to the **Selected fields** box by selecting each field in turn and clicking on the > button.

If you wish to add all the fields in the table to the form then click on the button.

You may set the order in which the fields appear on the form by selecting them in the order you desire. The $\boxed{<}$ button will remove a highlighted field and

$\boxed{<<}$ will remove all the fields from the form.

Once you have added the required fields to the form continue by clicking on the $\boxed{\text{Next>}}$ button.

Choose a Columnar, Tabular, Datasheet or Justified form. The layout of these was discussed above.

You are then asked what kind of style you want for your form and are given a choice. An example of the style is shown to the left of the dialog box. Click on each style in turn to see what it would look like. On the first occasion you create a form choose **Standard**; the style can be modified later. The next thing you are asked for is a title. Key in an appropriate title for your form into the text box. Now click on the $\boxed{\text{Finish}}$ button to display the form with data in it.

Saving and closing a form

Save a form by choosing **File-Save** or clicking on the $\boxed{\text{Save}}$ button. If this is a new form that you have not yet saved then Access will prompt you for a file name with a File-Save As dialog box. If you wish later to save this form with a different name then use **File-Save As** and fill in the appropriate details in the dialog box.

mber that there is a distinction between the name and the title of a form. The isplayed at the top of the form window. The name you give when saving the e form's file name which you need to be able to recognise when you want form for use again. These names appear in the database window when tab is selected.

be closed by using **File-Close** or the $\boxed{\text{Close}}$ button of the form win-form or the latest modification has not been saved you will be prompted en a form is closed its name (the one you gave to it when saving) will in the database window when the $\boxed{\text{Forms}}$ tab is selected.

To open a form from the database window, click on the $\boxed{\text{Forms}}$ tab, select the name of the form required and click on the $\boxed{\text{Open}}$ button.

Task 1: Creating a columnar membership form using AutoForm

In this task you will create a single column membership form which can later be modified to look like the form shown in FIGURE 14.1. The order in which the fields are selected for the form are important, as will become apparent when the form is used to enter data. To create this form:

1 From the database window click on the $\boxed{\text{Forms}}$ tab and click on the $\boxed{\text{New}}$ button.

2 Display the list of tables in the New Form dialog box and select **Membership** from the list of tables. Select **AutoForm: Columnar** and click on `OK`.

 Access creates a form with a title and a list of field names in one column with a corresponding list of data for the first record in another column. Notice that there are some differences between this form and the one shown in FIGURE 14.1. Customising the form will be considered in Unit 15.

3 Choose **File-Save** and give the form the name *Membership*.

4 Close the form.

Creating a tabular form

A tabular form is one that displays more than one record on the screen. The field names form headers for columns and the records are shown below in a table. The number of records displayed will depend upon the size of the window and the number of records in the table. If there are a lot of fields in a record it is unlikely that you will be able to see the complete record on the screen and you will need to scroll to the right to display more of the fields. This type of form is suited to records with only a few fields, such as those in the **Membership Category** table. The advantage of this form is that it displays more than one record at a time.

A tabular form may be created either using AutoForm or Form Wizard. The ing task considers creating a tabular form using the Form Wizard.

Task 2: Creating the membership category form

No data has been entered into the **Membership Category** table, this a form which can later be used for this purpose.

1 First close any open form.

2 From the database window with the `Forms` tab selected click on

3 In the New Form dialog box select the **Membership Category** table.

4 Select **FormWizard** and click on `OK`.

5 Add all the fields to the form and click on the `Next>` button.

6 Choose a **Tabular** form with a standard style.

7 Give it the title *Membership Category*.

8 Click on the `Finish` button to display the form.

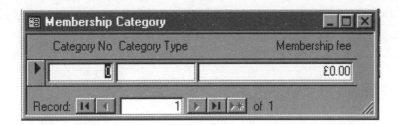

The difference between this form and the single column form is that the fields are arranged in columns. The top of the column is headed by the field name. There is no data in this form so there is only one blank record to display. When records have been added, as we shall see later, then more than one record is shown in the form.

9 Save the form as **Membership Category**.

10 Close the form.

Using a form

To use a form, first display the available forms in the database window by clicking on the Forms tab. Open the form either by selecting it and clicking on Open or by double-clicking on its name.

You can use the form to look at the data in the table (or query) upon which it is based. Whether it is a single column or tabular form use the record movement keys in the status bar or use the Edit-Goto menu to move around the records in your form. Using the *Page Up* and *Page Down* keys with a single column form will display the next/previous record whereas with a tabular form they will either page up or down a screenful of records.

Using the form to enter a new record into the table

Forms should be designed with this purpose in mind as it is their primary function. Entering data is a labour intensive task and the design of the form is important because it may be used for long periods by a person entering data.

To enter a new record using a form:

1 Go to the end of your records using the New Record button on the status bar. If your form is single column press the *Page Down* key and a blank form appears. If your form is tabular click in the first field of the blank record shown at the end of your records.

2 Enter data for another record by filling in the boxes for each field. When you have completed each text box (control) press *Enter* or *Tab* to move to the next one.

3 Check boxes are used for Yes/No fields. Checked is Yes, not checked No.

Task 3: Using a form to enter data into a table

In this task we shall enter data into the categories of membership table, using the tabular form just created.

1   Open the **Membership Category** form.

2   Enter data as shown below. As you enter each record it is saved to the **Membership Category** table.

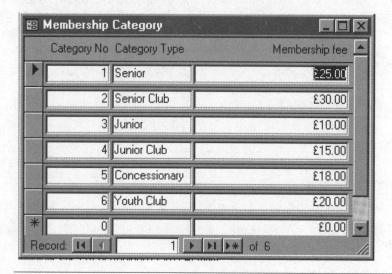

3   Close the form

4   Now there is data in the form use Tools-Relationships to create the link between the **Membership Category** and **Membership** tables. Drag **Category No** (**Membership Category**) to **Category No** on the **Membership** table. Check in the Enforce Referential Integrity check box. Refer back to Unit 8.

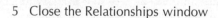

5   Close the Relationships window

Printing a form

Forms are designed primarily for screen use, i.e. they are intended for data to be entered via the computer and they display the data on screen. However, Access offers the facility to print from a form. Always preview a form before printing it. A form can be previewed from either the run or Design View mode.

Previewing

Previewing will display a miniature version of what is to be printed. This allows the layout to be assessed so that adjustments can be made before printing.

To preview a form:

1 Click on the **Print Preview** button in the toolbar, 🔍 and a miniature version of what is to be printed will be displayed.

2 To zoom-in and zoom-out simply click anywhere on the preview, or use the **Zoom** button. Clicking on the right mouse button will allow you to select the degree of magnification.

3 Choose **File-Page Setup** to make adjustments such as the orientation (portrait or landscape) the choice of printer and the width of the margins. Click on **OK** when the required adjustments have been made.

Printing

When satisfied that the preview is correct, printing may be done from either the preview screen or the form screen. To print from the preview screen:

1 Choose **File-Print**.

2 Select whether all or only certain pages of the form will be printed and the number of copies. Click on **OK**.

To print from the form screen follow the procedure above.

Task 4: Printing the membership category form

To print this form:

1 Open the **Membership Category** form.

2 Click on the **Print Preview** button.

3 Experiment with zooming-in and zooming-out.

4 Use **File-Page Setup** and/or **File-Print** to make adjustments before printing. If no adjustments are necessary, then click on the **Print** button.

5 Close the form.

Customising forms

What you will learn in this unit

 Forms are constructed from a collection of individual design elements, which are called controls. If you are familiar with Windows applications you will be familiar with dialog boxes and the controls that they contain. The controls that appear on the forms created so far are:

- labels, so that you know what each part of the form is for

- text boxes, for entering data.

 There are other controls, which will be introduced in Unit 21.

By the end of this unit you will be able to:

- display the customising tools (toolbox, palette, properties and field list)
- move and size controls
- align controls
- add text to a form
- add the date
- add headers and footers to a printed form.

Customising a form

A form may be modified so that it is easier for inexperienced users to enter information into the database. To modify a form you need to display the form in design mode (see following section). AutoForm or Form Wizard is a good way of quickly creating a form. However, the resulting form is rather standardised in terms of vertical spacing between controls, fonts and colours, so you are likely to wish to make modifications.

Components of a form in design view

Component	Description
Form Header	Contains text such as the form's title, but field headers and graphics may also be put into a header section.
Detail	Contains the controls (field labels, text boxes and check boxes) that display data from your table for which the form has been designed.
Form Footer	Similar in function to the Form Header and may contain information such as the date.

Right Margin	The position of the right margin is indicated by a vertical line on the right edge of the form. It can be moved by clicking and dragging.
Bottom Margin	A horizontal line that indicates the bottom margin of the form. This also can be positioned by clicking and dragging.
Scroll Bars	Vertical and horizontal scroll bars enable movement of the form within its window.

If you have used a Form Wizard to create the form, only the detail band and possibly the header band contain controls. The header band contains information which will always appear at the top of the form, usually the title. The detail band contains the controls for displaying the data.

Form design view

So far in this series of units a form has only been opened in 'form run' or data view. This is the mode in which forms are usually run where they display and more importantly, accept data. A form can also be shown in Design View, which allows modifications to be made to its layout. In Design View, which cannot be entered into the form, only the layout and appearance of the form can be changed. A form has a different appearance in Design View, as illustrated in FIGURE 15.1.

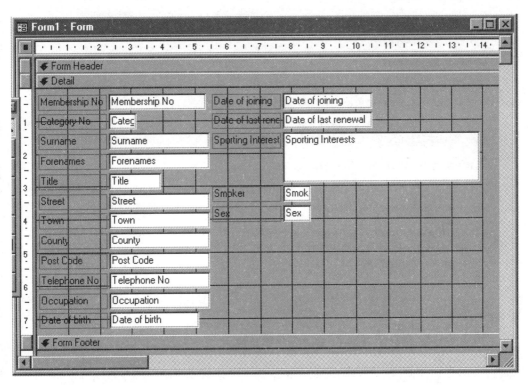

FIGURE 15.1

Instead of data appearing in the controls, the field names appear. Text or controls may be selected and moved to achieve the layout desired.

Label and text box controls

A field usually has two controls: a label control in which the field name appears and a text box control in which the data will appear when the form is run.

Extra windows

Other features of design mode are the availability of rulers and grid and design aids in the form of other small windows: the Toolbox, Field List and Properties Sheet.

The Toolbox offers a selection of tools by which controls and text may be added to the form; the Field List shows a list of fields in the table that the form was based upon; and the Properties sheet is a list of properties. The properties will depend upon what part of the form is selected. You will become familiar with these as you progress through the tasks. To display the Toolbox click on the **Toolbox** button or use **View-Toolbox**. To display the Field List click on the **Field list** button or choose **View-Field List**. To display the Properties sheet click on the **Properties** button on the toolbar or choose **View-Properties**.

The buttons are (from left to right) the **Field list** button, the **Toolbox** button and the **Properties** button.

Colour selection

 Colour selection can be made using the drop down buttons on the formatting toolbar. These will be considered in Unit 27.

Opening a form in design view

To open a form in Design View, from the database window, click on the **Forms** tab, select the name of the form required and click on the **Design** button.

Once a form is open you may switch between the form run (data) view and the design view by clicking on the button on the toolbar, or by selecting **View-Design View**, or **View-Form View**.

Form View   Design View

Moving and sizing controls

Before you can move or size a control you must select it. A control is selected by clicking anywhere on its surface. When selected the control is enclosed by an outlining rectangle with an anchor rectangle at its upper left corner and five smaller rectangles. These smaller rectangles are sizing handles. On columnar forms text boxes often have associated labels and when you select one of these objects they are selected together as a unit.

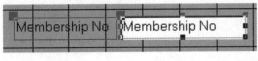

To...	Do this
Select a text box control and its label (if it has a label)	Click anywhere on either the label or the text box.
Move a text box control and its label (if it has a label)	After selecting, move the pointer over the label until it changes shape to a hand. Click and drag the label and entry box to new position.
Move label or text box control separately	After selecting, move the pointer over the anchor handle at the top left corner of either the label or text box control. The pointer should change shape to a pointing hand. Click and drag to new position.
Adjust the width and height of a control simultaneously	Move the pointer over one of the small sizing handles at one of the three other corners. It should change to a diagonal two-headed arrow. Click and drag to size required.
Adjust only the height of the control	Move the pointer over one of the sizing handles on the horizontal surface of the outline. It should change shape to a vertical two-headed arrow. Click and drag to height required.
Adjust only the width of the control	Move the pointer over one of the sizing handles on the vertical surface of the outline. It should change shape to a horizontal two-headed arrow. Click and drag to width required.

Selecting and moving a group of controls

You can select and move more than one object at a time. This is useful if you want to keep the relative spacing of a group of objects yet want to move them to another part of the form.

To select a group of objects, either:

■ imagine that the group of objects is enclosed by a rectangle (each object need only be partly enclosed by the rectangle); use the pointer and by clicking and dragging draw this rectangle on the form; when you release the mouse button all the objects within this rectangle will be selected, or

■ select one object, hold down the *Shift* key whilst selecting the next and subsequent objects (this is easier when controls are in close proximity).

To move:

- the whole group, with pointer as the shape of a hand then drag
- an individual control in the group, point to its anchor handle and drag.

To deselect:

- one object in the group, click on it while holding down the *Shift* key
- the whole group, click anywhere outside the selected area.

To move the group of objects click and drag the anchor handle of any of the objects in the group.

Using the ruler and the grid

The **View-Ruler** command will select whether or not the ruler is displayed. When a control is being dragged, indicator lines slide along both rulers to aid positioning of controls.

View-Grid will display or hide a grid, which is also an aid to the positioning of controls. The spacing of the grid can be adjusted by adjusting the setting of the **GridX** and **GridY** properties on the form's property sheet. To display the form property sheet use **Edit-Select Form** and click on the **Properties** button.

When **Format-Snap to Grid** is on, which is indicated by a tick by **Snap to Grid** in the menu, any new controls drawn on the form will have their corners aligned to points on the grid. When **Snap to Grid** is off, the control can be placed anywhere.

Aligning a group of controls

Once you start to move controls around the form they can become untidy as they become misaligned. By selecting a group of controls together they can be aligned. Select labels and text boxes separately for alignment purposes. To align labels:

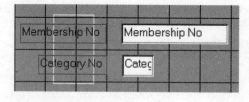 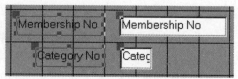

FIGURE 15.2

1 Select the labels by clicking on each label while holding down the *Shift* key. as illustrated in FIGURE 15.2. Alternatively, draw a rectangle that encloses part or all of all the labels you wish to select.

2 Choose **Format-Align** and as these are labels select **Right**. The selected group of controls should all align to the right.

To align text box controls:

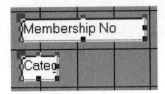

FIGURE 15.3

1   Select the text box controls by clicking on each text box while holding down the *Shift* key (FIGURE 15.3).

2   Choose **Format-Align** and as these are text boxes select **Left**. The selected group of controls should all align to the left.

Changing the form's area

The area of each section of a form – the header, detail and footer – may be altered individually. Also, the position of the right and bottom edge of a form may be adjusted. To alter the depth of a section of the form:

1   Move the pointer to the bottom edge of the section, where it will change shape

$\updownarrow$;

2   Drag down to increase the depth of the section.

To alter the area of the form drag the right and bottom edges to the size that you require.

Task 1: Customising the membership form

The aim of this task is to create the form shown in FIGURE 14.1. We don't give exact instructions as you can experiment with selecting and moving controls. You may find it useful to widen the form temporarily so that controls can be moved to temporary positions while you rearrange them on the form. If you wish to keep a group of controls together, select them as a group and then they can be moved as a group. Also try aligning groups of controls to achieve a tidy looking form.

1   Open the **Membership** form in design view.

2   If you inadvertently delete a field from the form see the following table for instructions on how to restore it.

3   When you have rearranged the detail section save the form design using **File-Save**.

Deleting or restoring fields from or to a form

To...	Do this
Delete a label or label and text box	Select the control and press *Delete* or use **Edit-Delete** to delete both label and entry box. To delete only the label click on it again before deleting.
	Note: if you delete a field you won't be able to use the form to enter data into this field. Use **Edit-Undo** if you unintentionally delete a field.
Restoring a label and field	Use **View-Field list** to display the list of fields available in the table. Click on the field name required and drag to the required position on the form. If the form is a single column form then both label and field will appear, although the label will require editing. If the form is a tabular one then just the field will be restored.

Changing the text of a field name label

The text of a field name label may be edited and, if required, additional text can be added to the form.

To...	Do this
Add a label	Click on the **Label** tool in the Toolbox window (see FIGURE 21.1), click on the form in the required position and type the text required.
Edit a label	Double-click on the label to display an insertion point in the text. Edit the text as required. Press *Enter* or click on a blank part of the form when finished.

Altering the size and font of controls

To alter the size or font of controls in a form.

1   Select the control(s) to be altered.

2   Open the **Font** list box in the toolbar and select the font required.

3   Open the **Point Size** list box and select the point size required.

4   Click on the left, centre or right alignment button in toolbar.

Note: if you increase the size of a font you may need to alter the size of the control and the size of the section.

Task 2: Adding text to the form header

In this task you will add text to the header section of the **Membership** form.

1 Open the **Membership** form in design mode.

2 Widen the Form header section.

3 Click on the **Label** tool in the Toolbox window.

4 Click in the space created for the form header and key in the text **Chelmer Leisure and Recreation Centre**.

5 Increase the size of the label and text. You may wish to change the font.

 6 Move and size the heading as in FIGURE 14.1, add the text **Membership Application Form**. If you wish you may alter the font or size of this text.

7 Save and close the form.

Task 3: Using the customised form to enter data

To gain a full appreciation of the modifications made to the **Membership** form then it should be used to enter data.

1 Open the form from the database window by clicking on the **Open** button.

2 Move through the records and display a blank form.

3 Compose data for a new member and using the form enter data into the next record.

4 Close the form.

Reorganising the field order

When data is entered into each field, *Enter* or *Tab* takes you to the next field. The order in which the fields are entered is defined by the order in which they were selected in the **Form Wizards**. Once the form has been modified then this order may need to be changed.

To change the tab order of the fields:

1 From the design view, choose **View-Tab Order** to display the **Tab Order** dialog box (FIGURE 15.4). This displays the order of the fields in the **Custom Order** box. In the **Section** box normally the Detail section is selected.

FIGURE 15.4

2   To alter the order of the fields select the field or fields to be moved and drag to the new position.

3   When the new order has been selected click on **OK**.

The **Auto Order** button will set the tab order according to the way in which the fields are set out on the form. They are ordered with the priority of left to right and then top to bottom.

Adding headers and footers

It is straightforward to add text into the header and footer sections of a form. Headers and footers are always displayed on the screen. Calculated text may be added to the header or the footer; for example the date can be shown.

If a form is to be printed the header section prints before the first record and the footer section prints after the last record. Extra sections – page header and page footer – can be added which will print on each page. You can control whether to display or print these sections. Calculated text may be added to show the page numbers. Page breaks may occur in the middle of records, if the record is in single column format. This can be avoided by adjusting the **Keep together** setting of the **Detail** properties from **No** to **Yes**; to display the Properties sheet check that the **Properties** button is depressed and click on the detail bar.

Task 4: Adding the date

The aim of this task is to put the date in the **Membership Category** form footer.

1   Open the **Membership Category** form in design view.

2   Choose **Insert-Date and Time**. Select a suitable date format and click on OK .
    The date and time will be inserted into the header.

3   Cut and paste to move the date and time into the footer.

4   Switch to run mode by clicking on the View button to see the result.

5   Close the form.

Task 5: Adding headers and footers to a printed form

When a form is printed the header is printed at the beginning and the footer is printed at the end of the records. To add a header and footer that print at the top and
bottom of each page of the **Membership** form when printed:

1   Open the **Membership** form.

2   Click on the Print Preview button.

3   Close the preview and display the form in Design View.

4   Choose **View-Page Header/Footer**. Two extra sections appear, Page Header and
    Page Footer.

5   Select all the title in the form header and use **Edit-Copy** (you need to select the
    label, not the text within the label).

6   Click on the Page Header bar and use **Edit-Paste**. Position the pasted copy.

7   Click on the Page Footer bar and choose **Insert-Page Number**. Choose a suitable
    format and click on OK .

8   Click on the Form Header bar. To display the **Properties** sheet, click on the
     Properties button on the toolbar.

9   In the **Section FormHeader** properties box select the All tab and click in the
    Display When box.

10 Open the list and select **Screen Only**.

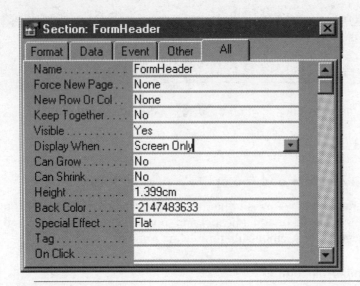

11 Click on the Detail bar and change the **Keep Together** property to **Yes** to prevent page breaks in the middle of records.

12 Preview and print the form.

Forms without Wizards

What you will learn in this unit

The previous units have considered creating forms using the Form Wizard. This method may be restricting when creating a custom form and forms may be created without using the Wizard.

By the end of this unit you will be able to:

- open a blank form
- choose the type of form
- add controls to the form.

Creating a blank form

If the columnar or tabular layout is not suitable for the intended form, then it may be easier to start with a blank form and create a custom design.

Choosing the type of form

If a form is created using AutoForm or the Form Wizard you are given the choice of the type of form. If a blank form is chosen then only a blank detail section is displayed. To create a blank form and choose its type:

1   Click on the **Forms** tab in the database window, click on **New** and highlight **Design View**.

2   Select the table upon which the form is to be based and click on **OK**.

3   Display the properties window by choosing **View-Properties** or clicking on the **Properties** button in the toolbar.

4   In the **Form Properties** sheet you should see the **Default View** property set to **Single Form**.

Adding header/footer sections

Choose **View-Form Header/Footer** to add the header/footer sections to the form. If you intend to print the form then page header/footer sections may also be added.

Adding a label to the form

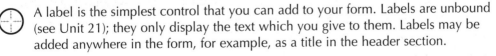

A label is the simplest control that you can add to your form. Labels are unbound (see Unit 21); they only display the text which you give to them. Labels may be added anywhere in the form, for example, as a title in the header section.

To add a label to a form:

1   Click on the **Label** button in the toolbox. Position the pointer in the form at the point where the label should go. The pointer becomes a symbol with two parts: the label symbol and the cross hair symbol used for box drawing.

2   Either click to put a small label box on the workspace, which will expand as you add text, or by dragging draw a box of the desired size. If you drag below the bottom or to the right of the particular section, this part of the form will expand to accommodate the size of label you require.

3   The label is outlined and a flashing insertion point appears inside it, ready for you to enter text. If you don't enter any text and click the mouse button the label will disappear.

4   The size and font may be adjusted by selecting the label and formatting using the appropriate list boxes in the toolbar.

Adding a text box

A text box is the most common type of control found on forms. The fields to which text boxes can be bound will be found in the field list compiled from the source table or query. To add a text box:

1   Click on the **Field List** button on the toolbar or choose **View-Field List** to display the field list window. Choose **View-Grid** to put a matrix of lines on the form to help with positioning the controls. Note that this grid is not visible when the form is run.

2   Click on the required field in the **Field List** and, holding down the mouse button, drag to the detail workspace. Whilst pointing in the workspace the pointer becomes a field symbol. The position of the field symbol indicates the upper left hand corner of the text box not the label so position the top left corner to allow room to the left for the label.

3   Click to place the label and field boxes. Position them by using the hand symbol to drag or by dragging the anchor handle and size by using one of the sizing handles.

4   If desired select the size and font of text in the control.

5   More than one field may be selected from the field list and they can be placed as a group. To select a contiguous selection click on the first field and hold down the *Shift* key while clicking on the last field in the group. To select a non-contiguous selection hold down the *Ctrl* key while making the selection.

6   The order in which the fields are selected determines the 'tab order' i.e. the order they will be filled in on the form. If this needs amending, from the form design screen choose **View-Tab Order**. In the dialog box use a drag and drop method to re-arrange the order of the fields.

Adding a multi-line text box

Multi-line text boxes are usually used to display memo fields. They are larger than the single line boxes. They also have a vertical scroll bar (visible when the control is selected whilst the form is being run) so that when there is too much text to be fitted into the text box then the scroll bar can be used to move through the text.

1   From the field list select a memo field. Drag the field list pointer to the lower middle part of the detail section and drop.

2   Adjust the size of the text box and position the label.

3   Click on the **Format** tab of the Text Box Properties window. The **Scroll Bars** property box will display **Vertical**, which adds a vertical scroll bar to your text box. Note that the scroll bar will only appear when you click in the text box whilst the form is run, indicating to Access that you are using this control.

4   You may wish to print the form to make sure that the whole memo field is printed. In the properties window change both the **Can Grow** and the **Can Shrink** properties to Yes. This will not affect the text box while it is being displayed on the screen.

Task 1: Creating a blank form

Although forms have been created either using AutoForm or Form Wizard, this task will explore using a blank form that will duplicate one of the forms already created. You will use the **Membership** table.

1   Click on the **Forms** tab in the database window, click **New**, then select **Design View**. Select the **Membership** table and click on **OK**.

2   Access creates a new form, showing the detail section.

3   Add header and footer sections by choosing **View-Form Header/Footer**.

4   You should see a matrix of lines on the form's workspace, if not then select **View-Grid** to display it.

5   Adjust the depth of the detail section by pointing to the top line of the Form Footer bar.

6   The pointer should change shape to a horizontal bar with double headed arrow. Click and drag downward to expand the detail section area.

7   Add all the fields, by clicking and dragging from the field list. Consider the order in which you select and place them. Try selecting and placing a group of fields.

8 Add a title to the form and save the form as **Membership 2**. (Remember that there is a distinction between the title of the form and the name it is saved under.)

9 Run the form and use it to add another record to the **Membership** table.

10 If the order of field entry does not match the form design, for instance if the fields were not selected in the right order, then the order can be changed by returning to Design View and choosing **View-Tab Order**. Save the changes.

Forms design: integrative tasks

The following tasks revise some of the topics covered in this and the last two units.

Task 2: Designing and using forms

There are two other tables that require forms to be designed: the **Classes** table and the **Bookings** table.

1 Use **AutoForm** and **Form Wizard** to create columnar forms for both these tables, saving them as **Classes** and **Bookings** respectively.

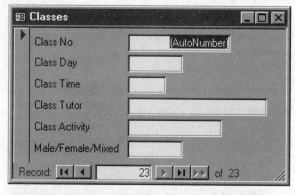

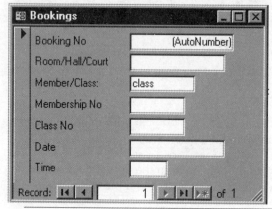

2 Use the forms to enter the data for these tables, shown in Quick Reference 2.
Note: when entering bookings data type *Yes* for a member and *No* for a class.
Remind yourself of the validation rules set in Unit 9 and try testing them while
entering the data.

3 Close the forms when the data has been entered.

Task 3: Adding a new table and creating a form

This task recaps on some of the activities met during this and the previous two units.
The aim is to create a new table and link it to the **Chelmer** database and create a
form to input data into this table. The table to be created is the **Tutor** table.

The Tutor table could comprise of the following fields: **Lastname, Initials, Title,
Street, Town, County, Post Code, Telephone No, National Insurance No, Date of
Birth** and **Qualifications**. Create this **Tutor** table, make all fields except for **Date of
Birth** and **Qualifications** text and choose suitable lengths for each. Use a short date
for **Date of Birth** and a memo for **Qualifications**. Set **Lastname** as the primary key.
However, note that this is not ideal: in a real situation an employee number would
be better. Save the table as *Tutor*. Create a link between this table and the **Classes**
table using **View-Relationships**.

Use **Relationships-Show Table** to add the **Tutor** table. Drag the field **Lastname** from
the **Tutor** table (the one side of the relationship) to the **Class Tutor** found in the
Classes table (the many side of the relationship).

Consider the pros and cons of checking the **Enforce Referential Integrity** check box.
If there is no data in the **Tutor** table you will not be able to enforce referential
integrity.

To design a form for this table:

1 Select the **Form** tab in the database window, then click on the **New**
button.

2 Select **Design View** for the **Tutor** table. Access creates a new form, showing the
detail section.

3 Inspect the **Form Properties** box to see that the **Default view** property is **Single
Form**.

4 Add a header and footer section by choosing **View-Form Header/Footer**. You
should see a matrix of lines on the form's workspace, if not then select **View-
Grid** to display it.

5 Adjust the depth of the detail section by pointing to the top line of the Form
Footer bar. The pointer should change shape to a horizontal bar with double
headed arrow. Click and drag downward to expand the detail section area.

6   Add all the fields to the form from the field list.

7   Add a title to the form and save the form as *Tutor*.

8   Select the text box for qualifications so that its properties sheet is displayed. Set the following properties for this text box: **Scroll bars - Vertical, Can Grow - Yes, Can Shrink - Yes.**

9   Save the form and run it.

10 Use it to enter the following tutor record: *Evans, P J, Mrs, 25 Lyme Green, Chelmer, Cheshire, CH2 1ED, 01777 560935, XZ 32 99 06B, 17/7/70, Y.M.C.A. Dance to Music, Certificate in Aerobics, First Aid (Red Cross).*

Using Report Wizard and AutoReport

What you will learn in this unit

This unit explores the basic design of printed reports that include data from an Access table. It explains how to create a report quickly using Report Wizard. Later units develop some of the themes in this unit more fully.

By the end of this unit you will be able to:

■ create a report using Report Wizard or AutoReport

■ save and close a report

■ use a report to print data from an Access table.

Reports are used to print information from a number of records. They can show the data from either a table or a query. As well as records, reports may also show summary information relating to the records displayed. Graphs created using Microsoft Graph may also be added.

Reports, then, are intended to allow you to select the data to be printed and then to present that data in an acceptable format. To emphasis the distinction between reports and forms: reports are intended to be printed, screen forms are normally displayed on screen, although the facilities often also exist for printing them.

In most applications you will create a number of different standard reports. For example, a mailing list of clients may simply show customer name and address, but a list showing outstanding orders to specific clients will also show details of the items customers have ordered, their value and other associated information.

Access allows you to create reports either to your own design using its wide range of tools for customising reports, or to start by using Report Wizard, which provides you quickly and easily with a basic report that you can later format and customise. We use Report Wizards here because they allow you to understand the basic concept of what a report is and how it works, before you grapple with customising specific features of the report.

Since forms and reports share many design and creation features, you will re-use some of the skills that you acquired earlier in designing a form.

Creating a single column report with Report Wizard

There are various types of report that can be created with Report Wizard. First we deal with the single-column report which is used most frequently and is relatively simple to create. A single column report places all the selected fields in a single column, with their field names to the left.

1 To enter Report wizard starting from the database window, either click on
   New in the database window when you are displaying reports, or click the
   New Object button on the toolbar and select **Report**. A **New Report** dialog
   box appears (FIGURE 17.1).

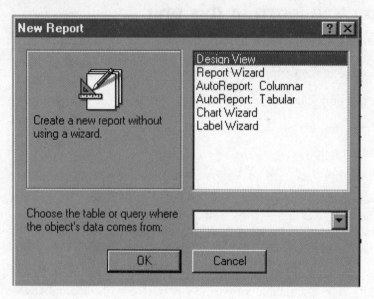

FIGURE 17.1

2 Select the **Report Wizard** option to create a report using Report Wizard.

3 Click on the down arrow button of the **Choose the table or query**... list box, to
   produce a list of tables and queries and select the table for which you wish to
   create a report.

4 Click on **OK**.

5 The next stage is to choose which fields are to be in the report. The possible
   fields are shown in the **Available fields** box (FIGURE 17.2).

6 These can be transferred to the report by selecting each field in turn and clicking
   on the **>** button.

7 If you wish to add all the fields in the table to the report then click on the **>>**
   button.

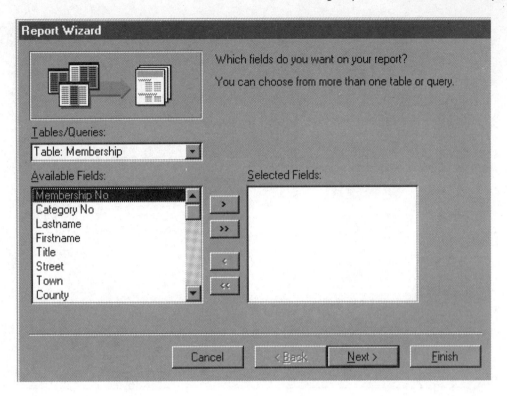

FIGURE 17.2

8 You may set the order in which the fields appear on the report by selecting them in the order that you desire. The `<` button will remove a highlighted field and `<<` will remove all the fields from the report.

9 Once you have added the required fields to the report continue by clicking on the Next> button.

 10 The next dialog box asks you to indicate grouping levels. Leave this for now and click on the Next> button. We shall return to this in Unit 18.

11 The next dialog box asks you to select the sort order. Select the fields you want the records to be sorted by. If you have only a small set of records just one sort field will be adequate. If you want records to appear in the same order as in the table or query it is not necessary to indicate a sort field. Click the Next> button.

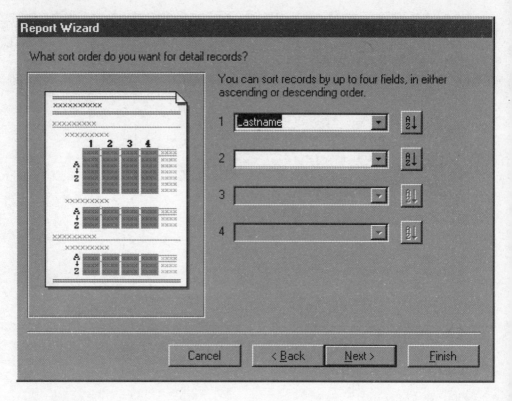

FIGURE 17.3

12 The next dialog box relates to the report's layout and orientation (portrait or landscape). The choice of layout depends on whether or not grouping is used. On the first occasion, if a grouping is used, choose **Outline 1** and **Portrait**. If no grouping is used choose **Columnar** and **Portrait**. Click on Next> .

13 You are then asked what kind of style you want for your report. You are given a choice of:

■ Bold

■ Casual

■ Compact

■ Corporate

■ Formal

■ Soft Gray.

14 The style determines the appearance of the field names and field contents in the report. An example of the style is shown on the left of the dialog box. Click on each style in turn to see what it would look like. On the first occasion a report is created choose **Corporate**. The style can be modified later. Click on the Next> button.

15 The next thing that you are asked for is a title. Enter a report title. Report titles are particularly important in flagging the purpose of the report to the reader, so choose something that conveys its contents.

16 With the option **Preview the report** selected, click on **Finish** . Note that Access has added a page number and the date at the bottom of every page.

Saving and closing a report

Save a report by choosing **File-Save**. If this is a new report that does not have a name, Access will prompt for a file name with a **File-Save As** dialog box. If you later want to save a report under another name use **File-Save As**, and enter the new name in the dialog box.

 Remember that there is a distinction between the name and the title of a report. The title is the text that is displayed at the top of the report when it is printed. The name you give when saving the form is the form's file name, which you need to be able to recognise when you want to open the form for use again. These names appear in the database window when the **Report** tab is selected.

Task 1: Creating a vertical (single column) report using Report Wizard

We wish to create a single column report which lists all the members in the database, showing the following fields.

■ **Membership No**

■ **Category No**

■ **Firstname**

■ **Lastname**

■ **Occupation**

■ **Date of Birth**

■ **Sporting Interests**.

We want the report to looks like the following extract.

Chelmer Leisure and Recreation Centre Members

Membership No	1
Category No	2
Firstname	Andrew J
Lastname	Walker
Occupation	Builder
Date of birth	12/3/52
Sporting Interests	Tennis, squash
Membership No	2
Category No	1
Firstname	Denise
Lastname	Cartwright

1 To enter **Report Wizard** starting from the database window, click on `New` when you are displaying reports, or click the `New Object` button on the tool-bar and select **Report**. A **New Report** dialog box appears.

2 Select the **Report Wizard** option to create a report using Report Wizard.

3 Click on the down arrow button of the **Choose the table or query..** list box, to produce a list of tables and queries, and select the **Membership** table. Click on `OK`.

4 Select the fields to appear in the report by clicking on the field names above in the **Available Fields** list box, and then clicking on the `>` button. The selected fields should appear in the **Selected Fields** list box. If you include any fields by mistake, use `>` to remove them. Click on `Next>`.

5 Do not indicate a grouping level; if Access has automatically created one (on **Category No**) then click on `>` to remove the grouping. Click on the `Next>` button.

6 Choose to sort by **Membership No** by entering it in the first box. Click on
`Next>`.

7 Choose **Columnar** and **Portrait** for the report layout.

8 Choose **Corporate** for the **Style** of the report. Click on `Next>`.

9 Enter the following report title: ***Chelmer Leisure and Recreation Centre Members***

10 With the option **Preview the report** selected, click on `Finish` to display the report on the screen.

11 Access will automatically save the report with the name **Chelmer Leisure and Recreation Centre Members**.

Using a report

To use a report, first display the available report names in the database window, then double click on the report name. The print preview window will appear showing a preview of how the report will appear when printed. Alternatively, click on the report name and then click on the `Preview` button.

To zoom in and out and to view a complete page on the screen, click on the report.

Note that a report picks up the properties of the table or query used when it was designed. Later, you change the properties of the table or query without changing the properties of the report.

Printing a report

Before printing any report always view the report in Print Preview.

Previewing

To preview a report:

1 Click the `Preview` button, and a miniature version of what is to be printed will be displayed.

2 To zoom-in and zoom-out simply click anywhere on the preview, or use the `Zoom` button. Click on the **Zoom Control** box to select a specific magnification for the preview.

3 Choose **File-Page Setup** to make adjustments such as the orientation (portrait or landscape), the choice of printer and the width of the margins. Some of the options in the **Page Setup** dialog box will be familiar since you will have used

them in printing tables and queries, but there are also special options for use when printing report, such as the number of items (records) across the page, item size, and item layout. Click on **OK** when the required adjustments have been made.

Printing

When satisfied that the preview is correct, printing may be done from either the preview screen or the design screen. To print from the preview screen

1 Click on the **Print** button in the print preview bar.

Alternatively, to print from the design screen:

1 Choose **File-Print**.

2 Select whether all or certain pages of the report will be printed and the number of copies. Click on **OK**.

Task 2: Using and printing a report

To use the report **Chelmer Leisure and Recreation Centre Members**, first select it from the file names displayed in the database window, by double clicking on the report name. The print preview window will appear showing a preview of how the report will appear when printed.

Now print the report.

1 Choose **File-Page Setup**. Now experiment with different Setup options, as follows:

2 Choose two columns across the page by selecting the **Columns** tab and entering *2* in the **Number of Columns** box. You may need to adjust the **Width** in the **Column Size** section to less than half your page width.

3 With two columns explore the effect of **Down, then Across** and **Across, then Down** in the **Column Layout** section.

4 Try increasing the column **Height**.

5 Close the **Page Setup** dialog box between each trial in order to view the new layout in **Print Preview**.

6 When you have a layout with which you are happy, print it, by selecting the **Print** button.

Creating a report using AutoReport

The really easy way to create a report is to allow Access to do all the work for you, by using AutoReport. This, however, does not allow any scope for specifying the contents or style of the report.

To use AutoReport:

1 Click on the **Reports** tab in the database window, and then on the **New** button.

2 In the **New Report** dialog box select either **AutoReport: Columnar** or **AutoReport: Tabular**.

3 Click on the down arrow button of the **Choose a table or query..** list box, to produce a list of tables and queries and select the table for which you wish to create a report.

4 Click on **OK** and the report will be created and displayed on the screen.

5 Use **File-Save** and give the report a name.

Task 3: Creating a tabular report using AutoReport

This task demonstrates how easy it is to create a report using AutoReport.

1 Click on **Reports** and the **New** button.

2 In the **New Report** dialog box select either **AutoReport : Columnar** or **AutoReport: Tabular**.

3 Click on the down arrow button of the **Choose a table or query..** list box, and select the table **Membership Category**.

4 Click on **OK** and the report will be created and displayed on the screen in preview mode.

5 Save the report as ***Membership Category*** and print it.

Grouped reports

What you will learn in this unit

This unit explores creating reports where records are arranged in groups according to the value of fields in a table or query.

By the end of this unit you will be able to:

■ create a report with grouped records.

Note: You may choose to omit this unit for the moment and return to it later when you are ready to design this kind of report.

Understanding grouped reports

A grouped report puts the fields you select into a row and groups the records according to the value of a field in the table or query. This approach can also be used simply to create a report in a table form with fields shown in columns, if you do not specify groups. The advantage of this type of report is that it displays more records to the page. However, is does not display records with several long fields which therefore cannot be accommodated next to each other on the page in parallel columns.

Records can be grouped by several different fields, although we shall use only one field for grouping.

Apart from the need to define how records will be displayed in groups, the process of creating a groups/totals report is similar to that for a single column report. The process is basically:

1   Select the fields to appear in the report.

2   Select how the records in the table or query will be grouped for the report. Groups are divisions within a report that include all records that have a value for a specific field.

3   Select the order in which you want the groups created (if you are using more than one group).

4   Select how the records are to be sorted for the report.

5   Select a layout.

6   Select a style.

7   Add the report's title.

8   Use Print Preview to display the report on screen.

9   Save the report.

10 Print the report, as appropriate, and subsequently, close it.

Task 1: Creating a grouped report using Report Wizard

We wish to create a grouped report that lists all the members for which there are records in the database, showing the following fields:

- **Category No**
- **Lastname**
- **Firstname**
- **Telephone No.**

The records are to be grouped according to **Category No**, i.e. all records with a given **Category No** are shown together. We wish to create a report which looks like the one below.

Members by Membership Category

Category No	Lastname	Firstname	Telephone No
1			
	Barrett	Martha A	01777 557822
	Cartwright	Denise	01777 552099
	Davies	Sandra M	01778 891441
	Jameson	Donna	
	Jones	Edward R	01777 567333
	Robinson	Rebecca	01777 568812
	Weiner	George W F	
2			
	Everett	Alan	
	Forsythe	Ann M	01777 569945
	Shangali	Imran	01777 561553

1   Enter Report Wizards by clicking the ▗New▖ button in the database window with the ▗Reports▖ tab selected.

2   Click on the **Report Wizard** option.

3   From the **Choose the table or query...** drop down list box select the **Membership** table. Click on ▗OK▖.

4   Select the fields to appear in the report by clicking on the fields names as indicated above, in the **Available Fields** list box, and then clicking on the 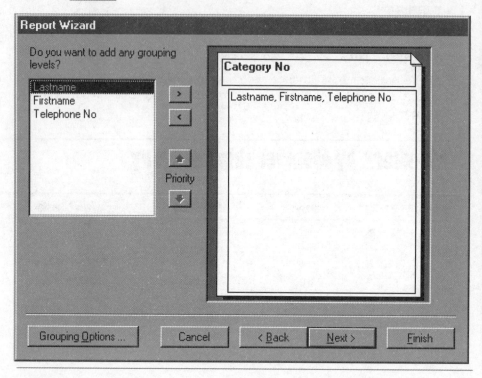 button. The selected fields should appear in the **Selected Fields** list box. If any fields are included by mistake use ▓ < ▓ to remove them.

5   Click on ▓ **Next>** ▓. You will probably discover that Access has automatically grouped the records by **Category No**. If not click on **Category No** in the list of fields and then click on ▓ > ▓ to display it in the heading box in the preview. Click on ▓ **Next>** ▓.

6   Sort records within groups alphabetically by the **Lastname** field. Click on ▓ **Next>** ▓.

7   Select **Stepped** and **Portrait** for the layout of the report. Click on ▓ **Next>** ▓.

8   Select **Compact** for the style of the report. Click on ▓ **Next>** ▓.

9   Enter the following report title: *Members by Membership Category*.

10 Choose **Preview the report** and click on ▓ **Finish** ▓. As the wizard was used to create the report it is automatically saved with the name of its title i.e. **Members by Membership Category**.

11 To print the report directly, click on the `Print` button. To change print options display the **Print** dialog box using **File-Print** and make the choices you require before clicking on `OK`.

Task 2: Creating a grouped report using more than one group

In this task you will create a grouped report which lists all the members for which there are records in the database, showing the following fields:

■ **Category No**

■ **Lastname**

■ **Firstname**

■ **Town**

■ **Telephone No**.

The records are to be grouped according to **Category No** and **Town**, so that, all records with a given **Category No** are grouped together and within this grouping all records with a given **Town** will be grouped together. We wish to create a report which looks like the one shown below.

Membership by Membership Category and Town

Category No	Town	Lastname	Firstname	Telephone No
1				
	Chelmer			
		Jameson	Donna	
		Jones	Edward R	01777 567333
		Robinson	Rebecca	01777 568812
		Weiner	George W F	
	Meriton			
		Barrett	Martha A	01777 557822
		Cartwright	Denise	01777 552099
		Davies	Sandra M	01778 891441

1 Follow the first five steps as for the previous task. You will probably discover that Access has automatically grouped the records by **Category No**. If not click on **Category No** in the list of fields and then click on `>` to display it in the heading box in the preview.

2 To add **Town** to the grouping select it and click on `>`. Click on `Next>`.

3 Sort records within groups alphabetically by the **Lastname** field. Click on
   Next> .

4 Select **Stepped** and **Portrait** for the layout of the report. Click on Next> .

5 Select **Compact** for the style of the report. Click on Next> .

6 Enter the following report title: ***Members by Membership Category and Town.***

7 Choose **Preview the report** and click on Finish . As the wizard was used to
   create the report it is automatically saved with the name of its title i.e. **Members
   by Membership Category and Town.**

8 To print the report directly, click on the Print button. To change print options
   display the **Print** dialog box using **File-Print** and make the choices you require
   before clicking on OK .

Task 3: Selecting the order of grouping

1 Create a report that is the same as the one in Task 2, with the records grouped
   according to **Category No** and **Town**. This time show all records with a given
   Town grouped together and within this grouping show all records with a given
   Category No grouped together.

2 Create this report as in Task 2, and when you have added **Town** as a grouping,
   click on the **Priority** up arrow to change the priority of grouping.

3 Continue as before but title this report ***Members by Town and Membership
   Category.*** Note the difference between this report and the previous one.

Mailing label reports

What you will learn in this unit

Mailing label reports allow the creation of mailing labels, from, say, a table of names and addresses. A mailing label report fits the fields you select into a rectangle that is designed to print labels. Unlike other Report Wizard reports this type does not show field names. It does, however, make it easy to add text such as commas and spaces.

By the end of this unit you will be able to:

■ create a mailing label report

■ use a query in the process of creating a Report Wizard report

■ perform a mail merge to create an accompanying letter.

Creating a mailing label report

The procedure for creating a mailing label report is similar to that for creating any other type of report, except that you use a special Label Wizard.

To create a mailing label report:

1   With **Reports** displayed in the database window, select **New** .

2   Click on the **Label Wizard** option and select a table or query to provide the data for the labels report. Click on **OK** to display the first of the **Label Wizard** dialog boxes (FIGURE 19.1).

3   Select the size of labels from the list. Label sizes are listed according to their Avery number. If you do not know the Avery label number for a given label size, look at the Dimensions and Number Across columns to find the label size that matches your labels.

4   Select **Unit of Measure** and **Label Type** and click on **Next>** (FIGURE 19.2).

5   Select the **Font name**, **Font size**, **Font weight** and **Text color**. You may also check **Italic** and/or **Underline**. Click on **Next>** .

6   Select fields as with other report types, so that they appear on the prototype label but remembering that more than one field can be added to a line.

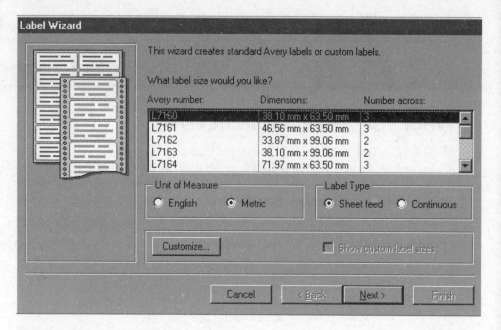

FIGURE 19.1

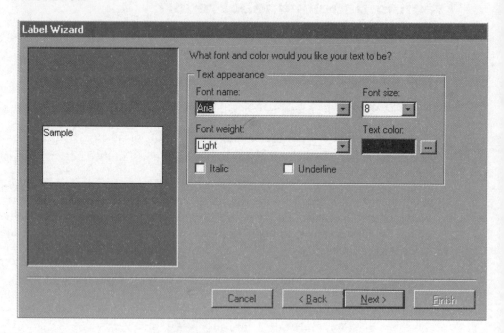

FIGURE 19.2

7   Add text, fields and punctuation to a line and then advance to a new line by pressing *Enter* (FIGURE 19.3). When you have created the label, click on Next> .

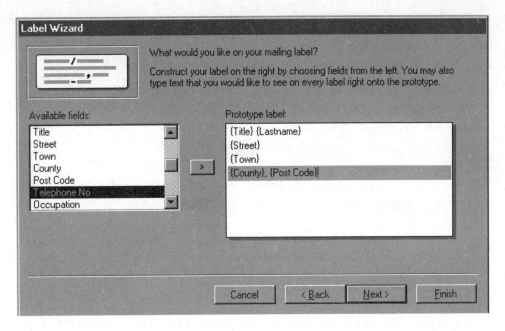

FIGURE 19.3

8   Select how the records are to be sorted, i.e. the order in which mailing labels are to be printed. Click on **Next>** .

9   Either accept the suggested name or type in a different name for the report. With **See the mailing labels as they will look printed** selected click on **Finish** to display labels on screen.

10 Save the report.

11 Print and close the report as appropriate.

Task 1: Creating a mailing label report wizard report based on a query

We wish to create a mailing label report which lists all members who have joined since 1/1/95. An extract from such a report is shown below. First we need to define and execute a query to select the appropriate records, and then we need to define the mailing label report that is to be used to display this set of records.

Mr Gray
4 The Parade
Chelmer
CHESHIRE, CH1 7ER

Miss Robinson
16 Lowton Lane
Branford
STAFFS, ST10 2DZ

Query design and execution were introduced earlier, and you may wish to review this topic at this point.

To define the query:

1 Starting from the database window, click on the `Queries` tab, and click on the `New` button to create a new query.

2 Select **Design View** and click on `OK`.

3 The **Show Table** dialog box appears. Select the table **Membership** and click on the `Add` button and then click on the `Close` button.

4 Next choose to include all fields in the query by double clicking on the title bar of the **Field List** box of the table in the upper section of the window. Click anywhere in the selected area and drag to the field row to transfer all the fields to the lower section.

5 In the **Date of Joining** criteria cell enter the query criteria **>1/1/95**. To view the result of this query click on the `Run` button on the toolbar.

6 Save the query by choosing **File-Save**.

7 In the **Query Name** box of the **Save As** dialog box, enter the Query Name: *New Members*.

8 Close the query.

Now that you have defined a query, you need to design a report to display the records retrieved by the query.

1 Click on the `Reports` tab in the database window and click on `New`.

2 Select the **Label Wizard** option to create a report using Label Wizard.

3 From the **Choose a table or query...** drop down list box select the query **New Members**. Click on `OK`.

4 Select the size of the labels. You may need to experiment with different label sizes. Try metric Avery number **L7160** first. Click on `Next>`.

5 Leave the font as default and click on `Next>`.

6   Select the fields to be included. These are, in the order that follows.

Title

Lastname

Street

Town

County

Post Code

7   Add the field **Title** followed by a space and then the field **Lastname** to the first line. Click on the *Enter* key to move onto the next line.

8   Add **Street** to the next line.

9   Add the remainder of the fields, each on a separate line, with the exception of **County** and **Post Code** which should be on the same line separated by a comma and a space. Click on **Next>** .

10 Choose to order the records in alphabetical order according to **Lastname**.

11 Accept the title **Labels New Members**. The report is automatically saved.

12 With **See the labels...** selected, click on **Finish** to display the report on the screen.

13 To print the report directly select the **Print** button. To display the **Print** dialog box use **File-Print**.

Mail merging

When a circular is to be sent out, creating mailing labels takes the tedium out of addressing the envelopes. The process can be further automated by using Access in conjunction with Word to perform a mail merge. In Word a standard letter can be produced and Access can provide the data (usually names and addresses) to be merged with the standard letter.

Task 2: Mail merging

For this task you will need both Access and Word. A standard letter will be sent to all the fitness instructors informing them of the times of opening over the Easter holiday. If you have not already done so you will need to complete, say, four records in the **Tutors** table (names of fitness instructors are in the **Classes** table).

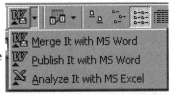

1   With the **Tables** tab selected, highlight the **Tutor** table in the database window.

2   Open the **Office Links** drop down list (on the toolbar) and select **Merge It with MS Word**.

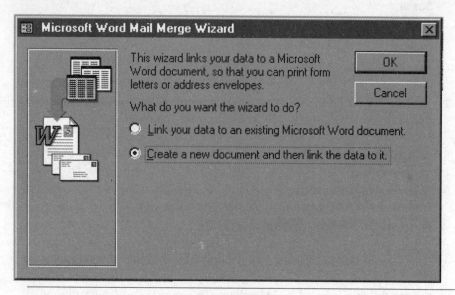

3   Choose the option to create a new document and click on **OK**. This causes Word to be loaded in mail merge mode. **Note**: ensure that there is data in at least one tutor record otherwise this will not work.

4   Next create a standard letter as shown overleaf. The parts of the letter that are replaceable fields are shown enclosed in double chevrons. To insert a replaceable field click on the **Insert Merge Field** button on the mail merge toolbar and select the required field from the drop down list.

5   It is best to check the merge for errors first; do this by clicking on the **View Merged Data** button. Check the merged data. Save the document.

6   To complete the task design a mailing label report to accompany the letters produced.

Chelmer Leisure and Recreation Centre

Tel: 01777 563444

Park View Road

Fax: 01777 560112

Chelmer

Cheshire

CE9 1JS

19 March, 199X

<<**Street**>>

<<**Town**>>

<<**County**>>

<<**Post Code**>>

Dear <<**Title**>> <<**Lastname**>>

Please note the following times when the Centre will be open during the Easter break.

Good Friday	9:00am to 5:00pm
Easter Saturday	9:00am to 1:00pm
Easter Sunday	Closed
Easter Monday	9:00am to 5pm
Tuesday	Normal hours

If you wish to reschedule any classes please let me know as soon as possible.

Yours sincerely

G V Richards

Manager

Customising a report

What you will learn in this unit

This unit explores some of the basic tools for designing customised reports instead of using the standard reports that can be created using Report Wizards.

By the end of this unit you will be able to:

- appreciate the component parts of a report
- create a blank report as a basis for later design work
- move and size controls
- change the report's area
- delete, add and restore fields to a report
- change the text of a field name
- add headers and footers.

Understanding customised reports

Although Report Wizard produces a useful basic report, eventually you may wish to design or create your own design from scratch, so that you can exercise greater control over the report design. If you examine the Report Wizard reports that you have created recently you will note that they have the following limitations: the title length is restricted; the spacing is fixed horizontal spacing that makes it difficult to distinguish between records; and the fixed format gives the same standard appearance time and time again.

This unit explores some of the simple tools for customising a report. These may be applied either to a report created initially with Report Wizards, or to create your own report. Before attempting to create or modify a report it is useful to identify the components of a report. These are listed and described below. If you examine the reports that you have just created using Report Wizards, you should recognise that they have these components. If you display an existing report in Design View, by clicking on the **Design** button with the report selected in the database window, the report will be displayed with these areas clearly marked.

Components of a report

Component	Description
Report header	Contains any headings or other introductory text that might appear at the beginning of the report.

Component	Description
Page header	Contains headings that will appear at the top of each page, such as a running title and page numbers.
Detail	Shows data from the records in the database. Sets up the format for records in general which is then used for every record included in the report
Page footer	Appears at the bottom of each page.
Report footer	Contains information at the end of the report, such as a final summary or a statement such as 'this is the end of the report'.
Group header	Marks the beginning of a group; usually introduces the group that the report will display.
Group footer	Marks the end of a group and often contains sections that summarise the records that are part of a group.

Working with report design allows you to adjust the content, size and position of everything that appears on the report. As with forms, each small piece of a report is called a *control*. Controls include a field's data, text, picture and calculations. Again, many of the features relating to forms that you experimented with earlier also apply to reports.

Modifying an existing report

To customise an existing report it must be selected in design mode thus:

1   Select the report in the database window and then click on the Design button; or

2   Click on the report name using the right mouse button and choose Design from the shortcut menu.

Creating a new blank report

To create a new report, without the aid of Report Wizard:

1   Click on the Reports tab in the database window and on New. ; or

2   Choose **View-Database Objects-Reports** and then click on the New button in the database window; or

3   Click on the drop down New Object button on the toolbar, then select **Report**.

4   Select the **Design View** option to create a report without using Report Wizard.

5   Click on the down arrow button of the **Choose the table or query..** list box, to produce a list of tables and queries and select the table or query for which you wish to create a report.

6   Click on   **OK** .

Extra windows

When you create a new blank report the Toolbox window will be displayed. This is useful for adding controls to the report. There are a number of such windows which you will encounter as you advance in report design. These are:

Window	Description
Properties sheet	to change different features of the report's contents
Field list	to add controls bound to fields
Toolbox	to select the design tool required (can be dragged to left of screen where it 'locks' as a toolbar)

All of these windows can be moved or closed in the same way as any other window. They can also be opened and closed from the **View** menu.

Task 1: Examining the components of a report

1   Examine one of the reports that you have created with Report Wizards in Unit 18.

2   With the database window displayed, click the   **Reports**   tab, and then the   **Design**   button. Note that Report Wizards creates reports with default settings in many areas.

3   Examine the report that you have displayed. Click on each control in turn. What are the default settings for the following?

   ■ **Report Header**

   ■ **Page Header**

   ■ **Detail**

   ■ **Page Footer**

   ■ **Group Header**

   ■ **Group Footer**

   ■ **Report Footer**

Task 2: Creating a blank report

Create a blank report for the **Classes** table, showing all of the fields in the table, thus:

1   Click on the   **Reports**   tab in the database window, and then the   **New**   button. Select the **Classes** table from the **Choose the table or query..** drop down list box.

2   Select the **Design View** option. Click on **OK** .

3   Consider the layout and decide where to put title, field labels and the fields
    themselves.

4   Add all the fields to the report from the field list. Display the field list; double-
    click on the field list title bar to highlight all the fields.

5   Click and drag the highlighted fields onto the Detail section of the report.
    Controls for all the fields should appear.

6   Save as ***Classes*** and close.

Moving and sizing controls

Moving and sizing controls is the basic activity for improving the appearance of the
report.

In order to move a control, it must first be selected. It can then be moved by dragging. The different types of controls can be selected in the same way as they are
selected and moved on forms. If you need a reminder, see Moving and sizing controls in Unit 15.

Task 3: Moving and sizing controls on an existing Report Wizards report

We wish to improve on the design of the report **Chelmer Leisure and Recreation
Centre Members**, so that the final report looks like this.

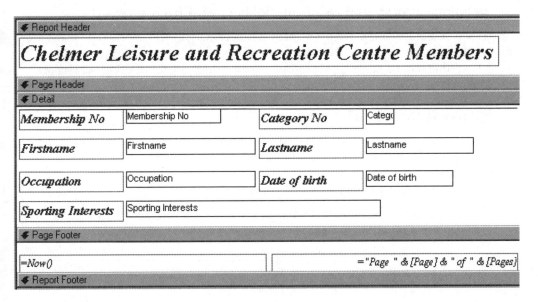

1 First open the existing report. Select the report **Chelmer Leisure and Recreation Centre Members** in the database window and then select the **Design** button.

2 Now move the controls on the report until it resembles the design screen shown above, using the instructions above for selecting and moving controls. If the tool-box is in the way, remove it by using **View-Toolbar**.

 You may get into a muddle in your first attempt to move controls. Remember that controls can be deleted by selecting them and using the *Delete* key. If all else fails, close without saving and start again.

3 View the new report on screen using **Print Preview**.

4 Save the report as *Members2* using **File-Save As**.

Customising a report

Changing the report's area

The area of each section of a report, the header, detail and footer, may be altered individually. It is also possible to adjust the position of the right and bottom edge of a form. To alter the depth of a section of the form:

1 Move the pointer to the bottom edge of the section, where it will change shape. Drag the pointer to a new location.

2 To alter the area of the report drag the right and bottom edges to the size that you require.

Deleting, adding and restoring fields to and from a report

When you create a report from scratch it is necessary to add appropriate fields from a selected table or query. You may also wish to add or delete fields when changing an existing report. Again, procedures are similar to those for deleting, adding and restoring fields to or from a form.

Changing the text of a field name label

The text of a field name label may be edited and if required additional text can be added to the form. Again,m procedures are similar to those for forms.

Task 4: Creating a customised report

We wish to open the report that we created earlier, **Classes**, add fields and modify field labels, in order to create a report like the one shown opposite.

Chelmer Leisure and Recreation Centre. Sports, Fitness and Exercise Classes

Classes

Number:		1	Class Tutor:	Evans
Class Day:	Monday		Class Activity:	Ladies' Aerobics
Class Time:		10:00	Male/Female/Mixed:	Female

Number:		2	Class Tutor:	Franks
Class Day:	Monday		Class Activity:	Weight Training
Class Time:		11:00	Male/Female/Mixed:	Male

1 First open the report called **Classes** by selecting the **Reports** tab in the data-base window, and then selecting the **Design** button.

2 Click on the fields and their labels and move them into a more satisfactory position. Rearrange them as necessary. You may wish to use **Format-Align-Left** to align a group of controls. (Select them as a group first.)

3 If you inadvertently delete a field, display the **Field List** window and drag the field onto the report .

4 Edit the field label **Class No** so that it reads *Number*, by selecting the field label control, clicking where the text editing is required and modifying the field name label. Modify other labels as necessary in the same way.

5 Press *Enter* or click on another part of the report to complete changes.

6 Try aligning groups of controls to achieve a tidy looking form.

7 Next create a report header and a report footer by choosing **View-Report Header/Footer** so that a tick is placed beside this option.

Next create a control box into which you can insert the text, thus:

8 With the toolbox displayed click on the **Label** tool (see FIGURE 21.1 Unit 21). Place the pointer in the **Report Header** box and drag it to create a box large enough to accommodate text.

9 Type the following text into the report header band: *Chelmer Leisure and Recreation Centre - Sports, Fitness and Exercise Classes*.

10 Repeat these steps to insert text in the report footer, page header and page footer bands.

11 Print preview the report, save **Classes** and close it.

You have now created a report showing all of the basic information, but clearly there is much scope for improvements to its format. A few of these are explored in the last tasks in this unit, but the majority are the subject of the next few units.

Reformatting a report

Altering the size and font of controls

To alter the size of font of the controls on a report:

1 Select the controls to be altered.

2 Click on the **Font** list box in the toolbar and select the font required.

3 Click on the **Font Size** list box and select the point size required.

If you increase the size of a font you may need to alter the size of the control and the size of the section.

Adding headers and footers

Page headers and footers can be easily added to a report. With the toolbox displayed click on the **Label** tool. Place the pointer in the appropriate header or footer box and drag it to make a box large enough to accommodate the text.

Task 5: Reformatting a report

This task reformats the report created in the last task using a number of additional features that have been introduced above.

1 Open the report called **Classes** in Design mode.

2 Select the controls in the **Report Header**, open the **Font Size** list box and select an appropriate larger point size. Click on the **Bold** button to make the text bold. Click on the **Centre** button to centre the text within the control. If necessary stretch the control box to display all of the text.

3 Move the field labels into the page header band by first selecting them as a group. Choose **Edit-Cut** and click anywhere in the page header. Then choose **Edit-Paste**.

4 Rearrange the labels in the page header to make column headings. Select these as a group and format them by making them bold, italic and slightly larger.

5 Adjust the size of the page header so that it just accommodates the labels by dragging the bottom of the page header.

6 In the detail band, re-arrange the controls to align with the labels in the page header. If necessary expand the boxes to accommodate the longest field value. For example make sure that the control box for **Activity** accommodates **Badminton**.

7 In turn select the text boxes for **Class No** and **Time** and left justify them by clicking on the ▌ **Align Left** ▌ button. Select the ▌ **Male/Female/Mixed** ▌ control box and delete it by pressing the *Delete* key.

8 Select and format the report footer in bold and italics.

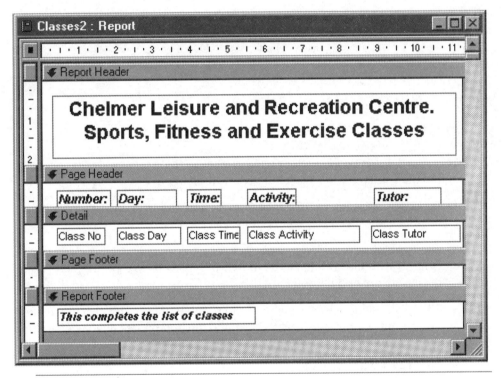

9 Note that it will probably be necessary to move back and forth between print preview and design mode a few times as you make changes and would like to view the results of those changes.

10 Print preview, save as **Classes2**, close and print as required.

Chelmer Leisure and Recreation Centre.
Sports, Fitness and Exercise Classes

Number:	Day:	Time	Activity	Tutor:
1	Monday	10:00	Ladies' Aerobics	Evans
2	Monday	11:00	Weight Training	Franks
3	Monday	15:00	Body Conditioning	Latham
4	Monday	19:00	Step Aerobics	Wheildon
5	Tuesday	10:00	Men's Multi-gym	Jackson
6	Tuesday	14:00	Ladies' Multi-gym	Adams
7	Tuesday	19:00	Family Multi-gym	Jackson

Tools

The report design window has a number of tools that you have been benefiting from in designing a report. It is useful to review these briefly.

1   The **Ruler** measures the distance from the top and left corner of the report. It can be removed or replaced by choosing **View-Ruler**.

2   The **Grid** appears in design view. Access automatically aligns moved or sized controls with the grid. It can be moved or replaced by choosing **View-Grid**. To deactivate the grid choose **Format-Snap to Grid**.

3   The **Align** option. Use **Format-Align** to position controls relative to each other. Select controls, choose **Format-Align** and the appropriate alignment e.g. Left.

Integrative tasks

Use the following tasks to practise the report creation skills you have gained from this and the last three units.

Task 6: Creating a single column report using Report Wizard

You require a report, based on the **Membership** table, which lists the following details for all members who are smokers.

- **Membership No**

- **Category No**

- **Title**

- **Firstname**

- **Lastname**

- **Occupation**

- **Date of Birth**

- **Sex.**

1   First define a query which allows you to select the records for the members who are smokers.

2   Save this query and then use it in the design of a report using Report Wizards. Don't forget to save the report, as ***Smokers***, and print preview it on screen before printing.

Task 7: Creating a groups/totals report using Report Wizard

You wish to create a report that lists all the classes offered by the centre, based on the **Classes** table. The report is to be organised in groups according to **Class Activity**. All fields in the **Classes** table are to be included.

1   Produce a second groups/totals report, based on the **Classes** table, which details all the information in the **Classes** table.

2   Sort the report in classes order.

3   Save this report as ***Classes List***.

Task 8: Creating a customised report

Instead of using Report Wizard to create the report in Task 6, attempt to create the same report independently of the Report Wizards tool, i.e. as a customised report.

Types of form controls

What you will learn in this unit

This unit describes the additional features that you can add to forms and reports.

By the end of this unit you will be able to:

■ identify the tools in the Toolbox

■ understand the function of the different types of control.

So far you have met forms and reports created by AutoForm, AutoReport and the Wizards, which tend to use limited controls. In this unit we will introduce the range of controls that can be added to both forms and reports. The level of sophistication that can be given to controls adds to the professionalism of the database application that is being created.

Types of form controls

In creating forms and reports you will have met labels and text box controls. If you are familiar with Windows applications you will be aware that there are other types of control, which you will have met when using dialog boxes. These include list boxes, check boxes and option buttons.

There are three categories of control.

1 *Bound controls.* A bound control is associated with a field in the table or query that was used to create the form. We have met text boxes, which are the most common type of bound control. Through a bound control, data can be displayed or altered.

2 *Unbound controls.* An unbound control is independent of the data in the form's table or query. Labels used as titles are examples of unbound controls.

3 *Calculated controls.* A calculated control is an expression. Usually the expression performs a calculation upon data in the form's table or query.

The Toolbox

The Access Toolbox allows you to add control objects to forms and reports. The Toolbox only appears when you are in design mode. If it is not visible in design mode then use **View-Toolbox** to make it visible. The Toolbox is composed of a set of buttons. Each button gives access to a different tool, the icon on the button indicates the function of the tool, as outlined in FIGURE 21.1. When you click on a button that particular tool becomes available.

Pointer — Control Wizard
Label — Text Box
Option Group — Toggle Button
Option Button — Check Box
Combo Box — List Box
Command Button — Image
Unbound Object Frame — Bound Object Frame
Page Break — Tab Control
Subform/Subreport — Line
Rectangle — More Controls

FIGURE 21.1

Tool	Function
Pointer	This is the default tool when the Toolbox is displayed. Click on it to deselect a previously selected tool and return the mouse pointer to its normal function.
Label	Allows you to draw a rectangle (frame) on the form into which text can be inserted.
Option Group	Creates a frame of adjustable size into which controls can be placed. Only one of the controls within the frame can be selected. Usually the controls are of the same kind, e.g. option buttons or check boxes. When a control within an option group is selected all others in the group are deselected.
Option Button	Creates a round button that switches between on and off when clicked with the mouse. Option buttons are most commonly used within option groups to select between values in a set.
Combo Box	Creates a box which is a combination of a text box and a drop down list box. This gives the choice of either selecting from a list or keying in an entry.
Command Button	Creates a command button to which you can assign a macro which will execute when the button is clicked.
Unbound Object Frame	Adds an OLE (Object linking and embedding – see Unit 31) object, that is something created by another application which supports OLE, for example, a

Microsoft Excel spreadsheet.

Page Break	Causes the printer to start a new page at the location of the page break on the form or the report.
Subform/Subreport	Adds a subform or subreport to a main form or report. Don't use this unless the subform or subreport already exist. See Unit 33 for more details.
Rectangle	Creates a rectangle that can be sized and relocated. Select width, colour and fill from the properties and palette.
Control Wizards	When this button is depressed it enables the control wizards so that if, say, the button tool is selected then the button wizard comes into operation. If the wizards are not required then check that this button is not depressed.
Text box	Creates a frame in which text is displayed or edited. This is the most common form of control.
Toggle Button	Creates a button that switches between on and off when clicked with the mouse.
Check Box	Creates a check box that toggles on and off. Multiple check boxes can be used in groups, but not within an option group, so that more than one check box can be selected.
List Box	Creates a drop-down list box from which an item or value can be selected.
Image	Creates a frame for displaying a static picture on a form or report. Once added to a form or report the picture cannot be edited. Useful for a company logo.
Bound Object Frame	Where the data table contains OLE objects, for example, digitised photographs in a personnel table, this tool is used to create an object control in a similar way to the text box control.
Tab Control	Creates a tabbed dialog box allowing you to divide data into sections that can be presented in a series of overlapping parts of a dialog box.
Line	Creates a straight line that can be sized and relocated. The colour and width of the line can be changed using the properties and palette.
More Controls	Displays a list of further controls.

Adding controls to forms

What you will learn in this unit

Controls on forms can be made more versatile by the use of list boxes, option buttons, option groups, etc; features encountered in dialog boxes. If the entry for a control can be selected from a list, for example, rooms in a leisure centre, then data entry can be made more efficient by providing a list box. The person entering the data simply selects from the list rather than having to key in the entry. This has the advantages of reducing error and maintaining consistency.

Calculated controls may be added to either forms or reports. They display information calculated from existing data. The example used in this session is that of calculating which members have not renewed their membership.

By the end of this unit you will be able to create:

■ a calculated text box

■ a list box

■ an option group

■ a combo box

■ a check box.

Adding controls to forms

This activity uses the Toolbox to add controls to forms. If the Toolbox isn't visible in form design mode choose **View-Toolbox** to display it. Move it by dragging its title bar to a suitable place on your screen. As the best way to see how to add controls is by experimentation, this unit consists entirely of tasks. By completing these tasks you should acquire the skills with which to attempt a form design of your own.

Task 1: Creating a calculated text box

In this task the calculated control that is to be created is one which flags members whose renewal is due. This control will be added to the **Membership** form created in Task 1 in Unit 14. Before continuing with the task it will probably be necessary to review and amend the dates of joining and the dates of renewal to make this task realistic.

When people join Chelmer Leisure and Recreation Centre they pay for one year's membership from that date. They renew their membership annually. To calculate whether the member's subscription is overdue then the renewal date is compared with today's date. If the renewal date is before today's date then the fee is overdue. To create a realistic number, say, three members overdue, amend or add records to the **Membership** table with appropriate dates for renewal.

1 Open the **Membership** table using the **Open** button to display the data.

2 View each record in turn and look at the **Date of Last Renewal** field.

3 Make amendments, if necessary, to the **Date of Last Renewal** field so that some members have a date of renewal before exactly one year ago from today and others after that date.

To add the calculated text box:

4 Open the **Membership** form in Design View.

5 Click on the **Text box** tool in the Toolbox.

6 Click on a suitable place on the form for the text box and its label.

7 Edit the label to read *Subscription*:

8 Click in the text box and key in the expression

   =iif(DateAdd("d",365,[Date of last renewal])<Date(),"Overdue","Up to date")

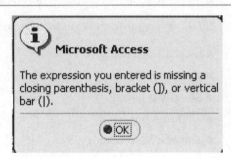

If you miss out a bracket, when you press *Enter* Access will display an information box. Click on **OK** d you will be returned to the control so that you can edit the expression. If you have trouble seeing this expression you can display it in a zoom box by selecting Control source in the Properties sheet and pressing *Shift+F2* to open the zoom box for editing.

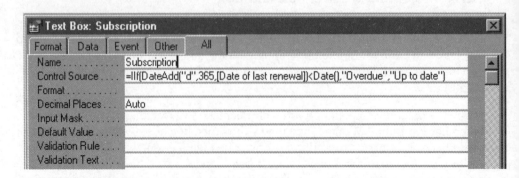

9 Click on the  tab in the text box property box and change the Name to *Subscription*.

10 Run the form. If you have errors return to the design view and check that you have keyed in the expression correctly. For example, if you have misspelt the control name, then the message **#Name?** appears in the control. Check all control names carefully and correct them.

Note: If you rename a control in an underlying table then this kind of error may result and the names in the expression will need to be amended accordingly.

The expression is an in-line IF....THEN.....ELSE statement. DateAdd adds one year to the date of the last renewal. This is compared to today's date. IF the result is less than today's date THEN the subscription is overdue ELSE it is up to date.

11 Save the form.

If you wish to create your own expressions refer to the Access Office Assistant for lists of functions available.

Formatting displayed values

Font and size formatting have already been discussed in Units 14 and 15. Type enhancements (bold, italics, underlining) and alignment (left, centre, right) can be chosen from the toolbar. Formatting can also be applied to the controls introduced in this session.

Task 2: Adding a list box

List boxes are useful for picking values from a static list of options that you create. You may define a list or use a table as a source of the list. The example that will be considered is that of adding a list box to the bookings form. The list box will be defined for the **Room/Hall/Court** field and use a static list. This static list is a list of rooms at the leisure centre. At Chelmer Leisure and Recreation centre there are six bookable rooms: the Fitness Suite, Sports Hall 1 and 2, and three courts.

To add a list box to the **Bookings** form:

1 Open the form in design mode.

2 Select and delete the **Room/Hall/Court** text box.

3 Open the **Field List** window and choose **Room/Hall/Court**.

4   Check that the **Control Wizard** button in the Toolbox is depressed and click on the **List Box** tool.

5   Click and drag the **Room/Hall/Court** field symbol to the former position of the **Room/Hall/Court** text box. Adjust the controls on the form so that there is room to have a list box approximately deep enough to show all the six rooms. If the list box is made smaller it will be shown with a vertical scroll bar. You may wish to try a slightly different layout as illustrated later in this task.

6   The **List Box Wizard** dialog box displays (provided the **Control Wizard** button in the toolbox is depressed). Select the option **I will type in the values that I want** and click on **Next>**.

7   Enter **1** into the **Number of columns** box. Click in the first cell (under **Col1**) and type **Fitness Suite**. Complete the column with **Sports Hall 1, Sports Hall 2, Court 1, Court 2, and Court 3** so there are six rows in column 1. Click on **Next>**.

8   Choose the option **Store that value in this field** and click on **Next>**.

9   Accept the label for the list box, which should be **Room/Hall/Court** and click on **Finish**.

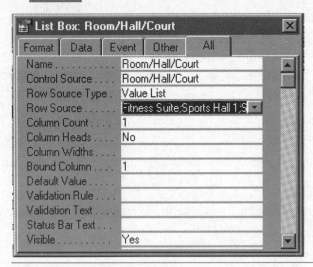

10 Click on the form **View** button on the toolbar to display the form. If adjustments to the position of controls are needed then return to the design mode to make them. The form could look something like:

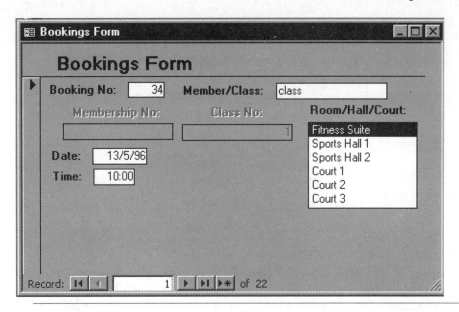

11 Save the form as ***Bookings2***. Try using the form to enter a booking. You may wish to amend the Tab order depending upon your design.

Task 3: Adding option groups

Option buttons are commonly employed in Windows applications to select one option from a set of choices. They are best used where the value of the option is numeric, for example, the categories of membership. To illustrate this, an option group will be added to the **Membership** form. Open the form in design mode. Adjust the area of the form to allow room for the option group at the bottom or side of the form.

To create an option group:

1 Check that the **Control Wizard** button in Toolbox is depressed. Click on the **Option Group** frame tool in the Toolbox.

2 Choose **Category No** from the **Field List** and drag to the form. Dragging is important as it links the control with the field. Release at a suitable position.

3   Enter the label names as shown in the illustration and click on **Next>** .

4   Select the option **No, I don't want a default** and click on **Next>** .

5   The default values are correct so click on **Next>** .

6   Choose the option '**Store the value in this field: Category No**' and click on **Next>** .

7   Choose the **Option** buttons type of control with an **Etched** style and click on **Next>** .

8   Give the option group the title ***Category No*** and click on **Finish** .

9   To test the form click on the **View** button. The already existing **Category No** text box control should serve to confirm the entry in the option group. Data could be entered into this field using either of the controls. Experiment by entering a new member's record.

10 Save the form as ***Membership***.

Task 4: Adding a combo box

In this task you will add a combo box for the choice of county to the **Membership** form. Three counties will be listed but the text box will accept an alternative that may be keyed in.

1   Open the **Membership** form in design view.

2   Select and delete the **County** text box.

3   Check that both the **Field List** window and the Toolbox are displayed. Check that the **Control Wizard** button in the Toolbox is depressed.

4   Click on the **Combo Box** tool in the Toolbox. Click and drag the **County** field from the field list onto its former location on the form.

5   Using the Wizard, opt to type in the values and set the number of columns to one.

6   Enter the list of counties, ***Staffs, Derbyshire***. Cheshire need not be included in the list as it is the default value.

7   Choose the store in **County** field option and edit the label if required. Click on **Finish** .

8 Click on the ▋ View ▋ button on the toolbar to display the form. The **County** text box should have a ▋ List Box ▋ button, which when clicked will display the list of counties. Notice that, when entering a new record, Cheshire is still the default county. If adjustments are needed return to design mode. When complete save the form. Experiment with entering data.

Task 5: Check box controls for logical fields

In this task the **Sex** and **Smoker** controls in the **Membership** form will be changed to check box controls.

1 Display both the Toolbox and the Field List.

2 Delete the **Smoker** field.

3 Select the ▋ Check Box ▋ tool in the Toolbox. Click on the **Smoker** field in the Field List and drag onto the form.

4 Repeat for the **Sex** field. Save the form.

Using filters to select records

What you will learn in this unit

Filters are used in conjunction with tables, queries and forms as a means of displaying selected records. A filter will 'filter out' those records that match specified criteria and display only these records. When a filter is created it is stored with the table, query or form and can quickly allow the user to view the data using the filter criteria, without having to resort to creating a query. Trends in data may be identified using this method of data filtering. Information concerning, for example, poor membership in a certain category, or room usage can be easily obtained. Only one filter is stored with the table, query or report but it may be changed if necessary. If you make changes to a filter and do not want to save them then, when you close the table, query or form, say No to the save changes question.

By then end of this unit you will be able to:

■ use a filter to select records using one field as a criterion (Filter by Selection)
■ use a filter to select records using more than one field as criteria (Filter by Form).

A common business need is to select out a particular set of data, e.g. a list of customers of a particular type, say small businesses. A datasheet or form displays all the records in its underlying table or query; by attaching a filter only selected records will be displayed. Using the buttons on the toolbar the filter can easily be switched on or off.

As we have already seen queries can display a selected set of data. The advantage that a filter offers is that it can be designed whilst viewing the form, table or query. If records are being amended then it can be useful to select certain records, for example, to change a room for a particular activity.

Filter by Selection

A filter created by this method will select records that match the value of the field selected. To filter by this method:

1   Select a field displaying a value, which is your criterion, e.g. Meriton in the **Town** field. Click on the `Filter by Selection` button in the toolbar. The filter control buttons are shown below.

Filter By Selection   Apply/Remove Filter

 2   Only the records with that value in the field will be displayed. To sort the records displayed via the filter use the sorting buttons on the toolbar as shown in Unit 6.

3   To remove the filter click on the `Remove Filter` button.

Task 1: Selecting with a filter

In this task you will filter the **Membership** form to display only those records where the **Town** field is Meriton.

1 Open the **Membership** form in Form View.

2 Move through the records until you find one for Meriton.

3 Click in this field and click on the **Filter By Selection** button.

4 When you move through the records now you will see only the Meriton ones.

5 Click on the **Remove Filter** button to display all the records.

6 Close the form.

Filter by Form

A filter created by this method will select records that match the value of more than one field. Alternatives may be included, for example Meriton and Branford in the **Town** field.

Filter By Form

To filter by this method:

1 Click on the **Filter by Form** button in the toolbar. This displays a filter form, the one illustrated in FIGURE 23.1 is for the **Membership** table.

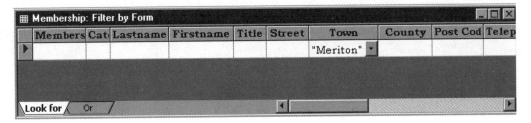

FIGURE 23.1

2 Using the filter form specify the criteria for record selection. When you select a field you can open a drop down list that displays all the different values used for that field in the underlying data.

3 You may specify 'AND' criteria by setting values in one or more fields, say all men in category 1.

4 You may specify 'OR' criteria using the 'Or' tab. This will display another sheet of the form filter. The rules of 'AND' and 'OR' logic apply to sheets of the form filter in the same way as rows in the query QBE grid.

5 Click on the **Apply Filter** button on the toolbar.

6 To remove the filter click on the **Remove Filter** button.

Task 2: Selecting with a filter form

In this task you will apply a filter to the **Membership** form. When filtering a form Access uses your form design for the filter form so you will see this rather than the form illustrated above, which is used when the table is being filtered. Open the **Membership** form in form view. The filter buttons should be in the toolbar. To select records using a filter form:

1 Click on the **Filter By Form** button and the filter form window appears.

2 In the **Town** field select **Branford**. Click on the **Or** tab and select **Meriton**.

3 Click on the **Apply Filter** button to see the selected records displayed in the **Membership** form.

4 To order the records by **Category No** select the category number field and click on the **Sort Ascending** or **Sort Descending** button.

Editing a filter

If you create a filter using Filter By Selection this filter will be saved with the form. To change it to use a different field value for selection purposes simply select that field value and click on the **Filter By Selection** button. If you wish to Filter By Form instead then click on the **Filter By Form** button and specify your criteria in the form.

The same procedure is used to edit a filter that was created using the filter by form technique.

Task 3: Editing a filter

This follows on from Task 2.

1 Click on the **Filter By Form** button to re-display the form filter.

2 Remove the town criteria by deleting them. Set criteria in the **Category No** field to filter out categories 3 or 4.

3 Click on the **Apply Filter** button to see the records.

4 Experiment with different filter forms, selecting using criteria for different fields.

5 Remove the filter and close the form.

Using controls in reports

What you will learn in this unit

In reports ordering is achieved by using the **Sorting and Grouping** button on the toolbar. Sorting and Grouping enhances the presentation of data in reports. The addition of a group header and footer identifies the group within the report. The field that is being used for grouping usually has its control in the group header acting as a heading. Calculated controls can be added to group footers to produce subtotals or averages for the group. Records may be displayed in different orders within groups, for example, members may be listed alphabetically by last name within category grouping; bookings may be listed in time and date order within room grouping.

Saving a form as a report

If you change a form to a report then you have more control over the ways in which the data can be formatted for printing, for example you can create a Group/Totals report from the data. To save a form as a report:

1 From the database window click on the **Forms** tab.

2 Click on the form you want to save as a report with the RIGHT mouse button.

3 Choose **Save As Report** from the shortcut menu, and click on **OK**.

4 Click on the **Reports** tab and you will see the report listed. The report has the same controls and property settings as the form, for example, if the **Keep Together** property of the detail section is set to **Yes** then page breaks will not occur in the middle of records.

Task 1: Saving a form as a report

In this task you will save the **Bookings** form as a report.

1 In the database window click on the form **Bookings** using the right mouse button.

2 Choose **Save As Report** from the shortcut menu, and click on **OK**.

3 Click on the **Reports** tab in the database window.

4 Select the **Bookings** report and preview it.

5   Use **Sorting and Grouping** to group by room and to sort in date and time order. (You may wish to refer back to Unit 18.)

6   Make any adjustments to the design before printing.

Adding controls to reports

Calculated controls

Calculated controls are useful in reports. For example, if a report has been produced from a table that contains data about stock in the form of quantity sold and price then the sales revenue can be calculated by multiplying the quantity sold by the price.

Task 2: Adding a calculated control to the Members2 report

A calculated control was used in the Membership form to find out whether a member's subscription was overdue. In this task this control will be copied and pasted into the report **Members2** customised in Unit 20.

1   Open the **Membership** form in Design View. Select the calculated control and copy it, using **Edit-Copy**. Close the form.

2   Open the report **Members2** in design mode.

3   Click on the Detail bar and use **Edit-Paste** to paste in the control. Move it to a suitable place and, if necessary, rearrange the other controls.

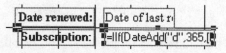

4   Save the report, preview and print it. The new control should print either **Up to date** or **Overdue** as illustrated in the extract below.

Date renewed: 4/10/96

Subscription: Up to date

Controls in grouped reports

The most usual way of grouping records is by category. An example used in Unit 18 was that of the categories of membership. To group by category the best way is to choose to group by a particular category when constructing the report using the Report Wizard.

To alter the grouping properties once into design mode of the report use the **Sorting and Grouping** dialog box. This dialog box can be used to add group headers and footers. Calculated controls can be added so that, for example, group sub-totals or averages can be added to the report.

Task 3: Adding calculated controls to a grouped report

1   Display the **Members2** report in design mode.

2   Click on the **Sorting and Grouping** button in the toolbar and set the sorting and grouping as illustrated below. This report sorts the members into alphabetical order within the category number groups. For **Category No** set the **Group Header** and **Group Footer** to **Yes**, and set **Keep Together** to **With first detail**, which will prevent a page break between the group heading and a following detail.

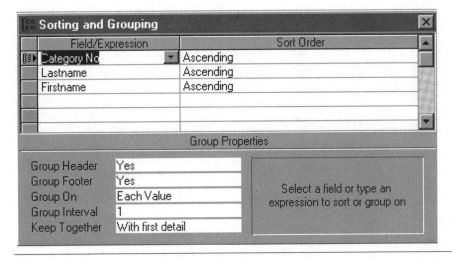

3   Move the control for the **Category No** to the **Category No Header**. Select the control, use **Edit-Cut**, click on the Category No header bar and use **Edit-Paste**.

4   In the Category No Footer add a text box control and key into it the expression *=Count([Membership No])* which will display the total number of members in each category.

5   Add the label ***Number of Members***.

◆ Page Header											
◆ Category No Header											
Category	Category N										
◆ Detail											
Membership No:		Membership									
	Firstname:	Firstname			**Lastname:**		Lastname				
					Date of Birth:		Date of birl				
	Occupation:	Occupation									
		Sex		Smoker							
Sporting Interests:		Sporting Interests									
◆ Category No Footer											
				Number of Members:		=Count([Membershi					
◆ Page Footer											
			="Page " & [Page]								

6 Preview the report, save and print it. A selected part of the print-out is shown following. **Note**: you may have to view more than one page.

Membership No: 10

    Firstname: George W F   **Lastname:** Weiner

    Occupation: Electrician   **Date of Birth:** 10/2/58

                Male   Non-Smoker

Sporting Interests: Weight training, squash

              Number of Members: 7

Task 4: Groups within groups in a report

Continue with the previous task. The aim is create a report that groups by town within each category group. Display the report in design view and display the sorting and grouping dialog box.

1 In the fourth row add the field **Town**. Select this row and drag it to below the first row. Priority of grouping can be changed by rearranging the rows in the **Sorting and Grouping** dialog box.

2 Select Yes for **Group Header** and **Group Footer**.

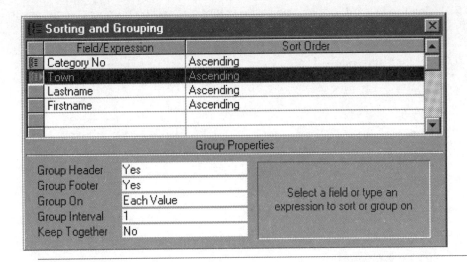

3   In report design mode move the control for **Town** to the **Town Header**.

4   Copy the calculated control for number of members from the **Category No Footer** and paste the copy into the **Town Footer**. Amend the labels for both these controls so that you know which is which.

5 · Preview the report, save and print it.

6   Experiment with different sorting and groupings.

Controls design: integrative tasks

The following tasks revise some of the topics covered in this and the previous two units.

Task 5: Adding a combo box to the classes form

In this task you will add a combo box for the choice of tutor to the **Classes** form. Six tutors will be listed but the text box will accept an alternative which may be keyed in.

1   Open the **Classes** form in Design View.

2   Select and delete the **Class Tutor** text box.

3   Check that both the Field List window and the Toolbox are displayed.

4   Check the **Control Wizards** button is depressed in the Toolbox. Click on the **Combo Box** tool in the Toolbox. Click and drag the **Class Tutor** field from the field list onto its former location on the form.

5 Using the Wizard, opt to type in the values and set the number of columns to one.

6 Enter the list of tutors.

■ Adams

■ Evans

■ Franks

■ Jackson

■ Latham

■ Wheildon

7 Choose the **Store that value in this field** option and edit the label if required. Click on **Finish** .

8 Click on the **View** button on the toolbar to display the form. The **Class Tutor** text box should have a list box button, which when clicked will display the list of tutors' last names. If adjustments are needed return to design mode. When complete save the form. Experiment with entering data.

If you complete the **Tutor** table (compose the records yourself) then the tutors' last names are held in this table. It could be used as the source for the combo box. This has the advantage that as tutors leave or new ones are employed the list in the combo box reflects the tutors' last names in the **Tutor** table. To make this change:

1 After dragging the **Class Tutor** field to the **Classes** form, choose '**I want the combo box to look up the values in a table or query**'.

2 Select the table **Tutor** and select **Lastname** from the available fields list.

3 Adjust the width of the column and continue with the wizard as usual.

Task 6: Adding a calculated control to a report

Use the **Classes3** report created in Unit 20 and group it by **Class Tutor**.

1 Move the **Class Tutor** control to the **Class Tutor Header**.

2 Add a calculated control in the **Class Tutor Footer** that will count the number of classes. **Hint**: count the **Class No** field.

3 Within the **Class Tutor** grouping try to group by activity and count the number of classes of each activity held by each tutor.

4 Save and close the report.

Adding lines and rectangles

What you will learn in this unit

This unit is the first of a series that focuses on features that allow you to adjust the appearance of the information on a report or form, and to make their presentation more exciting. Access offers a wide range of tools for formatting both screens and reports and supports the imaginative creation of interesting screens and reports. Whilst all these features can be applied to both forms and reports, some are used more often with forms and others with reports.

By the end of this unit you will be able to:

■ add lines and boxes to forms and reports.

Understanding design

These units focus on those tools concerned with screen and report design. You will already have used some of these features briefly in the last few units. Forms and reports created using Wizards use some of these features to a limited extent, but by the time you have completed these units you should be able to improve on Wizard designs.

Although the tools we explore in these units allow you to be very adventurous with your designs, remember that good design hinges on the appropriate and sparing use of objects such as boxes and lines, and upon the use of only a limited number of different fonts. In addition most organisations will wish to establish a house style which might be applied to all screens and groups of similar reports. We are not this consistent in the forms and reports that we generate in these units, because they have been used to demonstrate the wide range of features and designs that can be adopted. When, however, you do need to create a house style, form and report templates are one means of doing this and we introduce these briefly in later units. The tips below act as a reminder of good design features.

Design tips: forms

1   Keep the form simple and easy to read. Don't use unnecessary text and graphics, but do use fonts and font sizes that are easy to read on the screen.

2   Use colour sparingly, to make forms interesting, but choose colours that are comfortable for those working at the screen for a long period.

3   Design the form taking into account how it will be used, i.e. where data needs to be entered and ease of movement between data entry boxes.

4   Maintain a consistent appearance for related forms. This looks more professional and makes it easier for a user to acclimatise to a series of forms.

Design tips: reports

1 Keep the report simple. Make the data easy to read by choosing font sizes and types that print well. Use fonts and graphics to help to convey important messages in the report.

2 Design in the knowledge of the capabilities of the printer. In particular, a colour printer can produce much more intricate detail than a non-colour printer.

3 Consider the application of the report. Who are the readers and why will they be using it?

Adding lines and rectangles to forms and reports

Lines and rectangles can be added to emphasise portions of the form or report or to separate one part from another.

Lines are added thus:

1 Select the **Line** tool in the Toolbox.

2 Point to where you want the line to start.

3 Drag the pointer. The **Line** tool draws a line from where you start dragging the pointer to where you release the mouse.

Rectangles are added thus:

1 Select the **Rectangle** tool in the Toolbox.

2 Point to where you want the line to start.

3 Drag the pointer to where you want the opposite corner to be.

Changing control layers

When you add rectangles to a form or report, they are initially placed on top of any other controls, but as their default fill is transparent any controls already on the form or report that are bounded by the rectangle will still be visible.

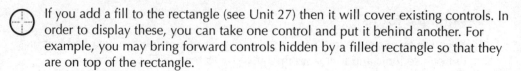 If you add a fill to the rectangle (see Unit 27) then it will cover existing controls. In order to display these, you can take one control and put it behind another. For example, you may bring forward controls hidden by a filled rectangle so that they are on top of the rectangle.

1 To move a control from the front to below other controls, select it and choose **Format-Send to Back**.

2 To move a control from behind other controls and to put it on top, choose **Format-Bring to Front**.

Task 1: Adding lines and rectangles

Open the form **Classes**. Experiment with adding lines and rectangles to the form as suggested above, until it looks similar to the form shown below.

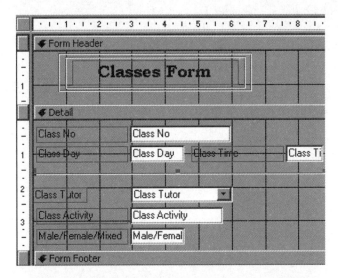

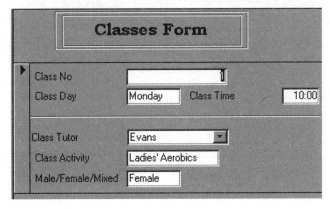

FIGURE 25.1

More specifically:

1   Move and size the controls so that they are in the position shown in FIGURE 25.1.

2   Edit the text of the labels appropriately.

3   Place two rectangles around the text in the form header.

4   Select one of the rectangles by clicking on it and practise deleting it by pressing the *Delete* key. You are likely to need to delete lines or rectangles that you have placed in the wrong place before you have finished!

163

5   Recreate the rectangle. Note that if you later choose a fill for either or both these rectangles you will need to use **Format-Send to Back** to send the filled rectangle behind the existing controls on the form.

6   Insert a line underneath the controls for **Day** and **Time**.

7   Save the form as ***Classes3***.

Style enhancements

What you will learn in this unit

Style enhancements include alignment, colour, three-dimensionality, fonts and borders. These properties are listed in the bottom half of the property sheet window and may also be set using buttons on the toolbar. When a control is selected that uses any of the style enhancements described in these units, the middle and right sections of the toolbar change to show the buttons in the table listed below.

Bt the end of this unit you will be able to:

- use different alignments
- use different fonts
- set dimensions
- set colours
- set borders.

Setting alignment and font

This activity explores the use of the toolbar to set alignment and font. First select the control to which you wish to add style, then click on an appropriate icon on the toolbar as required below.

Alignment

▤	left aligns text
▤	centres text
▤	right alignment

Font

 font name which sets the style of characters

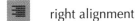 font size which sets the size of the characters

B bold, which sets characters as bold.

I italics, which sets characters as italic

<u>U</u> underline, which underlines characters

Alignment determines whether the characters that appear in the control start at the left side of the control, end at the right side of the control or are centred in the control's position. The defaults are right alignment for data fields containing numbers and dates, and left alignment for all other controls.

It is useful to examine the alignment of controls during the design phase. To do this, select the control by clicking on it and examine which of the alignment buttons is depressed. The best alignment depends on how the controls have been arranged on the form or report. For example, in a report showing data in columns with field labels in the Page Header, set the alignment of the headers to the same as that for the entries below them in order to align the headings with the data.

A **font** is a collection of features that describes how the text appears. Using two or three different fonts, and using a larger font size or bold or italics can emphasise parts of a report, and make your form or report more interesting.

Note: Although it is possible to set every control to a different font, good design requires that you are selective in the use of fonts. In particular you might consider the following:

- do not use more than two or three fonts on one report or form

- select a font that is appropriate for the application. For example, script and other fancy fonts are not often used in business applications, and where they are it is usually to achieve a particular effect

- it is usual to use screen fonts for screen display and printer fonts for printing. If you use, for example, a screen font for printing a report, Windows makes the closest possible substitution and there will be a difference between what you see on the screen and what is printed on paper. If you have True type fonts, use them. They appear the same printed and on the screen

- Access remembers the printer that is currently selected when you create a form or report and uses fonts specific to the selected printer.

Task 1: Setting alignment and fonts on forms

Open the form **Classes3**. Set the alignment and font of the text of the labels as shown in FIGURE 26.1. More specifically:

1　Increase the font size of **Class No**, **Class Day** and **Class Time**. You may also need to increase the size of the controls in order to accommodate the text of the labels and the data in the larger size.

2　Click on each control in turn and check its alignment. Left align controls for all fields except **Class No** which should be right aligned.

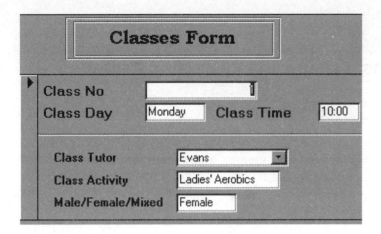

FIGURE 26.1

Task 2: Borders, lines, alignment and fonts on reports

The last two tasks have involved forms. In this task you are required to apply borders, lines, alignment and fonts to a report.

Design a new report *Classes4* based on the **Classes** table. Format the report so that it looks like this.

Design View:

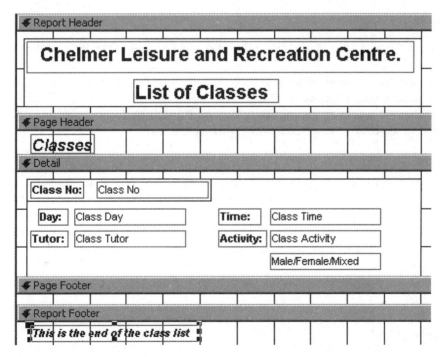

Print Preview:

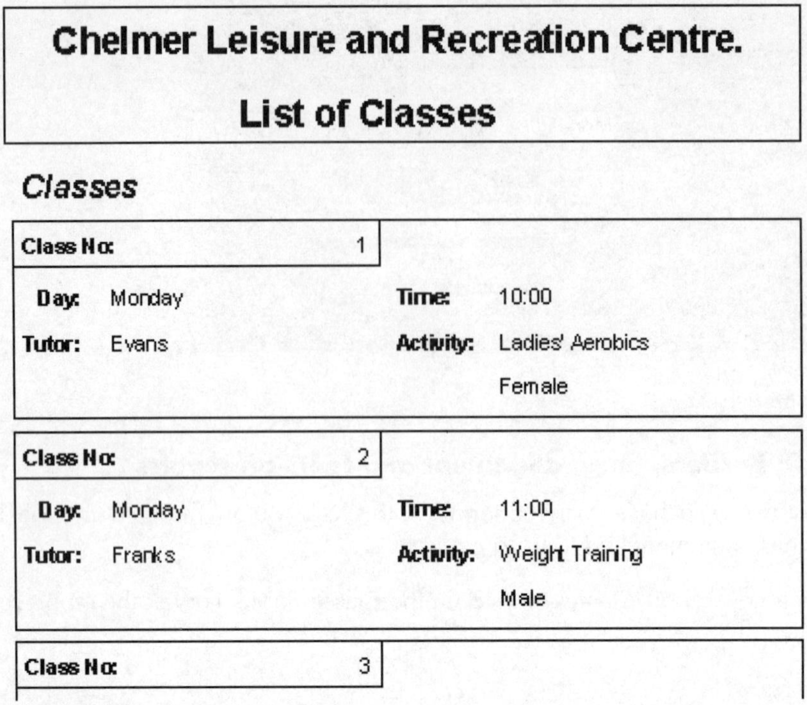

```
┌──────────────────────────────────────────────┐
│                                                │
│    Chelmer Leisure and Recreation Centre.      │
│                                                │
│             List of Classes                    │
│                                                │
└──────────────────────────────────────────────┘
```

Classes

Class No:	1

Day: Monday   Time: 10:00

Tutor: Evans   Activity: Ladies' Aerobics

Female

Class No:	2

Day: Monday   Time: 11:00

Tutor: Franks   Activity: Weight Training

Male

Class No:	3

FIGURE 26.2

View the report on screen and, save the report as *Classes4*. More specifically:

1　In the Report Header insert two controls and type in the text shown in FIGURE 26.2. Move the controls to centre them. Centre align the text in the controls. Format the text to an appropriately large size and bold. Insert a box around the text. Use **Format-Send to Back** to re-display the text.

2　In the Detail band, first add the controls using the **Field List**. Click on the field list window title bar to select all fields, and then drag one of the fields to where you want the fields to start within the Detail band. Fields and their field names will be added to the Detail band.

3　Edit the field names so that they match those shown in the illustration.

4　Move the controls to match the arrangement in the illustration.

5　Format the text in the controls to a slightly larger size and size the controls appropriately.

6　To align a group of controls select the group and apply **Format-Align-Left/Right**. Most of these controls are left aligned with respect to each other.

7   Next examine the alignment of text within the controls. Ensure that all controls are left aligned, and, in particular, remember to left align **Time**.

8   Insert a box around the **Class No** controls. Insert a further box to enclose all text in the Detail band.

9   In the Page Header band type in *Classes*. Format this text and place a line underneath it.

10 At the top of the Page Footer band insert a line.

11 Examine the report in Print Preview, noting especially that you have made your controls large enough to display their information.

12 Make any necessary adjustments, Print Preview again, and save the report as *Classes4*.

Special effects, colours and borders

What you will learn in this unit

You can make a control look three-dimensional, add colour or change border widths to make reports and forms look more exciting. Remember that since most reports are not printed in colour, colours are most likely to be useful for on-screen forms and do not normally need to be set for reports. Equally, three-dimensional controls are particularly useful on forms, where they may be used to highlight labels or to mark out a button.

By the end of this unit you will be able to:

■ set dimensions

■ set colours

■ set borders.

Using the Formatting (Form/Report Design) tool-bar

Special effects, colours and borders can be set using the Formatting (Form/Report Design) toolbar.

An alternative way to set these properties is through the property sheet window. This can be displayed by double-clicking on the control or area whose properties are to be viewed and changed. Generally, it is easier to use the formatting toolbar so we shall restrict ourselves to its use here.

The drop down buttons allow the control of Fill/Back Color, Font/Fore Color, Line/Border Color, Line/Border Width and Special Effects.

Back, fore and border colours

A control can have separate colours for back (ground), fore (ground) and border. To set a colour:

1 Select the control.

2 In turn, click on the drop down arrow of: **Fill/Back Color** , **Font/Fore Color** and **Line/Border Color** buttons to drop down the colour selection box, and choose an appropriate colour.

3   If the **Transparent** button in the colour selection box is clicked, the selected
control becomes transparent so that the control shows whatever controls are
behind it.

Experiment with different colours until you have chosen a colour combination that
is legible and draws attention to appropriate parts of the screen.

Border widths

All controls have adjustable borders. Some, such as the labels for
check boxes, option buttons and text boxes have as a default not to
display any border. Other controls, such as option groups, list boxes
and combo boxes, have as a default to display a thin black border.

To select a border width click on the drop down arrow of the
Border Width button on the toolbar. From the selection shown
choose an appropriate border width.

Special effects

Special effects can be set as one of the following: Flat, Raised, Sunken,
Etched, Shadowed, and Chiselled. These options are displayed by
clicking on the drop down arrow of the **Special Effects** button on the
toolbar.

Notes

■ When you select Raised, Sunken, Etched, Shadowed or Chiseled, the control
adopts the same colours as buttons on the toolbar and command buttons to
achieve the effect. These colours are set by the Windows Control Panel. It is only
possible to change the fore and back colours.

■ When a control is shown as Raised, Sunken, Etched, Shadowed or Chiseled
changing the border width will cause the control to revert to Flat.

Task 1: Setting dimensions and borders

Open the form **Classes3** and experiment with setting dimensions colours and borders. For example, try:

1   Setting all the field labels as Raised.

2   Setting the Form Header as sunken.

3   Increasing the width of the line in the Detail band.

4   Apply some colours to different parts of the screen to add interest.

Control default properties

What you will learn in this unit

In earlier units we have set the properties of controls after adding them to the form. It is also possible to set defaults for controls, which then apply to all controls of that type that you add to the current form or report. If you want to use a set of default control properties for multiple forms or reports, you can create templates that store default settings, and then use these templates whenever you create forms and reports. Templates will be explored in the next unit.

By the end of this unit you will be able to:

- examine the default properties of a control

- set default properties of a control.

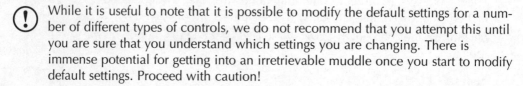 While it is useful to note that it is possible to modify the default settings for a number of different types of controls, we do not recommend that you attempt this until you are sure that you understand which settings you are changing. There is immense potential for getting into an irretrievable muddle once you start to modify default settings. Proceed with caution!

Setting property defaults

To set property defaults for a form or report you follow similar steps to those for property setting.

1   Click a tool in the toolbox, whilst the property sheet window is displayed. Use **View-Properties** to display the property sheet for that tool.

2   The property sheet window changes to show only the properties that you can set as the default for controls of the selected type, e.g. text, date or number.

3   The title bar changes to Default and the name of the object. Most of the properties listed you should recognise from earlier activities when you were setting the properties of the individual controls.

4   Change the properties in the property sheet window as you would change the properties for specific parts of forms or reports.

5   Any control of that type that you subsequently add to the form or report uses the new settings you have made for the control.

FIGURE 28.1 shows the **Default Properties Box** for a section in a form, showing the **Special Effect** property drop down list box.

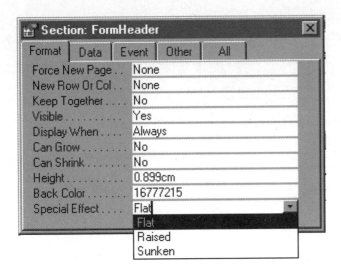

FIGURE 28.1

Default text box

Clicking on the `Text Box` button in the toolbox with the property sheet window open (use **View-Properties** to display it) will display the default **Text Box** window.

Most of the property settings in the property sheet window will be familiar, but there are five new properties that are specific to default control setting.

These are:

Property	Description
Auto Label	Causes labels to appear with, for example, text boxes.
Add Colon	Causes colons to appear at the end of labels.
Label X and Label Y	Set the relative distance from the upper left hand corner of the selected control.
Label Align	Sets the position of the text in the label.

Task 1: Examining the default properties of a control

To minimise the danger of you modifying the default settings in ways in which you did not intend and thereby finding it difficult to follow later activities in this book, this task concentrates on examining the existing default settings rather than modifying them. **Note that adjustments to default settings will apply thereafter until they are changed again.**

1 Open any form or report.

2 Select a section control by clicking on it. Click on the label button in the toolbox. Open the property sheet window. Examine the default properties for this tool.

3 In a similar way, examine the property sheet window for a text box control

4 Again, similarly, examine the property sheet window for a box or a line.

What are some of the differences between the defaults that are set for these different types of controls?

unit 29

Report and form templates

What you will learn in this unit

When a form or report is created without using a Wizard, Access uses a template to define its default characteristics. A template for producing reports or forms can be used in order to maintain a house style in form or report design, or, more simply, to avoid having to format all sections on each occasion. For example, you may choose to set a range of default settings for specific parts of a form. Alternatively, you may have an earlier version of a report design which you need to upgrade and from which two similar, but different, reports might be created. A report template can be created from the first report, and that template used as the basis for the design of the two subsequent reports.

By the end of this unit you will be able to:

- create a form template
- create a report template.

Understanding templates

A template determines the default settings for form, report, section and control properties, section sizes and whether the form or report includes headers and footers.

To create a template from an existing form or report:

1 Create a form or report with control settings you want.

2 Display the form or report header and footer and page header and footer, if you want these to be included in the default.

3 Set section sizes to determine their default size, if you want these included.

4 Save this form or report.

5 To use the form or report as a template, choose **Tools-Options** and click on the **Forms/Reports** tab.

6 Type in the name of the form or report in the **Form Template** or **Report Template** box. Click on **OK** .

When you next create a new blank report the selected report or form will be used as a template.

Note: The default for both form and report templates is **Normal**.

175

Task 1: Creating and using a report template

In this task we use a report that you have previously created to define the properties of a template. The most obvious properties that will be set are the section sizes (e.g. the size of the Page Header) and the presence or absence of various headers and footers. Other section and control properties have also been set.

1   First display the Database window.

2   To create a template based on the properties of the report **Classes4** choose **Tools-Options** and click on the **Forms/Reports** tab.

3   In the **Report Template** box at the bottom of the dialog box, enter the name of the report *Classes4*.

4   Click on **OK** , and this will be used as the default report template.

5   Now, create a new blank report based on a table or query of your choice without using the Wizard, i.e. by choosing **Design View**.

6   You should see that this report has the same headers and footers and section sizes as the new template. Close the report without saving.

Task 2: Creating and using a form template

In this task we will create a blank form and define the properties of the form to be stored in the template. The properties that will be redefined are those of the label tool.

1   Create a form design that will form a new template by clicking on the **Forms** tab, choosing **New** and clicking on **Design View** without basing the form on a table or query.

2   Display the form header and footer, to include these in the default. Adjust their size if desired. Set the label default properties to *Times New Roman, size 14*, bold, shadowed (see previous unit).

3   Save this form as *Chelmer* and close it.

4   Next, to use the form as a template, choose **Tools-Options** and click on the **Forms/Reports** tab.

5   In the **Form Template** box at the bottom of the dialog box, enter the name of the form *Chelmer*.

6 Click on **OK** , and this will be used as the form template.

7 Now, create a blank new form (note: form may be based on a table or query) without using the Wizard.

8 Note that the form has the same headers and footers and section sizes as the template. Use the label tool and note it has the properties as set in the template. Close this form without saving.

Task 3: Returning form and report templates to Normal

To return the form and report templates to normal:

1 Choose **Tools-Options** and click on the **Forms/Reports** tab.

2   In the **Form Template** text box, enter *Normal* and repeat for **Report Template**.

3 Click on **OK** .

Report and form charts

What you will learn in this unit

Analysis of the data in a database can often be effectively performed, and subsequently displayed with the aid of a chart. For example, it might be useful to examine the membership of the **Leisure Centre by Membership Category** or to look at the distribution of bookings and display this data as a chart.

Charts can be created by using Microsoft Graph, which is a component of both Access and Word. Here we introduce a few tasks that make use of Graph in order to demonstrate how it can be used to insert charts into a report or form. These tasks first take you step-by-step through the creation of a simple chart, and then demonstrate how that chart can be inserted in a report or form. If you require more detailed help on the use of Graph, consider using **Help** in Access or work through the relevant exercise in **Word 97 Basic Skills, by S J Coles and J E Rowley (Letts Educational, 1997)**.

By the end of this unit you will be able to:

■ add a chart to a report or form

■ edit a chart

■ understand the links between the database and the chart

■ use the clipboard to copy or move charts

■ add a chart to a report that is based upon a query.

Understanding charts

Charts are often most appropriate in reports where some summary data can be displayed pictorially. As such they will often be included in the report's footer.

Charts can also be added to forms. They may be used to chart items within individual records, in which case they can be included in the detail band. We start to demonstrate the process by creating a chart in a simple form, which we could display on the screen as a visual display of the prices for the various different membership categories. However, within the Chelmer database application, this is not a particularly illustrative example as you will see in the following task. If we had an inventory application with an Item table which contained the fields **Number in Stock** and **Re-order Level** then a chart comparing the values of these two fields would provide a visual indication of whether to re-order a stock item. To show summary data, it is best to create a blank form and insert a chart based on a table or query containing the data you wish to summarise.

Later we experiment with some simple charts that make use of queries to show counts of the occurrences of specific field values, for example to show the bookings by the room, hall or court that has been booked. We also experiment with moving charts between forms using the clipboard.

Adding a chart to a form

Charts can be used on forms to display data on screen at a glance. The simplest use is where the data comes from the tables, and the data from each record is shown on a separate chart for each record. This is the type of chart that we shall explore here, although as mentioned earlier the example is not particularly illustrative.

To use a chart in a form to display data from a table:

1 Display or create a form in design view. Insert a heading in the form header e.g. Chelmer Leisure.

2 Prepare to insert a chart in the detail band by ensuring that it is open, by clicking on it.

3 Choose **Insert-Chart**. Drag a chart box onto the Detail band area.

4 When you release the mouse button, Access presents a series of dialog boxes to help you define your chart.

5 Go through the dialog boxes making appropriate selections for fields to chart and labels for the chart, and insert a chart title.

6 To complete the chart, click on the ▉ **Finish** ▉ button.

7 Access now inserts a control in the Detail band which accommodates the chart.

8 Save and close the form. The chart is saved as part of the form.

Task 1: Adding a chart to a form

In this task we wish to add a chart to the Detail band in a form.

1 First open a new form in Design View. Choose to use the table **Membership Category**.

2 Click on in the Detail band to ensure it is open.

3 Choose **Insert-Chart**. Drag a chart box onto the Detail band area.

4 When you release the mouse button, Access presents a series of dialog boxes to help you define your chart.

5 Select a data source for your chart i.e. the table **Membership Category**. Click on ▉ Next> ▉.

6 Select **Category Type** and **Membership Fee** as the fields that contain the data you want for the chart. Click on **Next>**.

7 Select a chart type. Choose a column chart and click on **Next>**. Skip the preview chart step by clicking on **Next>**.

8 The next dialog box shows the link between chart and document as **Category No**. This link will mean that the chart display will change from record to record. Click on **Next>**.

9 Give your chart a title e.g. **Membership Fees**. Choose the option **No, don't display a legend**. To complete the chart, click on **Finish**.

10 Access now inserts a control for the chart in the Detail band.

11 To see the chart on the form click on the **View** button. You may need to adjust the size of the chart control in design view. The chart may need editing; this is discussed in the following section.

12 Save the form as **Fee Charts** and close the form. The chart is saved as part of the form.

Task 2: Creating a summary chart in a blank form

In this task the fee data will be charted as one chart in a blank form.

1 First open a new form in Design View. Do not select a table so that a blank form is created.

2 As for the previous task use **Insert-Chart** to create a chart box on the detail band area.

3 Continue as for the previous task, saving this form as **MemCatGraph**. View the chart; don't worry if you have made it too small, editing is discussed in the next section.

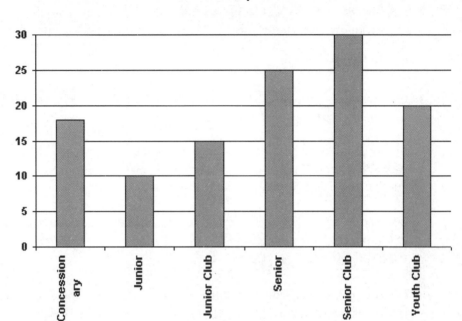

Membership Fees

Editing a chart

Charts can be edited in order to change the data that is displayed, or the way it is displayed. For example, in the chart displayed above the y axis numbers could be shown as £s. Graph is a powerful chart creation tool which allows a wide range of options for creating and designing effective charts. In the following task, we demonstrate how to use Graph to make a few simple alterations to a chart.

To edit a chart:

1 In Design View, double click on the chart.

2 Access starts **Graph** and displays the chart in the **Graph** application window.

3 Make any changes that you require.

4 Choose **File-Exit & Return** to **FormName:** *Form*.

5 Save and close the form or report. The chart is saved as part of the form or report

Task 3: Editing a chart

This task edits the form that you created in Task 2. We experiment with some basic editing techniques in order to demonstrate the principles. More specifically, we shall format the chart title and tick mark labels, and place a border around the chart.

1   Open the form **MemCatGraph** in Design View and add the header *Look how competitive our Membership Rates are*: as shown below.

2   Double-click on the chart control to start Graph. If you increase the size of the chart window then your chart will appear larger on the completed form. Note that, although you are working with the default chart data, the correct data will be displayed when you run the form.

3   Choose a different type of chart by clicking on the down arrow of `Chart Type` Button and selecting a **Bar Chart**.

4   Add or remove the gridlines by using **Chart-Chart Options** and choosing the `Gridlines` tab. Further gridline formatting may be achieved by selecting a gridline and using **Format-Selected Gridlines**.

5   Insert an axis label for the horizontal axis (y axis here), by choosing **Chart-Chart Options**, clicking on the `Titles` tab and adding the text *Membership Price* for **Value(Y) Axis**. Click on `OK`.

6   Double click on this label to call the **Format Axis Title** dialog box. Choose a larger font size and make the text bold and italic. Click on `OK`.

7   Click on the main title to select it and press *Delete* to remove it.

8   Click on the vertical axis; choose **Format-Selected Axis**. Make the axis text larger and bold italic.

9   Choose **File-Exit & Return to Form**.

10 If necessary, size the control by selecting it and dragging its border in order to display the edited chart. Note, you may need to return to Graph and alter the size of the Chart window.

11 Save the form as *MemCatGraph*. Close the form.

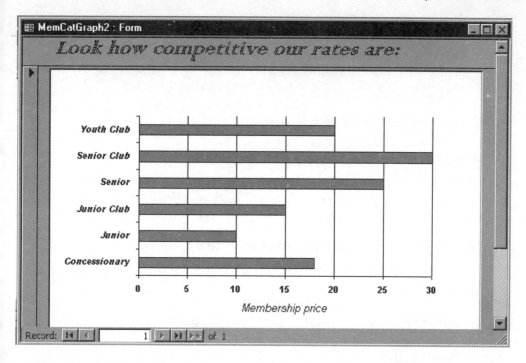

Demonstrating that charts are linked to the database

The charts that you create in Access and that use data in the database are updated when you update the data in the database. So, for example, the charts that we have just created should be automatically updated if we change the values in the **Membership Category** table.

Task 4: Testing links betwween the database and associated charts

1   In this task we wish to demonstrate how the chart changes to display new data in the **Membership Category** table. Suppose that we change the fees:

2   Open the **Membership Category** table in Datasheet View

3   Edit the values in the Membership Fee column to:

Category No	Membership Fee
1	£30.00
2	£35.00
3	£15.00
4	£20.00
5	£23.00
6	£25.00

4   Close **Membership Category**.

5   Open the form **Fee Charts**. Examine the charts and check that they are displaying the new data. Close the form and open the form **MemCatGraph** and view the chart, which should also reflect the changes to the data.

6   Leave the form **MemCatGraph** open for the next task.

Using the clipboard to copy or move charts

An easy way to insert a chart in a form or report, once you have created the report, is to use the clipboard to Cut or Copy and Paste the chart from one location to another.

Task 5: Using the clipboard to copy a chart

With the form **MemCatGraph** open as at the end of the last task, switch to **Design View** and click on the chart to select it.

1   Choose **Edit-Copy** to copy the chart to the clipboard.

2   Close the form.

3   Create a new grouped report based on the **Bookings** table, using the Report Wizard. Include all fields.

4   Group by **Room/Hall/Court** and sort in **Date** order. Access automatically names and saves the report.

5   Open the new report in Design View. Click on the report footer bar and choose **Edit-Paste** to insert the chart into this report from the clipboard. The chart should now be inserted in the report.

6   Close the report without saving.

Adding a chart to a report, with the aid of a query

The basic approach to creating a chart for a report is the same as that for creating a chart in a form. The above task demonstrates how to copy a chart into a report footer, but this is not a very useful chart to have in the footer of a report which lists bookings. A more useful chart would display bookings according to some category such as room, hall or court, or the category of membership. In order to create such a chart it is first necessary to create a query. Why?

If you think about the stages that you went through to create a chart in Task 2 you will remember that you needed to specify the two fields that were to be displayed on the chart. Suppose we wish to display the number of bookings for each room, hall or court. We need to display the values in the **Room/Hall/Court** field against the number of bookings for each of these. In order to do this we need a field called, say, **CountofBookings**. To create this field we need a query. The following task demonstrates how we might approach this.

Another interesting chart that we might add to a report which lists bookings is one which displays bookings by **Category Type,** i.e. how many bookings are made by each category of member? The creation of this chart would be more complex than the chart which we create below. Why? Because here we need to show **CountofBookings** by Category Type. This would involve creating a query which uses more than one table, and then basing the chart on that query. Which tables would you need to use in the query? Queries which use more than one table are introduced in Unit 32.

First it is useful to record the steps for adding a chart to a report.

To add a chart to a report footer:

1 Make 5 to 8 cm (2 to 3 inches) of space in the report footer section. Choose **Insert-Chart**.

2 In the grey area below the report footer section, draw a control that is about 5 cm (2 inches) deep and 15 cm (6 inches) wide.

3 When you release the mouse button, Àccess presents a series of dialog boxes to help you define your chart.

4 Go through the dialog boxes making appropriate selections for fields to chart and label for the chart, and inserting a chart title.

5 To complete the chart, choose the   **Design**   button.

6 Access now inserts a control in the report footer for the chart and resizes the footer to make room for the new control.

7 To view the chart on the report, click on the   **Report View**   button and move to the last page of the report.

8 When you have finished looking at the chart choose   **Close** .

9 Save the report and close it. The chart is saved as part of the report.

10 The same principles apply for adding a chart to any other part of the report, such as the Report Header.

Task 6: Adding a chart to a report using a query

In this task we wish to add a chart to the report footer in the report **Bookings**. First we need to create a query to use as the basis for the chart.

1   Create a new query using the **Bookings** table.

2 Add the fields **Booking No** and **Room/Hall/Court**.

3 Click on the ███ Totals ███ button to display the **Total**: row.

4 In the **Total** cell for the **Booking No** field insert **Count**.

5 In the **Total** cell for the **Room/Hall/Court** field insert **Group By** and in the **Sort** row insert **Ascending**.

6 Display the dynaset and check that the query counts booking in categories as you would expect it to.

7 Save the query as ***Bookings by Hall***.

Field:	Room/Hall/Court	Booking No	
Table:	Bookings	Bookings	
Total:	Group By	Count	
Sort:	Ascending		
Show:	☑	☑	
Criteria:			
or:			

Room/Hall/Court	CountOfBooking No
Court 1	2
Court 2	1
Court 3	1
Fitness Suite	8
Sports Hall 1	1
Sports Hall 2	9

Now we want to use this query to create a chart.

1 Open the booking report created in Task 5 in design view.

2 To remove the existing chart, click on it and press _Delete_.

3 Choose **Insert-Chart**. Drag a chart control in the report footer.

4 Access takes you through the creation of a chart using Chart Wizards.

5 Choose **Queries** and then **Bookings by Hall** as the data source for your chart. Add both fields to be displayed on the chart.

6 Choose a **Column Chart** type. Preview the chart.

7 In the **Linking Fields** dialog box choose <**No Field**> for both fields.

8 Give your chart a title or accept the suggested title i.e. ***Bookings by Hall***.

9 To complete the chart, click on **Finish**. Access now inserts a control in the report footer for the chart and resizes the footer to make room for the new control.

10 To view the chart on the report, click on the **View** button and move to the last page of the report.

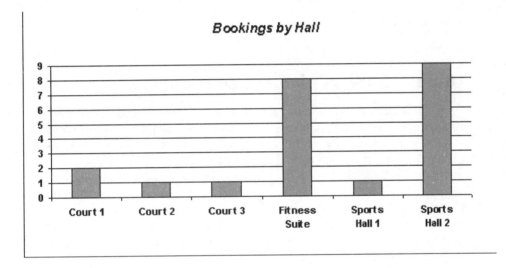

Bookings by Hall

FIGURE 30.1

Note: If you made the control too small to display a chart effectively, you cannot size the chart in Report Design View. You need to re-size the control that contains the chart in Design View, and to re-size the chart in Graph.

1 When you have finished looking at the report in print preview choose **Close** to move back into Design View.

2 Double click on the chart to take it into Graph and edit it as you choose. The chart in FIGURE 30.1 has been sized so that the tick mark labels display effectively, and the title has been formatted. Choose **File-Exit and Return to Bookings by Hall: Report** when you have finished editing.

3 Save the report and close it. The chart is saved as part of the report.

Forms and reports pictures

What you will learn in this unit

We have just experimented with adding charts to forms and reports. You can also insert other objects, including a picture from Windows 95 Paint, a worksheet object from Microsoft Excel, or any object from an application that supports what is known as object linking and embedding (OLE).

By the end of this unit you will be able to:

■ add pictures and objects to forms

■ add pictures and objects to reports.

Understanding pictures and objects

Here we briefly explore inserting a picture into a form or report. A picture can be created in Word or with Windows Paintbrush. We use Word to create a picture and insert it into both a report and a form. If a field on a form, for instance, uses an OLE object data type it is possible to display that object on the form. For example, in Membership we might have a field that accommodates a photograph of the member. This could be displayed on a form or printed on a report. Another application of a picture might be to insert a log into a form header and a report header. Since, typically, the same logo may be used on all forms and reports used by one organisation, in the tasks below we first create the logo for Chelmer Leisure and Recreation Centre, and then add it to a form and a report.

Task 1: Adding a logo to a form

1   Create the logo using Word, WordArt by selecting **Insert-Picture-WordArt**. Select the slanting **WordArt** style and click on **OK**.

2   Enter text for a logo, choosing a font and size for the text and click on **OK**.

3   Click on **AutoShapes** on the Drawing toolbar, choose the rounded corner rectangle shape from **BasicShapes**. Draw a rectangle around the text. Format the rectangle so that the line thickness is greater, say 6pt, and there is **No Fill**.

    (You may need to select **View-Toolbars** and click in the **Drawing** check box to display the Drawing toolbar.)

4   Adjust the rectangle to the required size. Select the **Pointer** tool on the Drawing toolbar, draw a rectangle around both the objects and use **Draw-Group**

to group them. **Note**: when you finish using the pointer tool deselect it by clicking on its button again.

5   Next, zoom in fully to the top corner of the logo and using oval and line tools draw a stickman. You may group the stickman objects so that you can move and size the stickman as one. Repeat to create another line drawing in the bottom right corner. Hint: the curve tool in the Lines group of AutoShapes is useful to create a wavy line.

6   When you are happy with the logo, group the objects by selecting them all using the pointer tool and using **Draw-Group**. Deselect the pointer and you can resize the logo into a size suitable for inclusion on the **Membership** form.

7   Copy it to the clipboard by selecting the drawing and using **Edit-Copy**.

8   Return to Access.

9   To add the logo to the form, open the form **Membership** in design view.

10 Click on the form header section.

11 Choose **Edit-Paste**, size the header section and position the logo.

12 Save the form and close it.

Integrative tasks

Task 2: Creating a chart for the Members by Membership Category report

The **Members by Membership Category** report was created in Report Wizards as a Groups/Totals report. It shows members grouped in categories. It might be interesting to create a simple chart which counts the members in each category and displays the number of members in each category. It would be even better if the category labels were shown as **Category Type** instead of **Category No**, but this would involve the use of a query which used multiple tables, and these are not introduced until later units.

To create this chart:

1   First create an appropriate query to count members by **Category No**. You will have created such a query earlier but probably did not save it.

2 Revisit Unit 13 to discover how to create a query which shows **Category No** and **CountofLastname**.

3 Save this query as ***Categories***.

4 Open the **Members by Membership Category** report.

5 Go through the steps necessary to create a chart in the report footer, choosing the query **Categories** as the data source.

6 Edit the chart as appropriate and save the report.

Task 3: Adding a logo to reports

In order to start to create some kind of house style to our reports, we would like to add the Chelmer Leisure logo to some of the reports generated from the **Membership** table. The easiest way to do this is to copy and paste the logo that we created in Task 1onto the clipboard, and then paste it into the report header.

1 Open the form **Membership** in Design View.

2 Click on the Chelmer Leisure logo to select it. Choose **Edit-Copy**.

3 Close the form.

4 Open the report **Chelmer Leisure and Recreation Centre Members**. Click on the report header, and choose **Edit-Paste**. The logo should appear in the report header.

5 Repeat this operation for the other reports you have created.

Using multiple tables in a query

What you will learn in this unit

This unit introduces queries that use more than one table. Tables are linked by their relationships and through these links can act as if they are one large table.

By the end of this unit you will be able to:

- add and delete tables from a query
- create queries using multiple tables.

In Unit 8 you saw how to set up relationships between tables, but these have not yet been used. The intervening units have introduced tables, queries, forms and reports. In the interests of simplicity these are based on one table or a query generated from one table. In this, and the next few units, using more than one table will be explored. Queries can use more than one table and these queries can produce forms or reports.

Through constructing queries using more than one table you should appreciate how versatile a relational database is. By keeping data in a series of linked but separate tables the need to duplicate data is reduced and it is simpler to update it. To illustrate this point, if the **Membership** table contained a **Fee** field, if the fee changed then every record would need amending rather than just the records in the **Membership Category** table.

Multiple tables in a query

When you use more than one table in a query there should be links between the tables chosen. This is a good opportunity to review the relationships between the tables in the Chelmer Leisure and Recreation Centre database. The **Membership** table is linked to the **Bookings** table through **Membership No**. The **Membership Category** table is linked to the **Membership** table through the **Category No**. The **Bookings** table is linked to the **Classes** table through the **Class No**. The **Tutor** table is linked to the **Classes** table through the **Lastname**.

If tables are added to a query and there is no relationship defined between them then Access will try to link them and this could be a time-consuming and unproductive process.

Joins between tables

Before you can use joins between tables, you must know the contents of their fields and which fields are related by common values. Assigning identical names to fields in different tables that contain related data is a common practice. This has been adhered to in the **Chelmer Leisure and Recreation Centre** database, for example,

Membership No is the link between the **Membership** and **Bookings** tables. There is an exception which is **Class Tutor** (**Classes** table) and **Lastname** (**Tutor** table), which could be remedied by using **Tutor No** as a field in both tables.

Knowing what is in your tables will help when you need to add tables to a query so that you add the tables containing the data you wish to access and also additional tables necessary to create links between tables. This is discussed in more detail at the beginning of each multiple table query used in this activity.

Joins are indicated in Access query designs by lines between field names of different tables, as illustrated in Task 1.

 Access allows different types of joins between tables, but only one type, the most common, will be considered here. This type of join is called an *equivalent* or *inner-join* and has already been created when the relationships were defined. Inner-joins display all the records in one table that have corresponding records in another table. This correspondence is determined by identical values in the fields that join the tables. In the case of the Chelmer Leisure and Recreation Centre database all joins are based on a unique primary key field in one table and a field in the other table in a one-to-many relationship (see Unit 8).

Adding tables to a query

When creating a query this is simply a matter of selecting more than one table from the **Show Table** dialog box. Tables are shown in the query window with lines between them indicating the relationships. If you omit a table then choose **Query-Show Table** to display the **Show Table** dialog box again.

Deleting Tables from a query

This a simply a matter of clicking on the title bar of the particular table and pressing the *Delete* key. However, check that the table was not providing an indirect link between two tables and also make any amendments to the query.

Task 1: Adding tables to the query window

In this task you will add all the tables in the Chelmer Leisure and Recreation Centre database to a query.

1 Starting at the database window, click on the ▐ **Queries** ▐ tab and click on ▐ **New** ▐. Select **Design View** and click on ▐ **OK** ▐.

2 From the **Show Table** dialog box add all the tables. These are **Membership**, **Membership Category**, **Bookings**, **Classes** and **Tutors**.

 3 By rearranging the tables, your query window will appear as illustrated below. If there are no lines or some missing indicating the relationships, abandon the query and check the relationships using **Tools-Relationships**. Refer to Unit 8.

4 A link may be displayed between **Lastname** in the **Membership** table and

Lastname in the **Tutors** table. This illustrates that the significance of field names should be considered when designing a table. However, the link can be removed by clicking on it and pressing *Delete*.

5   Delete the **Tutors** and the **Membership Category** tables. Consider why is it dangerous to delete the **Bookings** table.

6   Close the query without saving it.

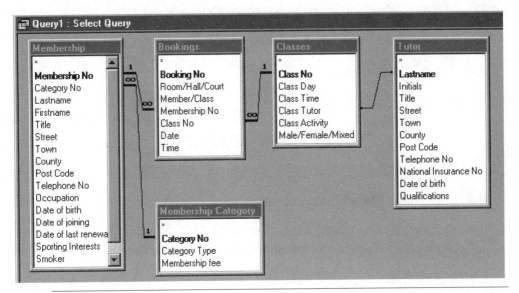

Using multiple tables

This section comprises a series of tasks in which questions are asked of the database and queries containing multiple tables are devised in order to answer the questions.

Task 2: Membership fees

Q. How much membership fee money has been collected in the last six months?

A. First decide which tables are needed. The data needed is the members who renewed their membership in the last six months, their membership category and the fee. This data can be found in the **Membership** table and the **Membership Category** table. Is there a link between these two tables? Yes, between **Category No** (primary key **Classes** table) and **Category No** (**Membership** table), so only these two tables will be required.

Before continuing you should review the dates of renewal in the **Membership** table and, if necessary, update them so that several members will be selected by this query.

To create the query:

1   From the database window click on the Queries tab and click on New. Select **Design View**.

2 From the **Show Table** dialog box select the **Membership** table and the **Membership Category** table. These two tables should be shown in the query window with a link between them.

3 Add the fields **Membership No** and **Membership Fee** to the query.

4 Create a calculated field which works out the time between the date of last renewal and today's date. In the first field cell enter the expression

   Rejoin: DateDiff("d",[Date of last renewal],Date())

   This calculates the number of days from the date of the last renewal to today.

5 Run this query to see the result.

6 Return to the query design. Add the criteria **<182** (i.e. less than six months - 182 days: you may need to check your records to see if this query will work) to find those with renewal dates less than six months old.

7 Run this query to check and then return to design mode.

8 Click on the **Totals** button to create totals.

9 In the **Rejoin** field select **Where** in the total cell and hide this field. In the **Membership No** field select **Count** and in the **Membership Fee** field select **Sum**.

10 Run the query. The result should be the number of members who rejoined in the last six months and the total of fees paid.

11 Save the query as *Recent fees paid*.

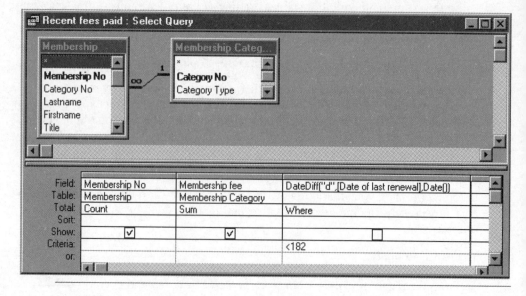

To create the report:

1 From the database window click on the **Reports** tab and click on **New**.

2 In the **New Report** dialog box select the query **Recent fees paid** and use **AutoReport: Tabular** to design a report.

3 Switch to design view and edit the labels so your report is similar to the one below. Save the report as **Recent fees paid**.

Fees paid in the last six months

No of members joining	*Total fees paid*
8	£176.00

Task 3: Class activities in the fitness suite

Q. What class activities are being held in the fitness suite?

A. The tables that are needed to answer this question are the **Bookings table** and the Classes table. There is a direct link between these tables through **Class No**.

To create the query:

1 From the database window click on the **Queries** tab and click on **New**. Select **Design View**.

2 From the **Show Table** dialog box select the **Classes** and **Bookings** tables. These two tables should be shown in the query window with a link between them.

3 Add the fields **Member/Class**, **Room/Hall/Court**, **Class Day**, **Date**, **Class Time** and **Class Activity** to the query.

4 In the **Member/Class** column set the criterion to No to select only classes and hide this field.

5 In **Room/Hall/Court** put *"Fitness Suite"* in the criteria row and hide this field.

6 Run the query.

7 Save it as **Activities in Fitness Suite**.

To create the report:

1 From the database window click on the **Reports** tab and click on **New** .

2 In the **New Report** dialog box select the query **Activities in Fitness Suite** and use **AutoReport: Tabular** to design a report.

3 Edit your design to create a report similar to the one illustrated. Save this report as **Activities in Fitness Suite**.

Class Activities in Fitness Suite

Day	Date	Time	Activity
Monday	13/5/96	10:00	Ladies' Aerobics
Monday	13/5/96	11:00	Weight Training
Tuesday	14/5/96	10:00	Men's Multi-gym
Tuesday	14/5/96	14:00	Ladies' Multi-gym
Tuesday	14/5/96	19:00	Family Multi-gym
Wednesday	15/5/96	10:00	Ladies' Aerobics
Thursday	16/5/96	15:00	Multi-gym
Friday	17/5/95	14:00	Men's Multi-gym

Task 4: Class attendance

Q. Which members are attending which classes?

A. Our database is unable to answer this question. Why? The data needed has not been recorded. The database could be modified so that this data can be added. What would be the best way to go about this? One method could be to introduce an extra field **Class** to the **Membership** table. However, this leads to problems if the member attends more than one class or a class is cancelled. A better alternative is to create another table that keeps lists of members in classes. This table would be linked to both the **Membership** and **Classes** tables. **Class List** would be a suitable name.

To create the **Class List** table:

1 From the database window click on the **Tables** tab and click on **New** . Select **Design View** and click on **OK** .

2 Create a table with two fields, **Class No** and **Membership No**. Make both fields

numeric of type long integer. This is so that they are of a type which will correspond to the counter types used by the fields **Membership No** (**Membership**
table) and **Class No** (**Classes** table) to which they will be related.

3   Each record is unique, that is the **entire** record not a field on its own. Therefore
the primary key must be both fields. To set both as the primary key select both
before clicking on the **Primary Key** button in the toolbar.

4   Save the table as **Class List** and close it.

5   Define two relationships as described below. In both of these relationships referential integrity is enforced. This will prevent a class or a membership number
being entered which does not exist in the **Classes** or **Membership** table, so a
non-existent member cannot join a class nor can a member join a non-existent
class.

6   Click on the **Relationships** button and then click on the **Show Table**
button. Add the **Class List** table.

7   Drag **Class No** from the **Classes** table to **Class No** in the **Class List** table. Check
the **Enforce Referential Integrity** check box.

8   Drag **Membership No** from the **Membership** table to **Membership No** in the
Class List table. Check the **Enforce Referential Integrity** check box.

9   Save the layout and close the relationships window.

10 Before a form can be created, a query which links the member's name to the
class activity needs to be created. A form can be created from this query which
lists the names of members in each class (this form will later become a sub-form
in a main/sub form in Unit 33):

11 From the database window click on the **Queries** tab and click on **New**.
Select **Design View** and click on **OK**.

12 From the **Add Table** dialog box select the **Class List** and **Membership** tables.
These two tables should be shown in the query window with a link between
them.

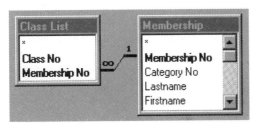

13 Add the following fields to the query: **Class No**, **Membership No**, **Firstname** and **Lastname**. Save the query as *Class Member List*. Close the query.

14 From the database window click on the `Forms` tab and click on `New`. In the **New Form** dialog box select the **Class Member List** query just created and use the **AutoForm: Tabular** to create a tabular form.

15 Display this form in design view and display the properties window. Click on each control in turn, except for the **Membership No**, and set the Locked property to **Yes** and the **Enabled** property to **No**. This prevents data being entered into these controls (this is unnecessary because this form is intended to be a subform). By setting the **Enabled** property to **No** this prevents the cursor going to these controls.

16 Add a title to the form as illustrated and save it as *Class Member List*.

 17 See Unit 33 for the creation of the main/subform.

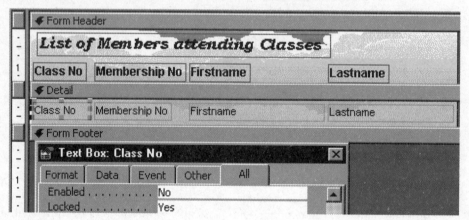

Main/sub forms and main/sub reports

What you will learn in this unit

Subforms and subreports are another way of making use of the links between tables. An example would be keeping academic information about students. A student may study several modules and for each one a performance record is kept. The details about the student, for example, Student No, Title, Surname, Forenames, Date of Birth, Date Enrolled, Personal Tutor could be kept in a **Student** table. The module results for all students could be kept in a **Results** table, with fields **Student No**, **Module No**, **Coursework Grade**, **Exam Grade**, **Overall Grade**, **Date Completed Module**. The tables **Student** and **Results** would be linked through the **Student No**.

A link between the **Student** and **Results** tables enables a main/subform to be designed for entering module results. By designing one form based on the **Student** table and another based on the **Results** table, the two forms can be combined into one known as a main/subform. This form would display the student details as heading information and results records for that student. A report can similarly be constructed. A Student report would be the main part of the main/subreport and a Results report would be the 'sub' part of the main/subreport.

By the end of this unit, you will be able to:

■ create and use main/subforms

■ create and use main/subreports

Creating and using main/subform forms

What is a subform? A main form is usually created from one of the primary tables in a database and a sub-form is a table that is related to it. This is best described by means of an example. Consider a wholesaler's database where there is a table of customer names, addresses, etc, and a table of purchase transactions made by customers. A form showing the customer's details plus a list of transactions made by that customer can be created using a main/subform.

The **Customer** table creates the main part of the form and that customer's transactions comprise the subform. This type of form is useful for all areas of transaction processing, such sales made by salespeople, or bookings made by members of a leisure centre.

A main/subform is created by inserting one form into another as follows.

1 Create the main form and the subform separately. Ideally these should be linked through an existing relationship. The main form should be created in single column format and the subform in tabular format.

2 Open the main form in Design View.

3   Use the **Window** menu to display the database window (shortcut key *F11*). If necessary click on the ▐ **Forms** ▌ tab to show the list of forms.

4   Click and drag the subform to the main form.

Task 1: Creating and using a main/subform

This task creates a main/subform for the **Class List** table. This form shows the class details and lists members enrolled in the class in subform. It can be used to book members into a particular class. Open the **Classes** form and use **File-Save As** to save the form as *Class Lists*, which is a copy of the **Classes** form that can be modified. Display this form in design view and set the **Locked** property for all the controls to **Yes**. This is the reason for making a copy of the form. The original **Classes** form can be used to enter classes data but this new form cannot.

1   Choose **Window-Tile Vertically** to display the **Class Lists** form window (in design view) and database window side by side.

2   Click on **Class Member List** (the sub-form created in Task 4 in Unit 32) and drag to **Class Lists** form.

3   A sub-form box appears on the form. You may wish to reposition and resize it.

4   Run the form and it should appear similar to the one illustrated below.

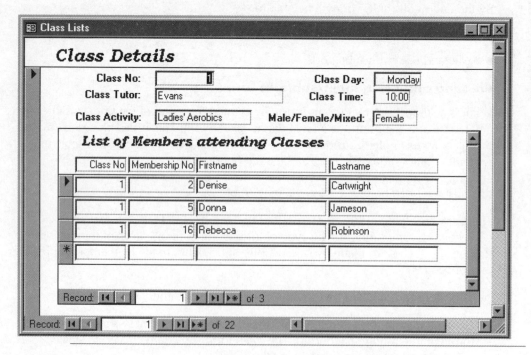

5   Save the form.

6 Try using the form to enter data. A class list can be created by entering the membership numbers of those members who are attending the class.

7 So that a report can be generated later enter data for three class lists as follows.

Class No	Membership No
1	2
1	5
1	16
4	4
4	6
5	7
5	10
5	1

Creating and using main/subreport reports

Like forms, reports can include subreports. An example of such a report is one in which a customer's details are shown in the main report and purchases made by that customer in the subreport. To insert a subreport into a main report:

1 Create the main report and the subreport separately as reports. Ideally these should be linked through an existing relationship.

2 Open the main report in design view. Use **Sorting and Grouping** to add a group footer, for example group by customer or group by company depending upon the nature of the subreport.

3 Choose the **Window** menu to display the database window (shortcut key *F11*). If necessary click on the **Reports** tab to show the list of reports.

4 Click and drag the subreport to the required section in the main report.

Task 2: Adding a subreport to a report

For this task check that you have a **Classes2** report created in Task 5 of Unit 20. Open it and save it as **Classes List2**.

In this task you will create a report of classes and the members enrolled on each of the classes. This is done by adding a **Class Member List** subreport to the **Classes List2** main report.

1 Save the form **Class Member List** as a report (see Unit 24) with the same name.

2 Open this new report in design mode.

3 Reorder the fields so that **Class No** is last in the row. Set the **Visible** property for this field to **No** so that it does not print. Remove the label for **Class No**.

201

4   Edit the header to read *List of members*.

5   Use the palette to alter the colour of fill and borders. Preview the report to check your settings.

6   Save the report and close it.

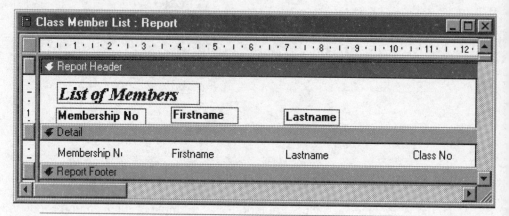

7   Open the **Classes Lists2** report in design mode.

8   Click on the **Sorting and Grouping** button and select **Class No** Ascending in the dialog box. Set the group header and footer to **Yes**.

9   If necessary, widen the group footer section to make room for the subreport.

10   Open the Window menu and choose **Chelmer Leisure: Database** to display the Database Window.

11   Click and drag the **Class Member List** report into the group footer section. You may need to re-arrange your windows so that you can readjust the position of the subreport.

12   In the subForm/subReport properties window note that the link between the two reports is **Class No**.

13   Set the **Can Shrink** and the **Can Grow** properties of the **Class No** Footer section to **Yes**. (Click on the section header to select the section.)

14   Delete the **Class Member List** label and adjust the size of the control as illustrated overleaf. Preview the report.

15   The report would look better if the field labels were in the **Class No** header. Cut and paste the headings from the page header to the **Class No** header as illustrated.

16 Preview, make final adjustments so that it looks similar to the following extract and save the report before printing it.

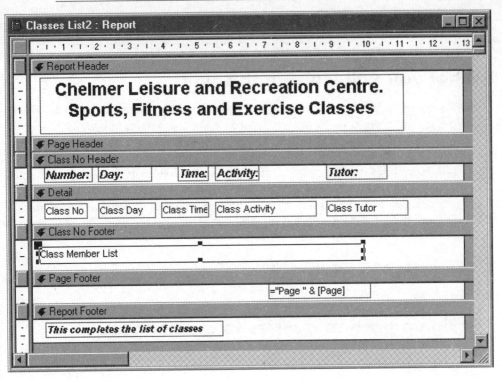

Action queries

What you will learn in this unit

Usually queries are passive in nature, i.e. they do not change any of the data, they only retrieve it in response to criteria. However, special queries known as *action queries* can be designed to change the data. An example could be a bank amending its customer credit limits. The bank wishes to amend the credit limit of customers whose present limit is £200 or less and who have been with the bank for six months or more. First, a query which selects the appropriate customer records would be constructed. By converting this search query to an action query the values in the **Credit Limit** field, for each selected record, would be updated with the new credit limit.

By the end of this unit you will be able to:

■ design action queries to modify data.

Designing action queries to modify data

Previously we have used queries to interrogate the database tables. Action queries can be used in a more powerful way to amend the tables. There are four types of action query: update queries, delete queries, append queries and make table queries.

An action query changes the data in your table or copies data from one table to another. Unlike the select queries we have already seen, an action query doesn't show the records it has retrieved for modification.

If you wish to see the result of the change made by an action query then will you need either to convert your action query to a select query or open the table (if you have created, appended to or deleted from it) to view the changes. The following activities explore the various action queries.

Make table and delete query

These two action queries will be used together to deal with members who have not renewed their membership for more than a year. This operation would be carried out periodically, say annually or every six months, to keep only current members in the **Membership** table.

Members who have not renewed their membership could simply be discarded or their information could be kept in a separate file for a further period as historical information. Chelmer Leisure and Recreation Centre follow the latter course and make a table of old members before deleting them from the current membership table.

(d.) A make table query does just what it says and creates one table from another or others. Data is selected by means of a query to create the new table. A delete query deletes a group of records from one or more tables. The query you design will select the records that are to be deleted. When you run the query, Access retrieves the records you asked for and deletes them from the table.

In this activity we will create a table in which to store old member details before deleting all the members whose last renewal date was in 1995 or before. So that some records meet these criteria open the **Membership** table and add a couple of records where the **Date of Last Renewal** is before the end of 1995. To prevent any problems with referential integrity, alter the date of renewal of the original records so that they are all after 1/1/96.

Task 1: Archiving and removing out of date members

1 Start a new query using **Design View**. Add the **Membership** table to the query.

2 Add all the fields from the table to the query by double-clicking on the table's title bar and dragging the highlighted area to the field cell.

3 In the **Date of Last Renewal** column enter *<1/1/96* into the criteria cell.

4 You may wish to run the query to see which records are selected.

5 To create the **Last renewed 95** table choose **Query-Make Table Query**, or click on the Query Type button and select **Make Table Query**. Key in the name of the table *Archive 95*. This table will go into the current database so don't change the option setting. Leave the check boxes at their default values. Click on OK .

6 Click on the Run button. A message box confirms the number of rows (records) that are being added to the new table. Click Yes to create the new table.

7 Next, change the query to a delete query using **Query-Delete Query**, or click on the Query Type button and select **Delete Query**. Check that the criterion in the **Date of Last Renewal** field is

Field:	Date of Last Renewal
Delete:	Where
Criteria:	<#01/01/96#

8 Click on the Run button. A message box confirms the number of records that will be deleted. Click Yes .

There is no need to save this query as it has performed its function.

9 View the tables to see the effect of the make table and delete actions.

Update query

An update query updates data in your tables. You choose the records and fields you want to update. When you run the query, Access retrieves the records you asked for (this is known as a dynaset) and makes the changes you specified. An example would be increasing the credit limit of all customers who have credit limits of less than, say, £2000.

Task 2: Update query

An example of an update query that Chelmer Leisure and Recreation Centre might use is when a member of staff changes. The update query can change the name of the **Class Tutor** in the **Classes** table.

1 Start a new query using Design View.

2 Add the **Classes** table to the query.

3 Create a query with three fields, **Class No, Class Tutor** and **Class Activity**. In the criteria cell for **Class Tutor** put *Franks*.

4 Choose **Query-Update Query**, or click on the **Query Type** button and select **Update Query**. An **Update To:** row appears in the grid in the lower part of the query window.

5 In the **Update To:** cell of the **Class Tutor** column type *Knight*.

An action query will change the data in your table. It is a good idea to check that your query will select the correct records before running it. You can do this by changing your action query into a select query.

6 First save the action query. Use **File-Save** and save it as *Update tutor*.

7 To change to a select query use **Query-Select Query**, or click on the **Query Type** button and choose **Select Query**.

The lower grid changes to the select grid.

8 Click on the **Datasheet** button on the toolbar to view the query's datasheet. The data that you see is the data that will be affected by your action query.

9 To change back to the action query, first display the query design (click on **Query Design** button in the toolbar) and choose **Query-Update Query**.

10 Click on the **Run** button on the toolbar. A message will appear telling you how many rows will be updated and giving you the opportunity to cancel. Click on **Yes**.

11 Close the query.

12 Create a select query using the new tutor's name as a criterion. Satisfy yourself that the action query has worked.

13 Delete the action query: in the database window click on the **Queries** tab, highlight the update query and delete it by pressing the *Delete* key.

Integrative tasks

The following tasks reinforce concepts introduced in this and the preceding units.

Task 3: Tutors' names and qualifications

Q. What are the names and qualifications of the tutors taking class on 13/5/96?

A. The tables needed are **Bookings** and **Tutors**. There is not a direct link between them so the **Classes** table must also be included in the query. Before creating this query, review the data in the **Tutor** table and create records for the tutors employed by the centre.

To create the query:

1 From the database window click on the **Queries** tab and click on **New**. Choose **Design View**.

2 From the **Show Table** dialog box select the **Bookings**, **Tutors** and the **Classes** tables. These three tables should be shown in the query window with links between them.

3 Add the fields **Date**, **Lastname** and **Qualifications**.

4 In the **Date** column set the criterion to *#13/5/96#* and hide this field. Run the query and save it.

5 Create a report based on this query.

Task 4: counting the number of non-smokers in aerobics classes

Q. How many members that attend Ladies' aerobics are non-smokers?

A. The tables needed are the **Membership** table, **Class Lists** table and the **Classes** table.

To create the query:

1 From the database window click on the **Queries** tab and click on **New**. Choose **Design View**.

2 From the **Show Table** dialog box select the **Membership**, **Class List** and **Classes** tables. These three tables should be shown in the query window with links between them.

3 Add the fields **Lastname**, **Smoker** and **Class Activity**.

4 In the **Smoker** column, set the criterion to **No** and hide this field.

5 In the **Class Activity** column, set the criterion to ***"Ladies' Aerobics"*** and hide this field.

6 Click on the **Totals** button, select **Count** for the **Lastname** field (only **CountofLastname** will show).

7 Run the query to discover the answer to the question.

8 Change the criterion for **Smoker** to find out the number of smokers attending Ladies' Aerobics.

Task 5: Attendance profile

Q. What is the attendance profile of classes on Wednesdays?

A. The **Classes** and **Class List** tables are required for this query. However, before constructing it use the **Class Lists** form to enter members into Wednesday's classes. A report containing a chart is a good method of presenting the answer to the query.

1 Create a query as illustrated. Click on the **Totals** button to display the **Total** row. Hide the **Class Day** field.

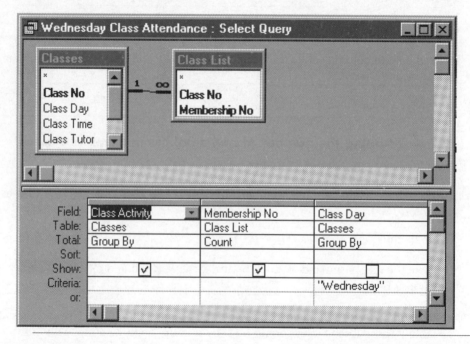

2 Save the query as *Wednesday Class Attendance*.

3 Create a columnar report based on this query using the Report Wizard. Add both fields, **Class Activity** and **CountofMembership No** to the report and sort on **Class Activity**.

4 Display the report in design view. In the report footer create a chart, using **Insert-Chart**. Base the chart on the **Wednesday Class Attendance** query. Select both fields for the chart.

5 Accept the options offered by the Wizard but choose no link between the chart and report and not to display the legend. Click on **Finish**. The chart can only be seen in Report View; in Design View only the default chart is seen. Some editing of the default chart in terms of size and scale can be achieved to produce a result similar to that shown below. As results of editing changes cannot be seen until the report is viewed, patience and perseverance may be required.

6 Save the report as *Wednesday Class Attendance*, and preview before printing.

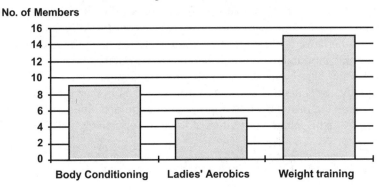

Wednesday Class Attendance

Importing databases

What you will learn in this unit

These next few units explore various issues associated with importing and exporting data.

By the end of this unit you will be able to:

■ understand the distinction between importing data and linking data

■ import data from databases created in earlier versions of Access

■ import data from other standard database packages such as dBase III, IV and 5, Microsoft FoxPro, Paradox and ODBC databases.

Understanding importing, exporting and linking files

Importing and exporting data is relatively straightforward with Access, especially between other standard packages and other packages in the Microsoft suite. Developers of the latest generation of database software have recognised that users now have significant databases established in earlier database packages and need to transfer data from these environments into any new database package that they acquire. Equally, users need to be able to integrate data in database, spreadsheet and word processing programs into appropriate documents. In general, no database or database product is stand alone; it must interface effectively with other related products.

You should select and attempt those activities for which you have the appropriate software and data.

Access offers two different approaches to making use of existing data compiled with other database software.

1 Linked data behaves as if it is part of the Access database although it is not. The data can be edited in both Access and the other application and can be viewed as an Access table, although no Access table is created. Linking is useful when you wish to maintain the data in its original file format, whilst creating Access forms and reports.

2 Imported data has been converted from its original format into an Access table. A copy of the data is placed in a table in an Access database.

Access supports linking and importing with dBase, FoxPro, Paradox, and ODBC databases.

Other database objects such as forms or reports can be imported from another Access database. When importing, all or a subset of these objects can be chosen. In this way a database created in an earlier version of Access can be imported to Access 97.

 If you want to add a table to an Access database this data can be imported into an existing Access database.

If you want to add data from an existing application to an Access table, you can append the data, as long as its format matches that of the existing table entries, i.e. it has the same fields with similar definitions.

Either link or import; do not do both, because this will create more than one copy of the data. With more than one copy of the data it is difficult to be sure which is the most recent and to maintain file integrity.

If importing an Access 7 (or earlier) database, create a new database using Access 97 first.

Exporting data puts Access data into a format that other applications can use and creates a separate file that contains the data stored in a table.

Importing data into an Access table

To import the data in a file into a table in the current Access database:

1   Display the database window.

2   Choose **File-Get External Data-Import** or click on the **New Object** button and choose **Table** and **Import Table**.

3   Choose the format of the data to be imported from the **Files of type** list box in the **Import** dialog box.

4   Select the drive from the **Look in** list box

5   Select the directory and then the file you want to import and click on the **Import** button.

6   When Access has imported the file you have selected, it displays a message to say that it has successfully imported the file. If Access needs some guidance on formatting the file as an Access table you will be prompted by a series of wizards.

7   Click on **OK** and **Close** .

If the database window is displaying the database's tables, the newly imported table should appear in the list of tables (FIGURE 35.1).

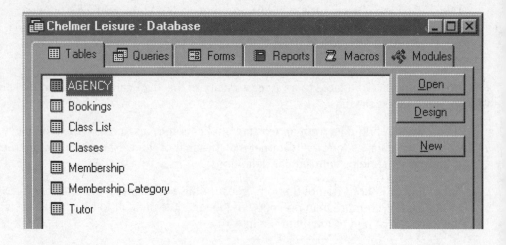

FIGURE 35.1

Importing Access database objects

You can import tables, queries, forms, and reports from another Access database whether or not the database was created in a previous version of Access. To import Access database objects:

1 Display the database window.

2 Choose **File-Get External Data-Import**.

3 Choose **Microsoft Access** from the **Files of type** list box in the **Import** dialog box.

4 Select the drive from the **Look in** list box

5 Select the directory and then the file you want to import and click on the **Import** button.

6 The **Import Objects** dialog box is displayed (FIGURE 35.2). Click the tab of the type of object you wish to import. Select one or more of the objects listed and click on **OK**.

7 The imported objects will be listed under the appropriate tab of the database window.

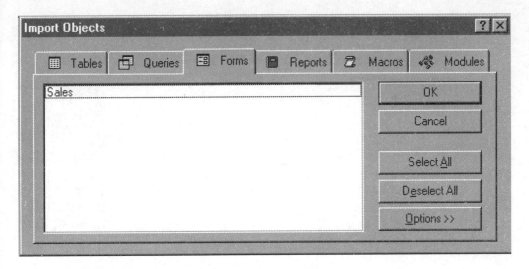

FIGURE 35.2

The **Options** button provides choices such as importing a table structure without the data or importing queries as tables.

Linking a table

To link data stored in another file as a table in the current database:

1   Display the database window.

2   Choose **File-Get External Data-Link Tables** or click on the **New Object** button and choose **Table** and **Link Table**.

3   Choose the format of the data that you want to import from the **Files of Type** list box in the **Import** dialog box.

4   Select the drive, directory and filename of the file that you want to link and click on **Link**. There may be a further dialog box, depending on the type of data you are linking, for example, links to index files used by dBase.

5   When Access has linked the file you have selected it displays a message saying the attachment is complete.

6   Click on **OK** and **Close**.

Linked tables are used in the same way as any other Access table. The link icon is displayed in the database window, showing that there is a link to that table (FIGURE 35.3). Simply click on the **Table** icon to use the table. Linked tables can be used with queries, forms and reports just like any other table. The link icon will reflect the type of database that holds the data; in the illustration a link to another Access table is shown.

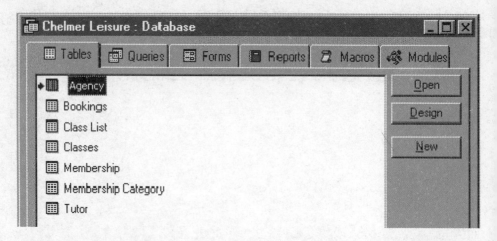

A linked Access table

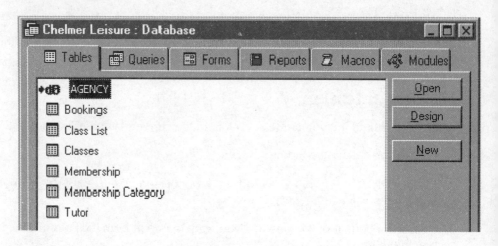

FIGURE 35.2 A linked dBaseIV file

To delete a linked table, if you no longer require the link:

1 Select the icon for the linked table that is to be detached.

2 Select **Edit-Delete**.

This deletes the link but the table remains intact, and could be re-linked at a later stage.

Differences between linking and importing

Imported and linked tables differ in the following respects.

1 They have different **icons**; compare FIGURES 35.1 and 35.2.

2 **Deleting a table**. When you delete an imported table, the table and its contents are deleted. When you delete a linked table, the link is broken between the

current database and the database that contains the table. The data is still available in the original database and any other databases that use the table as a linked table.

3   **Adding data**. Imported data can be added to an existing table or placed in a new table. Linked tables are separate from existing tables in the database.

4   **Speed**. Linked tables are not as fast as tables stored in Access files because the data from the linked table must be constantly read from the original file. Access to data in linked tables can be speeded up by appropriate use of queries and indexes.

5   **Table design**. Linked tables can only be modified to a limited extent in table design. Features such as field names, data type, the order of fields, adding new fields or deleting fields can not be performed on linked tables.

6   **Importing or linking?** If you link, the data remains in another database format and can still be used just as Access tables are used, for example, to edit data, create queries, forms and reports that use data. If you intend to use your data only in Access you should import it. Access works faster with its own tables and Access tables can be customised more easily.

Task 1: Importing, exporting and linking files

This task asks you to review some of the basic concepts associated with importing, exporting and linking files. Answer the following questions.

1   What are the advantages of importing a file compared with linking it?

2   How can you tell when viewing filenames with the database window, which files are imported and which files are linked?

3   Why should you not both link and import a file?

4   What does exporting do?

Using dBase data with Access

dBase III, IV and 5 files can be imported or linked using the steps outlined above. There are only two special points to note.

1   In an imported table dBase field types are changed thus:

dBase	Access
Character	Text
Numeric	Number
Float	Number
Logical	Yes/No

dBase	Access
Date	Date/Time
Memo	Memo

In a linked table, the table continues with the original dBase field types.

2   In linking a dBase table the speed with which Access operates with the data in the dBase file can be improved by selecting appropriate dBase index files.

Task 2: Importing and linking dBase data into/to Access

In this task you first import, and then link an existing dBase file into Access.

First you require a dBase file to import. Either create a file in dBase, or use an existing dBase file. You could create a file such as:

Field	Field Name	Type	Width	Dec	Index
1	AGENCYNO	Numeric	3		Y
2	SURNAME	Character	20		Y
3	INITIALS	Character	3		N
4	TITLE	Character	10		N
5	STREET	Character	30		N
6	TOWN	Character	20		Y
7	COUNTY	Character	20		N
8	POSTCODE	Character	10		N
9	DATEBIRTH	Date	8		Y
10	SEX	Logical	1		N
11	MARRIED	Logical	1		N
12	QUALIFICAT	Memo	10		N

This could be a dBase file held by an employment agency called **AGENCY.DBF**. Make a copy of this file so that you have two copies. You are going to use one of these copies to import and the other to **link**.

Import the first copy thus:

1   Display the database window.

2   Choose **File-Get External Data-Import**.

3   Choose the format of the data to be imported from the **Files of Type** list box in the **Import** dialog box, i.e. select dBase III, IV or 5 (*.dbf).

4   Choose the drive, the directory and the .DBF file that you wish to import and click on the **Import** button.

When Access has imported the file that you have selected, it displays a message that it has successfully imported the file.

5   Click on **OK** and **Close** .

You will now see **AGENCY** listed with the other tables in the database.

6   Open this table, set **AGENCYNO** as the Primary Key. Set the index for
SURNAME to Yes (Duplicates OK). Set the index for **TOWN** to Yes (Duplicates
OK). Set the index for **DATEBIRTH** to Yes (Duplicates OK). Format **DATEBIRTH**
to Short Date. **Yes/No** fields result in -1 for true and 0 for false. Set format for
SEX to *;"Male";"Female"* and that for **MARRIED** to *;"Married";"Single"*.

If the database window is displaying the database's tables, the newly imported table
should appear in the list of tables (it will be shown in upper case). Click on the table
name and in design view examine the table and observe that the field types have
been changed to be consistent with Access field types.

Use the second copy of the file to link. Link this table by following these steps.

1   Display the database window.

2   Choose **File-Get External Data-Link Tables.**

3   Choose the format of the data that you want to import from the **Files of Type** list
box in the **Import** dialog box, i.e. select dBase III, IV or 5 and click on OK.

4   Select the drive, directory and filename of the file that you want to link and click
on **Link** .

5   Select the dBase index files (.NDX or .MDX). Choose **Select** . Click on **OK** .

When Access has linked the file it displays a message saying that the link is
complete.

6   Click on **OK** and **Close** .

If the database window is displaying the database's tables, the newly linked table
should appear in the list of tables. It will be indicated by a linked table icon.

7   Try to modify the linked and imported tables.

Note that in table design an imported table can be modified in exactly the same
way as any other Access table. The linked table can only be modified to a
limited extent. You will find that you cannot change the structure, but the
following properties can be set: format, decimal places, caption, default value,
validation rule, and validation text. Try changing some of these.

Complete the task by deleting the link to the linked table:

8   Select the icon for the linked table that is to be unlinked.

9   Select **Edit-Delete** and choose **Yes** .

Importing text/spreadsheets

What you will learn in this unit

It is possible to import spreadsheet data and text files into Access, in the following spreadsheet and text formats.

- Excel (versions 3.0, 4.0, 5.0, 7(95) and 97)
- Lotus 1-2-3
- Delimited text (where text is separated into groups by commas, tabs or other characters)
- Fixed width text (where values are arranged so that each field has a certain width)
- HTML files.

By the end of this unit you will be able to:

- import spreadsheet data into an Access database
- import delimited text files into Access.

Importing spreadsheet data

When a spreadsheet or text file is imported, Access creates a new table to store the imported data.

There are a number of options for in importing spreadsheet data and text files, because you need to define how the table should be created from the imported data or text.

Before attempting to import spreadsheet data it is easiest if the data is in an appropriate format. The spreadsheet data must have the same type of data in each field and the same fields in every row as the Access table. In addition, it is preferable if column headings of an appropriate type are inserted in the first row of the spreadsheet so that these can be used as field names. Access will look at the first row of data and assign a data type for each field on the basis of this first row. For example, if the first value for a field is a date, then Access assigns date/time data type to that field and assumes that all values for that field will be dates.

To import spreadsheet data into Access:

1 Display the database window.

2 Choose **File-Get External Data-Import**.

3 Select the appropriate format for the data that you want to import (e.g. Excel) and the drive and directory that contains the file to be imported.

4 Select the name of the spreadsheet that you want to import and click on the
   Import button. Access will display an **Import Spreadsheet Wizards** dialog
   box (FIGURE 36.1).

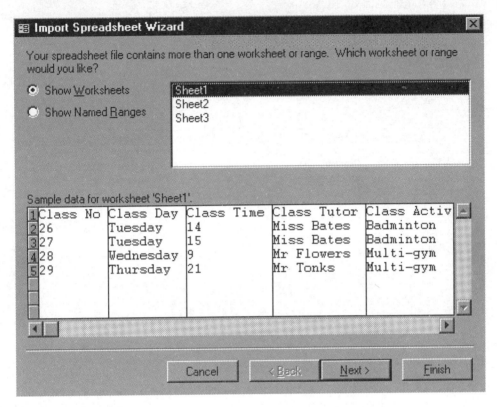

FIGURE 36.1

5 This dialog box allows you to select the required sheet or range. When you see
   the required data displayed in the sample area click on **Next>** to display the
   next dialog box in the Wizard (FIGURE 36.2).

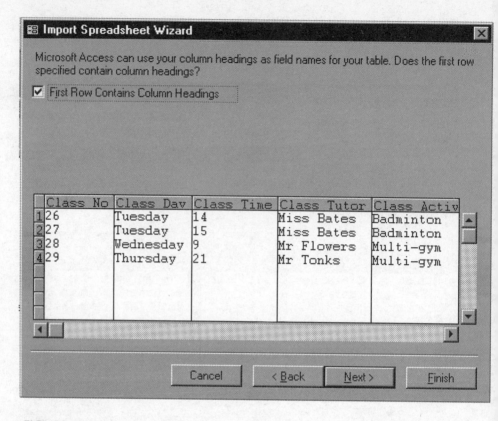

FIGURE 36.2

6 Tick the **First Row Contains Column Headings** check box if the spreadsheet range you are importing has labels in the first row that you want to use as the field names in the table. Click on **Next>** .

7 The next dialog box allows you to choose whether to import the data into a new table or add it to an existing one. If you opt to add it to an existing table then choose the table from the drop-down list.

8 If you are importing the data into a new table continue to work through the Wizard's dialog boxes: to set indexes for the fields being imported, set a primary key and name the table. Click on **Finish** .

9 When Access has imported the table, click on **OK** . If you have imported data into a new table then it should be displayed in the list of tables in the database window.

Task 1: Importing spreadsheet data

Note: To complete this task you need access to a copy of Excel or Lotus or other compatible spreadsheet package.

Create a spreadsheet in Excel or Lotus 1-2-3 into which you can enter data that matches the **Classes** table. Save this file as *Classes2*. As illustrated, enter the field names in the first row, and then enter some records for specific classes, one record per row, as required.

	A	B	C	D	E	F
1	Class No	Class Day	Class Time	Class Tutor	Class Activity	Male/Female/Mixed
2	26	Tuesday	14:00	Bates	Badminton	Female
3	27	Tuesday	15:00	Bates	Badminton	Female
4	28	Wednesday	09:00	Flowers	Multi-Gym	Mixed
5	29	Thursday	21:00	Tonks	Multi-Gym	Male

Open Access.

1 Display the database window.

2 Choose **File-Get External Data-Import**.

3 In the **Files of type** list box, in the **Import** dialog box choose the appropriate format for the data that you want to import (e.g. Excel) and the drive and directory that contains the file to be imported.

4 Select the name of the spreadsheet that you want to import. Click on the **Import** button. Access displays the **Import Spreadsheet Wizards** dialog box.

5 Tick the **First Row Contains Column Headings** check box. Click on **Next>**. Choose the option to import the data into a new table. Click on **Next>**.

6 The next dialog box allows you to specify information about each of the fields that you are importing. By clicking on each field in turn you can set: field name, indexed (or not) and whether the field is to be imported. Use the default settings (i.e. don't make any changes), and click on **Next>**.

7 You are prompted to choose the primary key for the new table. Choose **Class No** and click on **Next>**. Enter the table's name, e.g. **Classes2**, and click on **Finish**. When Access has finished importing the table it will display a message to that effect.

8 Click on **OK**. The new table should be displayed in the list of tables in the database window.

9 You may wish to repeat this task importing the data into the existing table **Classes**.

Note: If you choose to allow Access to analyse your table it will, when you ask, run the Table Analyzer Wizard, and inform you of the faults in your table design. Try this if you are interested. What is wrong with the design of this table?

Importing delimited or fixed width text files into Access

A delimited text file is one in which fields are separated by a special character, such as a comma or a tab. In a fixed width file, fields are aligned in columns with spaces between each field. Data in a text file intended for importing into a table must be in an appropriate format. As with spreadsheets, the text file must have the same type of data in each field and the same fields in every row. Again the first row may be used as field names, and Access uses the first row of data as a basis for assigning data types. Note that only delimited and fixed width text files, saved as .txt files can be imported. So, for example, if you create a file in Word, you must save it as a .txt file (using 'Text only' or 'Text only with line breaks') and not a .doc file if you wish to import it into Access.

To import a delimited text file:

1   Open the database window.

2   Choose **File-Get External Data-Import**.

3   Choose the appropriate format for the data you want to import (e.g. Text files) and the drive and directory that contains the file to be imported.

4   Select the text file to be imported and click on the **Import** button. The **Text Import Wizard** dialog box will be displayed.

5   Choose **Delimited** as the format. Click on **Next>**.

6   Specify the **text delimiter** that has been used, e.g. Comma or Tab. Click on **Next>**.

7   Specify whether you would like to store your data in an existing or new table.

8   Specify the following information about each of the fields you are importing: field name, data type, whether indexed, and whether the field should be included. Click on **Next>**.

9   Choose the Primary Key. Click on **Next>**. Choose the file name and click on **Finish**.

10 Access creates a new table with the same name as the original text file, unless you chose to append data to an existing file. Click on **Close**.

Task 2: Importing delimited text files

Note: To complete this task you need access to a copy of an appropriate word processing package, such as Word 97.

Create a delimited text file into which you can enter data that matches the **Classes** table. If you are working with Word 97 you may choose to do this by creating a table but you will need to convert the table to text before saving as a .txt file. Text delimited by commas or tabs may be saved directly as a .txt file. Save this file as **Classes3** and close it. Enter the field names in the first row, and then enter some records for specific classes, one record per row, as required, as shown below.

Class No	Class Day	Class Time	Class Tutor	Class Activity	Male/Female/Mixed
26	Tuesday	14:00	Miss Bates	Badminton	Female
27	Tuesday	15:00	Miss Bates	Badminton	Female
28	Wednesday	09:00	Mr Flowers	Multi-gym	Mixed
29	Thursday	21:00	Mr Tonks	Multi-gym	Male

1   Open Access and open the database window.

2   Choose **File-Get External Data-Import.**

3   In the **Files of type** list box, in the **Import** dialog box choose the appropriate format for the data that you want to import (e.g. Text files) and the drive and directory that contains the file to be imported.

4   Select the text file to be imported and click on the **Import** button. The **Text Import Wizard** dialog box will be displayed.

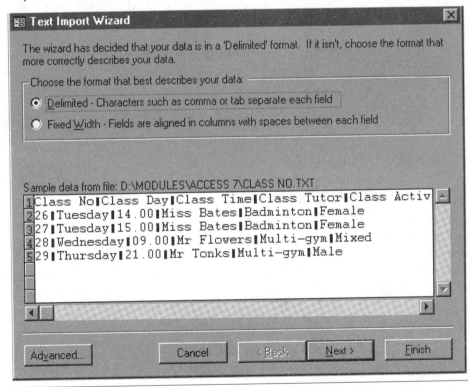

223

5   Choose **Delimited** as the format. Click on   Next> .

6   Specify the text delimiter that has been used, e.g. Comma or Tab.

7   Tick the **First Row Contains Field Names** check box. Click on   Next> .

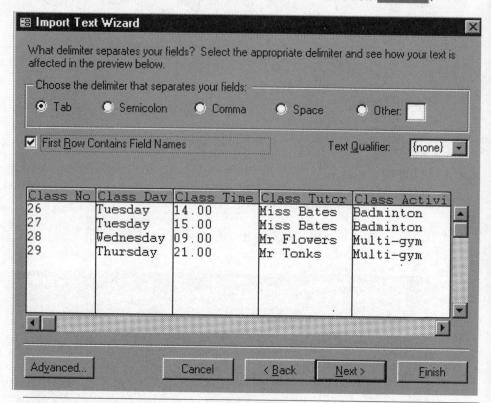

8   You may choose to import your data into a new table or an existing one. If you want to import the data to an existing table then specify the table using the drop down list. Choose the new table option. Click on   Next> .

9   Accept the data types for the fields. Click on   Next> .

10 Set **Class No** as the primary key and name the new table *Classes3*. Click on   **Finish** .

11 View this table in Datasheet View, and then in Design View. Change the data and data type of **Class Time** to a time format.

Notes

We have just explored a further way of creating text and entering it in a database. Normally, it is more satisfactory to enter data directly into a database, but on occasions an existing word processed file, say, in this instance of the classes on offer, or the names and addresses of some members, may usefully be incorporated into an Access database, either simply so that it is merged with other similar data, or because it is easier to sort, group and query the data in database format.

We do not describe importing fixed-width text fields here.

Exporting a table; publishing in HTML

What you will learn in this unit

Data can be exported from Access tables to text files, spreadsheets and to any of the database formats from which you can import data. Data can also be exported to a Word for Windows mail merge data file, which can then be used to create form letters, mailing labels and other merged documents. Data may be exported to other database applications so that it can be merged with other data in other files.

Another alternative is to make data available to others via the Internet, and Access provides a Wizard to enable you to do this.

By the end of this unit you will be able to:

- export a table to a database
- export a table to a spreadsheet
- export a table to a word processor
- use the Publish to Web Wizard.

Understanding exporting

Important note: Access allows table and field names that can contain up to 64 characters and can include spaces. Some other database packages and other applications work with shorter maximum table and field names, and may not allow spaces in names. When you export a table with table or field names that are not acceptable to another application, Access adjusts the names. For example, if you export data to a dBase table, Access truncates any names longer than 10characters. It is therefore important to check that after such truncation you will be left with a set of unique field and table names.

To export data in a table to a file in a format that other applications can use:

1 Display the database window, click on the tab for the object type you wish to export and highlight the name of the object, e.g. the **Membership** table.

2 Choose **File-Save As/Export**.

3 In the **Save As** dialog box choose **To an External File or Database**. Click on **OK**.

4 Choose the folder in which you wish to save the file.

5 Select the type of file to be created from the **Save as type** list box and give this version of the table an appropriate filename (FIGURE 37.1). Click on the **Export** button.

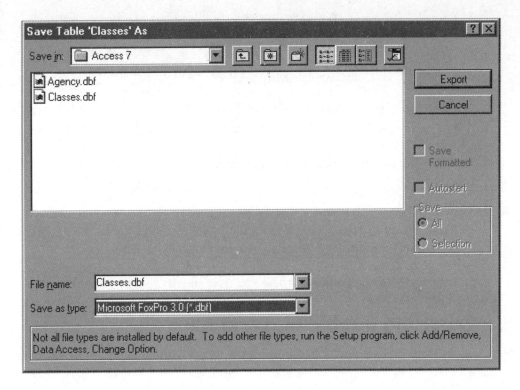

FIGURE 37.1

Exporting to a database or spreadsheet file

To export data to a database or spreadsheet file:

1 Open the database containing the table that you wish to export and select the table.

2 Choose **File-Save As/Export**. In the **Save As** dialog box choose **To an external File or Database**. Click on **OK**.

3 Choose the folder in which you wish to save the file.

4 Select the type of database file to be created from the **Save as type** list box and give this version of the table an appropriate filename. Click on **Export**.

Task 1: Exporting a table to dBase

Note: To complete this task you require dBase on your system. dBase field names are only 10 characters long so you may need to revise your Access field names.

Export the table that was imported in Unit 35, **Classes**.

1 Switch to the database containing the table **Classes** and highlight it.

2   Choose **File-Save As/Export**. In the **Save As** dialog box choose **To an External File or Database**. Click on `OK`.

3   Choose the drive and directory in which you wish to save the file.

4   Select the type of dBase file to be created from the **Save as type** list box and give this version of the table the name *Classes4*. Click on `Export`.

Task 2: Exporting a table to a spreadsheet

Note: To complete this task you require a spreadsheet package such as Excel or Lotus 1-2-3.

1   Export the table that was imported earlier, **Classes**, following the same steps as in the last task but this time selecting, say, Excel as the file type.

2   Enter the name of the file to where you want the data exported as *Classes5*.

Exporting a table to a text file

It may often be appropriate to select a set of records from a table and export them to a word processor for further formatting or for integration into a text based document.

To export an Access table to a text file:

1   Open the database containing the table that you wish to export and select the table.

2   Choose **File-Save As/Export**. In the **Save As** dialog box choose **To an external File or Database**. Click on `OK`.

3   Choose the folder in which you wish to save the file.

4   Select a text file type from the **Save as type** list box and give this version of the table an appropriate filename. Click on `Export`.

5   The Export Text Wizard will allow you to select the format of the text, i.e. delimited with a particular delimiter character or in a fixed width format.

Task 3: Exporting a table to a text file

Suppose we wish to create a brochure detailing the opportunities for Ladies Leisure and Recreational Activities available at Chelmer Leisure and Recreation Centre. This leaflet will be essentially a word processed document containing text about the activities and the Centre. However, embedded in the document will be a list of Body Conditioning and Multi-gym Classes for Ladies. In order to extract this information from our Access **Classes** table, and insert the data into the leaflet, we need first to select the appropriate records by the use of a query, convert the result of the query to a table, and then export the data in the table to a word processor file.

To execute the query:

1 Click on the Queries tab in the database window and click on the New button to create a new query, using **Design View**.

2 In the **Show Table** dialog box, choose **Classes**. Click on Add then Close .

3 Add the appropriate fields to the query.

4 Use criteria to select the required records.

5 Run the query to display the dynaset. Save and close the query, choosing an appropriate name.

To export the data to a word processor file:

1 Click on the Queries tab and select the newly created query.

2 Choose **File-Save As/Export**. Access displays the **Save As** dialog box. Choose **To an External File or Database**. Click on OK .

3 Choose the folder in which you wish to save the file

4 Select Text files from the **Save as type** list box and choose an appropriate file-name. Click on Export .

5 Work through the stages in the Export Text Wizard to select a delimited format with a tab delimiter. You can use Word to convert this to a word processed table.

Exporting Access data to another Access database

Exporting and importing are two sides of the same process. Data can be transferred between Access databases, either by importing or exporting. You import when the current database is the one where you need a copy of the table or other object and you export when you are in the database that contains the object or data you want copied to another database.

To export a table or other database object, follow the steps for exporting a table but to select an object other than a table click on the appropriate tab in the database window.

After exporting, the object is in both databases but there is no link between the two copies of the object. So, for example, if the object is updated in one database it will not be updated in another.

Publishing a database on the World Wide Web

Some or all of the data in a database may be information that could be made available to customers or clients. Access provides a Publish to the Web Wizard which allows any combination of tables, queries, forms and reports to be converted to HTML format. Many organisations use 'intranets' which are local 'Webs' that operate in the same way as the WWW except that published pages are only accessible to internal users. This is a useful way to make certain company data available to employees.

To publish Access objects (tables, queries, forms, and reports):

1   Choose **File-Save As HTML**. The Publish to Web Wizard starts.

2   Select the combination of objects by choosing the appropriate tabs and ticking the object or objects required.

3   You may select an existing HTML document as a template. This could be one with a company logo and background. Different templates may be used for different objects or you can continue without selecting a template.

4   You can select whether your page is static or dynamic. A dynamic page can reflect changes in your database but this facility is dependent on your WWW server. To begin with it is best to create static pages.

5   Select the folder into which the HTML document is to be saved. It is advisable to have a specific folder for HTML documents so that it is easy to keep them together for copying to a server. The **No, I only want to publish objects locally** option allows you to save to your folder.

6   You may choose to create a home page for your publication. If you have chosen to publish more than one object, a home page with links to pages for each of these will be created.

7   You may choose to save the publishing profile that you have selected so that the Web Wizard can use it again next time you publish an HTML file.

8   View your document with your browser. If you have an HTML editor and are familiar with its use you may wish to add links and make formatting changes.

Task 4: Using the Web Wizard

This is a simple task that introduces the basics of publishing in HTML format.

1   Follow the steps described above. Select the **Membership Category** table, **Wednesday Class Attendance** query, and **Classes2** report as objects to be published.

2   Continue choosing defaults and allow the Wizard to save the document in your **My Documents** folder, unless you wish to specify an alternative.

3 Tick the create a home page option and call it **Chelmer**. Follow the Wizard's instructions accepting the defaults through to **Finish** .

4 Using Explorer find the HTML files and double-click on **CHELMER.HTM** to open it, alternatively start your browser and use **File-Open** to open this file. You should see links to the three HTML documents; use the links to view them.

5 If you wish, experiment with creating other pages.

Using the clipboard to transfer data

What you will learn in this unit

In addition to transferring data between Access and other applications by importing, linking and exporting, information can be transferred between applications using the clipboard. Transferring data using the clipboard is very straightforward, provided the data is in an acceptable format. It is especially easy if you are working with Excel and Word alongside Access.

By the end of this unit you will be able to:

■ use the clipboard to transfer data.

Using the clipboard to transfer data

The clipboard is the Windows temporary area where it can store information from any applications designed to use it. The basic procedure is to:

1   Select the data to be moved.

2   Select **Edit-Copy** or **Edit-Cut** depending upon whether you want to retain the data in its original location or not.

3   Switch to the application into which you wish to import data.

4   Select **Edit-Paste**.

This procedure can be adopted, for example, for:

■ moving Access data into an Excel (or other) spreadsheet

■ moving Access data into a Word for Windows document in the form of a table.

■ moving Access objects from one database to another.

Task 1: Using the clipboard to move Access data into a Word document

Chelmer Leisure and Recreation Centre may find it useful to have a list of those members who are children, in other words to have a Membership Category of Junior or Junior Club. First we need to create a query to select appropriate records, and then we can select appropriate records on the screen and use **Edit-Copy** and **Edit-Paste** to insert those records in a word processed document.

To create a query:

1   Click on the **Queries** tab in the database window and click on the **New** button and **Design View** to design a new query.

2   In the **Show Table** dialog box, choose **Membership**. Click on Add and then Close.

3   Add the following fields to the query: **Category No, Firstname, Lastname, Date of Birth, Date of Joining, Sporting Interests, Sex**.

4   Use a criterion in the **Category No** field to select categories 3 OR 4.

5   Run the query to display the dynaset. Select the dynaset.

6   Copy the selection to the clipboard, switch to the word processor and paste the table from the clipboard.

7   Close the query without saving.

Another case where Chelmer Leisure and Recreation Centre would wish to move Access data into a document would be to create a list of classes intended for a publicity document such as a poster or leaflet.

To create a query:

1   Click on the Queries tab in the database window and click on the New button and **Design View** to create a new query.

2   In the **Show Table** dialog box, choose **Classes**. Click on Add then Close.

3   Add the following fields to the query: **Class Day, Class Time, Class Activity, Male/Female/Mixed**.

4   Run the query to display the dynaset. Select the dynaset.

5   Copy the selection to the clipboard, switch to the word processor and paste the table from the clipboard.

How could you amend the query to produce a leaflet targeted at male members?

Task 2: Using the clipboard to move Access data into an Excel spreadsheet

This task investigates how **Bookings** table data can be pasted into an Excel spreadsheet to perform additional analysis.

1   Create a query based on the **Bookings** table.

2   Add the fields **Booking No** and **Date**.

3   Click on the ██Totals██ button to create totals.

4   Select **Count** for **Booking No** and **Group By** for **Date**. Run the query.

5   Use **Edit-Select All Records** and **Edit-Copy**.

6   Switch to Excel.

7   Use **Edit-Paste** and the data is pasted in Excel.

The average number of bookings per day can be found, which could have been done using Access; however Excel could be used to calculate the median and mode of this data. Other more sophisticated statistical analysis could be used on Access data transferred to Excel, such as forecasting using a linear regression technique.

Creating and editing macros

What you will learn in this unit

(d.) This unit introduces macros. Macros are basically a list of instructions, rather like short programs. When using Access there may be occasions when the same series of actions is performed again and again. To save time these may be recorded as a macro so that one command, to run the macro, can replace the need to issue a series of commands.

By performing a series of actions macros can automate your database application. Macros in Access are powerful and perform many tasks that in other database management systems could only be achieved by writing a program. Creating macros, however, does require a clear understanding of your database application so that you can plan exactly what you want each macro to do. In this, and the following four units, you will be introduced to some macros, which while not being comprehensive should cover some of the basics.

By the end of this unit you will be able to:

■ create simple macros.

The macro window

Macros are entered in macro windows, just as you enter a query using a query window or a form using a form window.

The macro window is usually shown with two columns, **Action** and **Comment**, as illustrated in FIGURE 39.1. In the Action column the action for the macro is selected from a drop down list associated with that cell. In the Comments column you can add comments to act as a reminder of the function of the macro.

Task 1: A macro to open a form

This macro is easy to create and one which is frequently used. This task will consider construction of the macro stage by stage. At each stage relevant explanation is given.

1   Click on the **Macros** tab in the database window and click on the **New** button to display the macro window.

The first action of this macro is **OpenForm**. There are many actions to choose from, as you will discover when you open the list box of the Action cell.

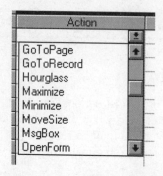

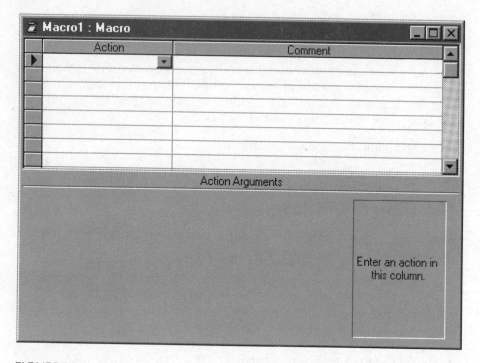

FIGURE 39.1

---

2 Open the **Action** cell list box. Scroll through the actions and select **OpenForm**. When you do this you will see that an argument section appears in the lower left of the macro window. Whatever action is selected, there will nearly always be an argument section to complete. Some actions require more arguments than others; refer to the section on 'Understanding actions and arguments' later in this unit.

---

3   Open the **Form Name** list in the **Action Arguments** section and select
    Membership. Leave the action arguments as their default values.

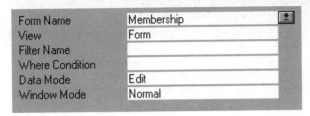

Form Name	Membership
View	Form
Filter Name	
Where Condition	
Data Mode	Edit
Window Mode	Normal

The **View** argument opens the form in form run mode. The **Data Mode** argument
of Edit allows the form to be edited. The **Where Condition** specifies which
record is displayed when the form opens. If this argument is left blank then the
form is opened displaying the first record.

4   Key into the **Comment** column the description *Open Membership form*.

5   Save the macro with the name *Chelmer*.

   Note: a macro must be saved before it can be run or executed. Choose File-Save
   or press *F12* to save the macro.

   Click on **OK** .

6   The macro can be tested by running it. Click on the **Run** button in the toolbar.
    The **Membership** form should be displayed with the first record showing.

   Note: There are several different ways in which a macro can be run or executed.
   Refer to the section 'Executing macros' for details of the different methods.

7   Close the form and close the macro. The macro name should be displayed in the
    database window.

Modifying a macro

A macro may need to be edited to change its actions or correct an error. All or part
of a macro may be copied from one macro window to another to save having to
repeat work that has already been done. Macros may also be copied from one database to another.

Normally a macro is edited to change its actions, usually to improve or refine them.
Display the macro window that you wish to modify. Editing may be achieved using
either the mouse or the keyboard.

Task 2: Editing a macro

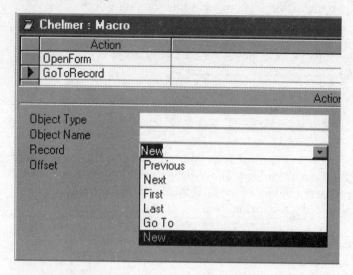

In this task the macro created in the last task will be opened and edited so that, when it opens the Membership form, it displays the form ready to accept a new record. This is useful when a new member's details are to be entered.

1   Open the macro **Chelmer** in design mode.

2   For the second action of the macro select the **GoToRecord** action.

3   To define which record to go to the **Record** argument is used. Open the list box associated with this argument and select **New**.

4   Save the macro and run it. This time the **Membership** form should be displayed ready to accept a new record.

5   Close the form and the macro.

Task 3: Sizing and positioning the form

To add a further refinement to the macro to open the form, the size of the form can be set. If the size is not set then the form will be displayed at the last size used when the form was displayed in design mode. Sizing and positioning a form from a macro gives consistency to your database application.

1   Open the macro **Chelmer** in design mode.

2   Insert a row in the macro sheet below the **OpenForm** action. Highlight the second row and use **Insert-Rows** to insert a blank row.

3   In the new row select the action **MoveSize**. Set the arguments as shown in the following table:

Right	The new horizontal position of the window's upper left corner, measured from the left edge of its containing window	4cm
Down	The new vertical position of the window's upper left corner, measured from the top edge of its containing window	1cm
Width	The window's new width	15cm
Height	The window's new height	12cm

4   Save the macro and run it.

5   You may need to adjust the sizes in the **MoveSize** arguments to suit your form. To do this, close the **Membership** form, edit and save the macro.

6   Save the changes and run the macro. The **Membership** form should display nicely and be ready to accept a new record.

7   Close the **Membership** form and the macro.

Understanding actions and arguments

The macro actions available in Access can duplicate commands that would be chosen from the menus, as well as control many processes such as synchronising the records that forms display. There are many actions available, so by means of illustration a few will be considered along with their associated arguments. If the action duplicates a command which would generate a dialog box then the arguments are the selections that would be made in that dialog box. Three of the many actions are illustrated below.

Action	Argument	Function
FindRecord	Find What	Finds the next record after the
	Match	current record meeting the
	Match Case	specified criteria. Searches
	Search	through a table, form, or dynaset.
	Search As Formatted	
	Only Current Field	
	Find First	

Action	Argument	Function
OpenForm	Form Name	Opens or activates a form in one
	View	of its views.
	Filter Name	
	Where Condition	
	Data Mode	
	Window Mode	
OpenReport	Report Name	Opens a report in the view
	View	specified and filters the records
	Filter Name	before printing.
	Where Condition	

By defining the arguments, for example, the name of a report in the Report Name argument, then the appropriate action is carried out.

Executing macros

You can run a macro in many ways. If you are creating quick macros for immediate use, you may want to run them by choosing them from the macro window or database window. To create a system that is more automated or one that is easier to use, you can run a macro in a variety of ways which are outlined briefly below and are discussed in more detail later.

Running from the macro window

A macro can be run from its macro window. This capability is useful for testing a macro. To run the macro click on the **Run** button on the toolbar or choose **Run-Run**. If the active macro window contains a group of macros, only the first macro in the window runs. To run a specific macro in a group of macros see Unit 40.

From any window

Choose **Tools-Macro Run Macro** and in the **Run Macro** dialog box select or key in the name of the macro. Click on **OK**.

From another macro

A macro can be run from another macro using the **Run Macro** action. The argument for this action is the name of the macro to be called. When the called macro has run, Access returns control to the next action in the calling macro. The macro may run repeatedly if either the **Repeat Count** or **Repeat Expression** is set.

From an event

The running of a macro can be 'triggered' by an event. An event can be the opening or closing of a form or report, or it can be the selection of a control. For example, a macro which opens a form can run when a field is selected. A macro that validates an entry can run when a field is exited. These kind of macro events make your database application much more professional in operation.

From a button

This is another way to make your database application more professional. Command buttons are a very easy addition to a form. By clicking on the button the macro can be performed, such as opening another form.

From a shortcut key

It is a good idea to assign frequently used macros to a short-cut key, for example *Ctrl-p* could be assigned to a macro that performs printing. By pressing the shortcut key combination the macro will run.

Creating macro groups

What you will learn in this unit

It is useful to keep related macros together and Access offers the facility to group macros. It is therefore possible to have more than one macro in a macro window. This has the added advantage that it reduces the number of macro windows. Many macros are small, only a few lines long, and if each required a separate macro window then it would be difficult to keep track of them all.

A macro can be assigned to a command button so that when the button is clicked the macro runs. Buttons may be added to existing forms that are based on tables or they can be added to blank forms. A blank form which does not have an associated table can be created; this is known as an **unbound form**. By adding buttons to the form it can become a menu form.

By the end of this unit you will be able to:

- create a simple macro group
- add buttons to a form
- assign macros to the buttons.

Creating macro groups

To distinguish macros in one window each has its own name. The macro name is entered in the **Macro Name** column of the window, which is displayed by clicking on the **Macro Names** button in the toolbar or by choosing **View-Macro Names**.

This column is displayed to the left of the Action column.

Each macro in the window begins with the action to the right of its name. The macro ends when it reaches the beginning of the next macro or it runs out of actions. There is no need for a particular end action.

When a macro window contains several macros then to refer to a specific macro within the group use the following syntax:

   macrowindowname.macroname

where a full stop separates the macro window name from the macro name, for example Chelmer.NewBooking. To run a particular macro in a group choose **Tools-Macro** and select the macro required from the drop down list; macro names are listed using the syntax described above. Note that if the macro name is omitted then the first macro in the group will run.

Task 1: Creating a macro group

In this task another macro will be added to the Chelmer macro. This will be another open form macro to open the booking form ready to take a new booking.

1   Display the **Chelmer** macro window.

2   Click on the Macro Names button in the toolbar.

3   Leave a couple of blank rows below the existing macro and in the Macro Name column put *NewBooking*.

4   On the next row select the action OpenForm. Set the Form Name argument to **Bookings**.

Macro Name	Action
	OpenForm
	GoToRecord
NewBooking	OpenForm
	GoToRecord

5   The second action is GoToRecord, with the argument of Record set to New.

6   Save the macro.

7   To run this part of the macro group select Tools-Run Macro.

8   In the Run Macro dialog box open the drop down dialog box and select **Chelmer.NewBooking** and click on OK .

9   Close the form and close the macro.

Adding command buttons to a form

A macro can be made convenient to run by assigning it to a button on a form, either existing or blank. The button can then be clicked to run the macro.

1   Open a form in design view and display it by the side of the database window.

2   Click the Macros tab in the database window.

3   Drag the name of the macro on to the form where the button is to appear and release.

4   The button will have the name of the macro. If you want, you can change it by editing the text on the button.

5   Save the form with the button.

6   Display the form in Run mode and click on the button to run the macro.

Task 2: Creating a blank form and adding buttons to it

In this task you will create an unbound blank form that will only contain two command buttons. The first will be one which when clicked on will open the **Membership** form ready to accept a new member's details. The second button will open the **Bookings** form ready to accept a new booking. To create a blank unbound form:

1   From the database window click on the **Forms** tab and click on **New**. Leave the 'Choose the table or query...' box empty as this form is not bound to a table or query. Choose **Design View**.

2   To add a command button, display the new blank form and the database window side by side.

3   Click on the **Macros** tab of the database window and select **Chelmer**.

4   Drag the macro onto the form. A button appears with the name Chelmer on it.

5   The name on the button can be changed by editing the **Caption** property. Edit the name of the button to read **New Member**. You should find that the **On Click** property is set to Chelmer, i.e. the first macro in the macro group **Chelmer** will run when the button is clicked.

6   Set the properties of the form as follows (if the form is not selected use **Edit-Select Form** to select it):

Property	Setting
Caption	**Form Menu** (the name that will appear title in the bar of the form)
Default View	**Single Form**
Scroll Bars	**Neither**
Record Selectors	**No**
Navigation Buttons	**No**

7   Save the form as **Form Menu**. Run the form and click on the **New Member** button you have just created. Close the **Membership** form.

8   Return to Design View of the **Form Menu** form.

9   Drag the macro onto the form. A button appears with the name Chelmer on it.

244

10 The name on the button can be changed by editing the **Caption** property. Edit the name of the button to read ***Make Booking***.

11 You should also edit the **On Click** property, which is set to Chelmer, to ***Chelmer.NewBooking*** so that the macro **Chelmer.NewBooking** will run when the button is clicked.

12 You may add a title and adjust fonts as illustrated below.

13 Save the form and try the new button.

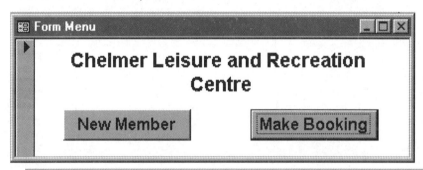

Task 3: Adding a button to a form

This will be a very simple macro to close the open object, which might be a form or report. In the preceding task, closing the form after adding a new member or taking a new booking would be simple if a button labelled **Close** was added to both the **Membership** and **Bookings** forms.

The macro to close an object is simple and it can be added to the **Chelmer** macro group. To add this macro:

1 Display the **Membership** form in design view. Check that the **Control Wizards** button in the Toolbox is depressed.

2 Select the **Command Button** tool from the Toolbox and click at the bottom of the form. The Command Button Wizard starts.

3 Select **Form Operations** from the **Categories** list and **Close Form** from the **Actions** list. Click on **Next>** .

4 Choose a picture or text for the button. Click on **Next>** . Give the button the name ***Close Membership Form*** and click on **Finish** .

5   Save the form.

6 Try out the macro; clicking on the **Close** button should close the form.

7   Add a Close button to both the **Bookings** form and the **Form Menu** form. Notice that the button's **OnClick** property is set to **Event Procedure**.

8   Save the forms and test your macros.

Assigning macros to keys

What you will learn in this unit

It is useful to be able to assign a frequently used macro to a keystroke as this gives the operator more choice when using the database. The example we shall consider is that of *Ctrl-n* to display the Membership form ready to accept a new member's record and *Ctrl-b* to display the Booking form. Examples of other shortcut keys that could be used are *Ctrl-x* to close or *Ctrl-p* to print.

By the end of this unit you will be able to:

■ assign macros to keys.

Assigning a macro to a key

A separate macro needs to be created in which the key assignments are set. All key assignments are kept in this macro as a group. So that Access knows this is a key assignment macro, it is saved with the name **AutoKeys**. In the AutoKeys macro each key combination has a name and this name must follow the naming convention shown in the table below.

Key Combination	Macro Name
Ctrl-*letter*	^*letter*
Ctrl-*number*	^*number*
Function key	{F1} and so on
Ctrl-*Function key*	^{F1} and so on
Shift-*Function key*	+{F1} and so on
Insert	{Insert}
Ctrl-Insert	^{Insert}
Shift-Insert	+{Insert}
Delete	{Delete} or {Del}
Ctrl-Delete	^{Delete} or ^{Del}
Shift-Delete	+{Delete} or +{Del}

To assign a macro to a shortcut key:

1 Create and save the macros and/or macro groups to which you wish to assign shortcut keys.

2 Open a new macro window and display the Macro Name column. This macro will become a macro group in which all shortcut keys are defined.

3   In the macro name column put the macro name, for example, **^p**.

4   The action for this macro will be a RunMacro action which will refer to one of the macros you have already created. See the following section for more detail on the RunMacro action.

5   State the macro name that you are calling in the **Macro Name** argument. Use the correct syntax, i.e. if the macro is in a group then use:

macrogroupname.macroname.

6   Use the **Comment** column to note which macro is being called.

7   Save the shortcut key macro as **AutoKeys**.

8   Any shortcut keys you wish to set up later must be added to this macro.

The RunMacro action

A macro can be run from within another macro by using the RunMacro action. The arguments for the RunMacro action are the name of the macro to be run, and the number of times the macro is to repeat. The macro may be set to repeat a set number of times or an expression can be used to test whether the macro has been performed the required number of times.

When the main (or calling) macro is run it performs its list of actions. When the RunMacro action is encountered the specified macro runs the required number of times. When that has finished Access returns control to the next action in the calling macro.

Task 1: Assigning shortcut keys

In this task the shortcut key *Ctrl-m* (^m) is to be assigned to the macro that opens the **Membership** form ready to accept a new member's record and *Ctrl-b* (^b) to open the **Bookings** form. To create an **AutoKeys** macro:

1   Open a new macro sheet. Display the **Macro Name** column.

2   Put **^m** in the **Macro Name** column.

3   In the **Action** column select the **RunMacro** action and set the **Macro Name** argument to **Chelmer** (this is the first macro of the **Chelmer** group of macros).

4   In the **Comment** column type **Opens Membership form for new record**.

5   In the next row of the **MacroName** column put **^b**.

6   In the **Action** column select the **RunMacro** action and set the **MacroName** argument to **Chelmer.NewBooking** (this is the **NewBooking** macro of the **Chelmer** group of macros).

7   In the **Comments** column put *Opens Bookings form for new record*.

8   Save the macro as *AutoKeys*.

9   Open the **Form** menu and try using the shortcut key.

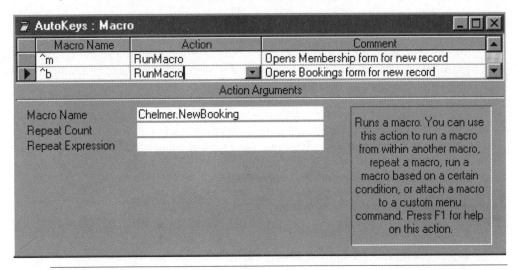

You may have noticed that in many Windows applications the shortcut letter in a menu or on a button is underlined. It is possible to do this, by displaying the form or report containing the button in design mode and editing the Caption so that an & precedes the letter to be underlined. For example, Make Booking would be typed as *Make &Booking* so that it appeared as **Make <u>B</u>ooking** on the button.

Assigning macros to events

What you will learn in this unit

Specific events in forms and reports can be used to 'trigger' the running of a macro. Examples are the opening of a form, the user selecting or exiting from a field control or the double-clicking on a field.

By assigning macros to events the database system becomes more professional as set procedures within the system become automated. Event driven macros can be used to open multiple forms together, print reports using specific queries, or create error checks that are more extensive than those available through control properties. There are more form events than report events.

By the end of this unit, you will be able to:

■ assign a macro to an event

■ use conditions to determine how a macro will run

■ use control reference correctly

■ appreciate that more complex procedures can be achieved using small programs or modules.

The events for a form or report can be found in the table of properties. Forms, controls and reports have different events associated with them. The following tables illustrate some of the events to which macros can be assigned.

Events in a form or record

Form property	Event	Example of use
On Open	Runs the macro when the form opens but before displaying a record	The macro may open or close other forms when the form opens
Before Insert	Runs the macro when the user begins to enter data into a new record	The macro can display extra information or a warning message
Before Update	Runs the macro after the user has finished changing or entering the record but before the record is updated in the database	The macro can display a dialog box asking the user to confirm that the record be updated.

Form Property	Event	Example of use
After Update	Runs the macro after the user has finished changing or entering the record but after the record has been updated in the database.	The macro can update other forms using the data in the new record.
On Delete	Runs the macro when the user deletes a record but before the record is actually deleted.	The macro may ask for confirmation as to whether the record should be deleted.
On Close	Runs the macro as the form is about to close but has not disappeared from the screen.	The macro may ask whether data may be transferred when the form is closed.

Events in a form control

Form control property	Event description	Example of use
On Enter	Runs the macro when a control is clicked i.e. just as it receives the focus.	The macro may ask for a password before allowing data entry.
On Click	Runs the macro when a command button is clicked.	The caption on the button usually indicates the function of the macro, for example Print.
Before Update	Runs the macro after the user leaves a control but before the control is changed.	The macro can validate the data that has been entered and ask for it to be corrected.
On Dbl Click	Runs the macro when the user double clicks on a control or its label	Can display a form with information regarding data entry.
On Exit	Runs the macro when the user attempts to move to another control but before the focus moves away.	Can define the next control using the GoToControl action.

Events in a Report

Report Event	Event Description	Example of use
On Open	Runs the macro when the report opens but before printing.	Displays a form in which to enter criteria.

To assign a macro to an event first create and save the macro. To assign it to the required form, report or control:

1 Open the required form or report in design view.

2 Select the form, report or control to which the macro is to be assigned.

To	Do This
Select a form or report	Click on the background in a form. Click outside a report section. Choose either **Edit-Select Form** or **Edit-Select Report**
Select a report section	Click on the section header
Select a control	Click on the control

3 Display the properties window by clicking on the **Properties** button in the toolbar.

4 Select the required event in the properties table.

5 Open the combo box and select the macro name to be assigned to this event. If the macro is part of a group, select the group's name and edit it to add a dot and the name of the macro.

6 Save the changes made and test the macro.

Using conditions

Your macros can have the capability to make decisions about how they operate. Macros can test whether a condition is true and if so they can run actions you specify.

By adding the condition column to the macro window, expressions can be added. You enter, in this Condition column, expressions that can be evaluated as true or false. If the expression is true, the macro action on its right runs. If the expression is false the macro action doesn't run.

Expressions test the values of control names, for example:

[Surname]="Smith"	True, when Surname control contains the text *Smith*.
[Membership Fee]<20	True, when the control *Membership Fee* is less than 20.

Task 1: Using conditions to control the focus in a form

In this task you will assign a macro to the Member/Class control in the **Bookings** form which will control whether the focus moves to the Membership No control or to the Class No control.

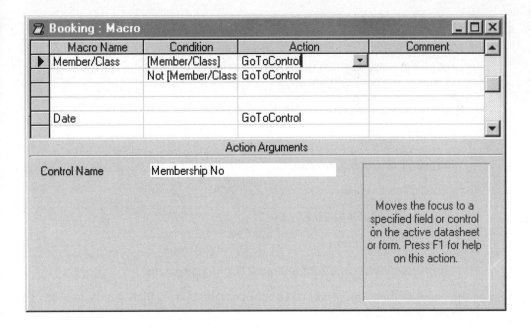

1 Create the macro group **Booking** as illustrated. Display the Condition column by clicking on the `Conditions` button in the toolbar. There are two macros in the group and they are named after the controls to which they will be assigned.

2 The **Member/Class** macro has two conditions, one if the Member/Class control is true and the other if it is false. If the Member/Class control is true then the GoToControl action specifies **Membership No** (as illustrated). If the Member/Class control is false then the GoToControl action specifies Class No.

3 To move the focus to **Date** after either a **Membership** or **Class** number has been entered, the macro **Date** is used. This macro uses a GoToControl action with the Control Name argument **Date**.

4 Save the macro group as *Booking*.

5 Display the **Bookings** form in design mode.

6 Click on the Member/Class control and set the On Exit property to Booking. This means that the first macro in the macro group **Booking** will run when this control is exited.

7 Set the On Exit control of **Membership No** to Booking.Date. Repeat for the Class No control.

8 Save the form and test the macro group by entering some data.

Control reference syntax

To be able to refer to a control name from within a macro the correct syntax must be used. If the way in which the control is referred does not follow the rules of syntax then the macro will not work.

The syntax for referring to controls is as follows.

For a control on a form

Forms!*formname*!*controlname*

For a control on a report

Reports!*reportname*!*controlname*

For a control on a subform

Forms!*mainformname*!*subformname.Form*!*controlname*

If the name of the form, report or control contains spaces then it must be enclosed in square brackets, for example:

Forms![Membership Category]![Membership Fee]

If the macro is run from the form or report containing the control then the control can be referred to by the control name alone, this is known as the short syntax, for example

[Membership Fee]

If you are in doubt always use the full syntax. If the short syntax is used in an inappropriate situation then the macro will not run.

Task 2: Using a form to enter report criteria

If a report is created that is based on a query then it is useful to be able to enter criteria for the report. The report that is to be used is the one based on the **When joined** query which listed members who have joined the centre during a defined period. This query was created in Unit 12. Use Report Wizard to create a single-column report from this query. Save the report with the name **When joined**.

A form will be created that will allow the start and end dates of the time period to be entered before the report is previewed.

The task involves creating an unbound form, a macro group, a module and also the underlying query and the report will be edited. This is a long task, so follow the steps carefully.

Step 1 is to create an unbound form.

1   From the database window click on the ▮**Forms**▮ tab and click on ▮**New**▮. Leave the 'Choose the table or query…' box empty as this form is not bound to a table or query.

2 Select **Design View** and click on **OK** .

3 In design view set the properties for the form.

Property	Setting
Caption	**Period under investigation** (the name that will appear in the title bar of the form)
Default View	**Single Form**
Views Allowed	**Form**
Scroll Bars	**Neither**
Record Selectors	No
Navigation Buttons	No
Dividing Lines	No

4 Add an unbound text box for each criterion you want to enter. There are two criteria to be entered so add two text boxes, use the completed form illustrated following as a guide.

5 Set the properties for the text boxes as follows.

Property	Setting
Name	Start Date (first text box)
	End Date (second text box)
	Use a control name that describes the type of criterion.
Format	Short Date (both text boxes)
	Use a format that reflects the data type of the criterion.

6 Edit the label of the first text box to read **Period beginning** and the second text box to read **Period ending**, as illustrated.

7 Add text to indicate the purpose of the form.

8 Save the form and give it the name **When joined**.

▦ Period under investigation	✕

Enter the start and end dates for the period under investigation

Period beginning [   ]
Period ending   [   ]

[OK   ]   [Cancel   ]

Your form will not look like this yet as you have only used design mode. The OK and Cancel command buttons will be added to the form after you create macros for them.

Step 2 is to create a module that is used by one of the macros.

Modules have not been introduced as they involve programming, which is beyond the scope of this book other than superficially as in this example. The module being created is a function which will return either 'true' or 'false' depending whether a specified form is loaded. Access modules may be standard, i.e. available globally, or they may be attached to a form or report. In this case the function will be attached to the **When joined** report.

1 From the database window open the report **When joined** in Design View. Click on the   Code   button in the toolbar to display a module window. Type the line

Function IsLoaded(MyFormName)

and press *Enter*.

2 Key in the rest of the module exactly as illustrated. The line End Function is pre-set and you add the lines in between. If you are familiar with Basic you will notice that a For...Next loop and an If statement are used to test the names of open forms against the name specified and to set the function to true if a match is found.

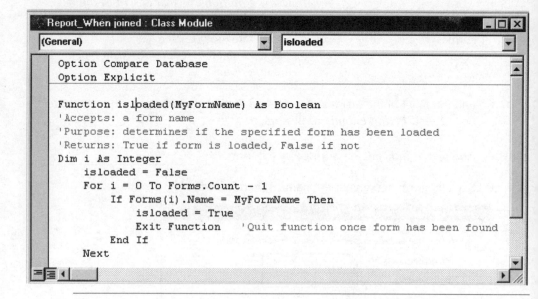

```
Report_When joined : Class Module                              _ □ ×
(General)                              ▼   isloaded                    ▼
    Option Compare Database
    Option Explicit

    Function isloaded(MyFormName) As Boolean
    'Accepts: a form name
    'Purpose: determines if the specified form has been loaded
    'Returns: True if form is loaded, False if not
    Dim i As Integer
        isloaded = False
        For i = 0 To Forms.Count - 1
            If Forms(i).Name = MyFormName Then
                isloaded = True
                Exit Function    'Quit function once form has been found
            End If
        Next
```

3 Save and close the window. The function will be automatically saved as part of the report when the report design is saved.

Step 3 is to create the macros for the form.

The four macros used by the form will be kept in one macro group as illustrated at the end of this step.

1· In the database window, click the ▊Macros▊ tab, and then choose the ▊New▊ button.

2 Create a macro that opens the unbound **When joined** form. Display the macro names column. Give the macro the name *Open Dialog*, and select the OpenForm action.

3 Set the action arguments for **OpenForm** as follows.

Argument	Setting
Form Name	When joined
View	Form
Data Mode	Edit
Window Mode	Dialog

4 Add a second action that cancels previewing or printing the report. This action will only take place if the form doesn't load. Click the ▊Conditions▊ button, and type the following expression in the Condition column: *Not IsLoaded('When joined')*, select CancelEvent as the action for this condition being true. The function IsLoaded checks whether the named form is loaded.

5 Add a macro to the group that closes the form. Give the macro a name such as *Close Dialog*. Select the Close action. Set the action arguments as follows.

Argument	Setting
Object Type	Form
Object Name	When joined

6 Create a macro for the ▊OK▊ button. This macro hides the form. Give the macro a name, such as *OK*, and select the SetValue action. Then set its action arguments as follows.

Argument	Setting
Item	Visible
Expression	No

7 Create a macro for the ██ **Cancel** ██ button. This macro closes the form. Give the macro a name, such as **Cancel**, and select the Close action. Then set its action arguments as follows.

Argument	Setting
Object Type	Form
Object Name	When joined

8 Save and close the macro group. Give the macro group a name that reflects the general purpose of the group; in this case, **When joined**.

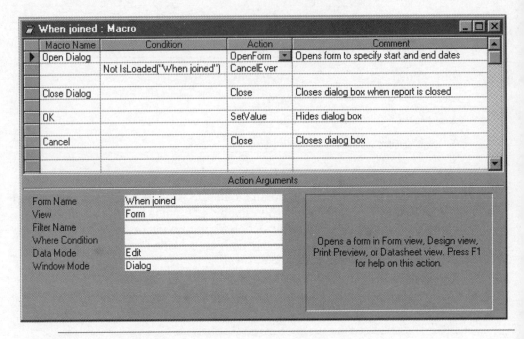

Step 4 is to add OK and Cancel command buttons to the form.

1 Re-open the unbound form **When joined** in Design View.

2 Using the Toolbox, add a command button for OK (without using the Wizard), and set its properties as follows.

Property	Setting
Caption	OK
On Click	When joined.OK (macrogroup.macroname)

3 Add a command button for Cancel (without using the Wizard), and set its properties as follows.

Property	Setting
Caption	Cancel
On Click	When joined.Cancel

4 Save and close the form.

Step 5 is to edit the criteria in the underlying query **When joined**.

1 Open the **When joined** query in Design View.

2 Replace the criteria for the **Date of Joining** field. In the new criteria expression, the controls in the **When joined** form are used. Enter the following replacement expression to refer to controls named **Start Date** and **End Date**:

Between [Forms]![When joined]![Start Date] And [Forms]![When joined]![End Date]

3 Save the changes and close the query.

Step 6 is to attach the macros to the **When joined** report.

1 In design view of the main report, set the following properties.

Property	Setting
OnOpen	When joined.Open Dialog
	(Name of the macro that opens the unbound When joined form)
OnClose	When joined.Close Dialog
	(Name of the macro that closes the unbound When joined form)

2 Try putting two unbound text boxes into the header so that the title reads *List of members that joined between* Start Date *and* End Date.

Macros for data validation

What you will learn in this unit

When a table is defined it is possible to set Validation Rules to validate data being entered. One rule used prevented a Category No of greater than 6 being entered as there are only six categories of membership. Validation rules are limited in the validation that they can perform, and macros can take validation one stage further. This unit demonstrates the use of macros for data validation.

By the end of this unit you will be able to:

■ use macros for data validation

■ run a start-up macro

■ use macros to select records.

Using macros for data validation

The kind of validation that a macro can perform is to check whether a member signing for a class is the right sex for that class. This will be considered in the following task. Another example is checking that a room is available at a certain day and time before a booking is accepted.

Task 1: Validating bookings for classes

This task uses a macro that will check whether a person booking a class is of the right sex. It will prevent a female member booking into a male class and vice versa. When a booking is made the **Class Lists** main/subform is used. The membership number is entered into the subform (**Class Member List**). To check whether the member is male or female the membership data needs to accessed. This can be done by opening the membership form at the record of the membership number just entered.

To prevent the membership form from displaying on the screen it can be opened as hidden by a validation macro that is assigned to the Before Update property of the Class Member List form. To create this validation macro:

1 In the database window, click the ███ Macros ███ tab, and then click on the ███ New ███ button.

2 Select the **OpenForm** action. Then set the action arguments for **OpenForm** as follows.

Argument	Setting
Form Name	Membership
View	Form
Where	[Membership No]=Forms![Class Lists]![Class Member List].Form![Membership No]
Data Mode	Read Only
Window Mode	Hidden

3 Add a second action that displays a message box. This action will only take place if the member is male and the class is female only. Click the **Conditions** button, and type the following expression (in one line) in the Condition column:

> *Forms![Membership]![Sex] And Forms![Class Lists]![Male/Female/Mixed]="Female"*

4 Select MsgBox as the action for this condition being true. Set the properties for the message box as follows.

Argument	Setting
Message	This is a female only class
Beep	Yes
Type	None
Title	Classes Validation

5 Add a third action that cancels the event. This action is also dependent upon the condition in the row above, and to indicate this an ellipsis, three dots in a row (...) are put in the condition column. Select the CancelEvent action.

6 The fourth action undoes the current record. Select RunCommand as the action and set its property.

Argument	Setting
Command	Undo

7 Put an ellipsis (...) in the condition column.

8 Add a fifth action that displays a message box. This action will only take place if the member is female and the class is male only. Click the **Conditions** button, and type the following expression in the Condition column:

> *Not Forms![Membership]![Sex] And Forms![Class Lists]![Male/Female/Mixed]="Male"*

261

9 Select **MsgBox** as the action for this condition being true. Set the properties for the message box as follows.

Argument	Setting
Message	This is a male only class
Beep	Yes
Type	None
Title	Classes Validation

10 Add a sixth action that cancels the event. This action is also dependent upon the condition in the row above, and to indicate this an ellipsis, three dots in a row (...) are put in the condition column. Select the **CancelEvent** action.

11 Add a seventh action that undoes the current record (as fourth action).

12 Put an ellipsis (...) in the condition column.

13 The final action is **Close**. Set its arguments as follows.

Argument	Setting
Object Type	Form
Object Name	Membership

14 Save the macro using the name *Male Female Validation*.

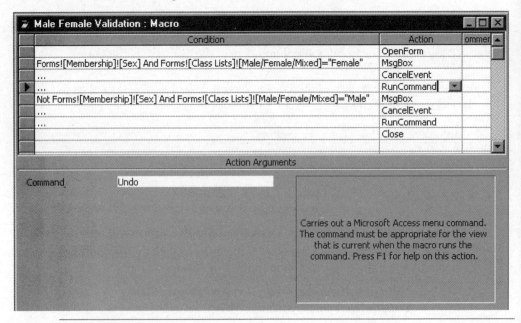

Condition	Action	ommen
	OpenForm	
Forms![Membership]![Sex] And Forms![Class Lists]![Male/Female/Mixed]="Female"	MsgBox	
...	CancelEvent	
...	RunCommand	
Not Forms![Membership]![Sex] And Forms![Class Lists]![Male/Female/Mixed]="Male"	MsgBox	
...	CancelEvent	
...	RunCommand	
	Close	

Action Arguments

Command   Undo

Carries out a Microsoft Access menu command. The command must be appropriate for the view that is current when the macro runs the command. Press F1 for help on this action.

15 Open the **Class Member List** form in design view. Display the form property sheet, open the **Before Update** property of the form (under the ▆ **Event** ▆ tab) and select **Male Female Validation**. Save and close the form.

16 Select the **Class Lists** main/sub form and open it. Try entering a female member into a male class and vice versa to test your macro. If it doesn't work it is likely that a name has been mistyped. Open the macro in design view and check it carefully.

Running a macro at start-up time

To give a database application a professional look a macro can be written which will run when the database is opened. This macro can open required forms and set any defaults. Typically a start-up macro would open a form which displayed a main menu for the database. This might have various buttons that the user can click depending upon the action they wish to take.

The macro to perform the start-up tasks is written as usual but to tell Access that it is the start-up macro it is saved with the name **Autoexec**. When the database is opened if there is a macro called **Autoexec** then it will be run.

It is possible to stop the macro **Autoexec** running if you wish to do some development work on the database by holding down the *Shift* key when the ▆ **OK** ▆ button is clicked or *Enter* is pressed to open the database.

Using macros to create a record amendment form

Once a table has been created, such as the **Membership** table, then the table will need to be maintained. In this activity we consider the amendment of records. A member may, for example, change his or her address or category of membership or supply information not previously given. Records can be edited simply, when viewing the table, by using the **Find** facility to find the right record and then making changes to the field or fields in that record. However, this is not a particularly friendly interface and a more sophisticated method is to create a form through which records can be located and amended. Such a form uses a list box displaying Membership numbers through which the desired record may be selected. The following task will create an amendment form for the **Membership** table as illustrated following.

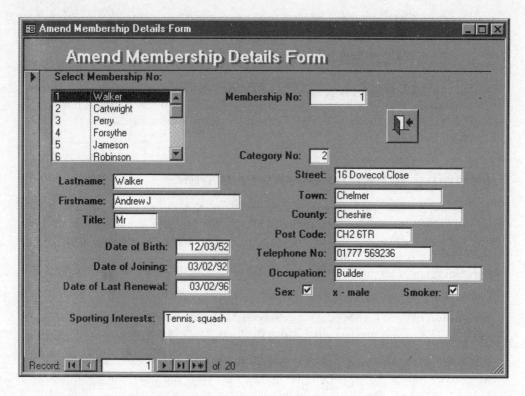

Task 2: Membership record amendment form

In this task a form and several small macros will be created.

1 Using **AutoForm: Columnar** create a single column form based on the
   Membership table. Give the Form the title *Amend Membership Details Form*.
   Display the form in design view and adjust the positions of the controls to allow
   room for the addition of the list box.

2 With the **Control Wizard** button in the Toolbox depressed click on the
   List Box button and click on the form at the place where the list box is to go.
   In the **List Box Wizard** dialog box select the **I want the list box to look up the
   values in a table or query** option. Click on **Next**.

3 Select the **Membership** table. Click on **Next**. Select **Membership No** and
   Lastname as columns in the list box by clicking on **>**. Click on **Next>**.
   Remove the tick from the **Hide key column** check box as we are using the key to
   search for members. Now you may adjust the widths of the columns in the list
   box. Click on **Next>** again and once more to accept that **Membership No** is
   the field to be used by the form. Click on **Next>**. Edit the label of the list box
   to read *Select Membership No:* and click on **Finish**.

4 Display the property sheet for the list box control and give it the name **Select Membership No.**

5 You may wish to make further adjustments to the positions of the controls on the form. When finished, save the form as **Amend Membership Details**. Close the form.

6 Open the macro **Chelmer** in Design View. Scroll down to the end of the existing macros and add a new one with the name **Find Record**. This macro has the following actions.

Action	Argument
GoToControl	Membership No
Find Record	= [Select Membership No]
GoToControl	Select Membership No

7 Save the macro. Open the form **Amend Membership Details** in Design View. Click on the list box, display its property sheet and assign the macro **Chelmer.FindRecord** to the list box's **After Update** property. Save and close the form.

8 Add another macro, **Amend Member Load**, to the Chelmer macro group. This macro has just one action.

Action	Argument
GoToControl	Select Membership No

9 Close and save the macro group. Open the **Amend Membership Details** form again, in Design View. Use **Edit-Select Form** and display the form's property sheet. Assign the macro **Chelmer.AmendMemberLoad** to the **On Load** property of the form.

10 Click on the **Membership No** control and set its **Tab Stop** property to **No**. Also set its **Locked** property to **Yes**.

11 Save the form. Try it out to search for member's records and make some changes. As a finishing touch you could add a **Close** button to this form.

You should find this form useful to search for records providing you know the member's membership number. If you only have a name then you will need to display the table and use the **Find** facility.

Integrative tasks

The following tasks draw on this and the last four units concerning the use of macros.

Task 3: A report menu

This task creates a form containing several buttons which when clicked will preview a certain report. The underlying macro for each button opens a report, an action similar to that for opening a form.

1 Display the **Chelmer** macro window.

2 In the next convenient row put **Membership Report** as the name of this macro.

3 Open the Action cell list box. Scroll through the actions and select the **OpenReport** action. Set the arguments for this action as follows.

Argument	Setting
Report Name	Members2
View	Print Preview

4 Key into the Comment column the description *Preview Membership Report*.

5 Save the macro group.

6 In a similar fashion create macros to open the **Labels New Members**, **Classes4**, and **Bookings** reports.

7 Create a blank unbound form. Add to it a title, e.g. *Reports Menu* and add four buttons, one for each macro just created.

8 Label each button and assign the appropriate macro to it. Remember to use the correct syntax, e.g. Chelmer.Mailing for the On Click property. Save the form as *Reports Menu* and run it.

Task 4: A query menu

This task creates a form containing several buttons which when clicked will run a certain query. The underlying macro for each button opens a report, an action similar to that for opening a form.

1 Display the **Chelmer** macro window.

2 In the next convenient row put *Sporting Interests* as the name of this macro.

3   Open the **Action cell** list box. Scroll through the actions and select the **OpenQuery** action. Set the argument for this action as follows (leave the others at their default settings).

Argument	Setting
Query Name	Members' Sporting Interests

4   Key into the **Comment** column the description ***Sporting Interests Query***.

5   Save the macro group.

6   In a similar fashion create macros to open the **Member Ages**, **Fitness Suite Bookings**, and **When joined** queries.

7   Create a blank unbound form. Add to it a title, e.g. ***Queries Menu*** and add four buttons, one for each macro just created.

8   Label each button and assign the appropriate macro to it. Remember to use the correct syntax, e.g. Chelmer.Sporting Interests for the On Click property. Save the form as ***Query Menu*** and run it.

A database application

What you will learn in this unit

In the earlier units we have explored the creation and use of tables, queries, reports, forms and macros. In order to create a fully operational database system, known as an application, it is necessary to link all of these components together. In this unit we explore some of the issues associated with the creation of a working application.

By the end of this unit you will be able to:

■ understand the issues and stages in the design of an application

■ use forms and macros to create a series of linked menus

■ create a simple application for the use and maintenance of one table

■ appreciate the complexity of relational database design.

A major underlying objective of this unit is to attempt to begin to draw the various components of the Chelmer Database that you have created in this book into a partial application. In order to retain this integrative focus, this unit, unlike most others in this book, will not seek to explore the wide range of features that can be used in the design of applications, such as drop-down menus, menu bars and pop-up forms, but will instead use some of the basic features and focus on the integration of the database components into a basic application, which the reader is welcome to refine later.

Understanding applications

Why do we need applications? Earlier units have introduced you to the creation of the component parts of applications: tables, forms, reports, queries and macros. (Modules might also be included in an application but we have not attempted these in this material.) You may think that you have already created an application! Indeed, through the database window you are able to select tables, call up a form, edit data in tables, perform queries on tables and produce reports. This might be adequate for a relatively small personal or in-house database, but real applications are tailored for specific environments. A Leisure Management System would not access the database components through the database window. Users expect to start the system up and view a main menu which offers them one or a series of options, such as add a new member or make a booking. They do not want to have to remember the name of the table which needs to be accessed in order to perform these actions. Users expect to be able to click on a button or choose a menu option and move straight into the form that allows them to perform the appropriate data entry. So for example, an opening or main menu screen might appear as in FIGURE 44.1.

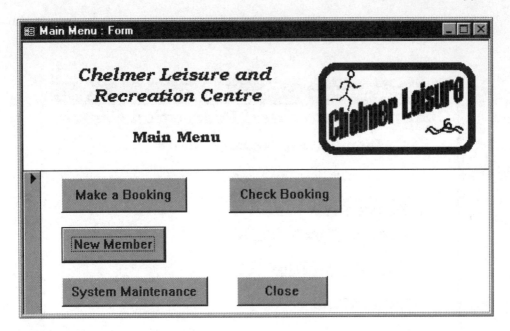

FIGURE 44.1

When the user clicks on the first option a form, such as **Bookings**, would be displayed.

When the user clicked on **System Maintenance**, an additional menu would be displayed which would offer further options, perhaps as displayed in FIGURE 44.2.

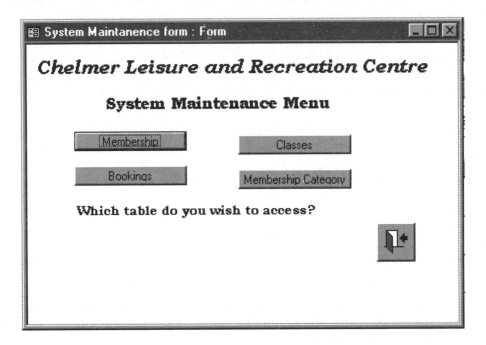

FIGURE 44.2

Clicking on one of these buttons would, for instance lead to a further menu for the actions that can be performed on **Membership** table, as for example, in FIGURE 44.3.

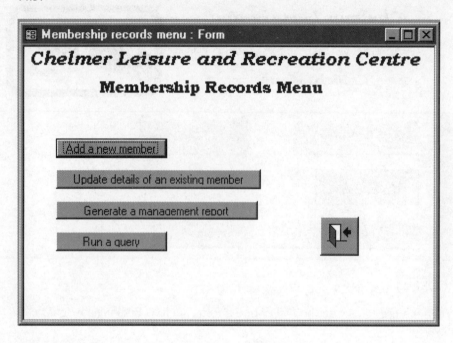

FIGURE 44.3

What then is a database application? The *Access User's Guide* offers a succinct definition.

> 'A Database Application is a set of related Microsoft Access database objects that you can use to accomplish a particular database task. For example, if you use a certain set of forms and reports frequently, you can create an application that gives you easy access to these forms and reports and displays them conveniently in the Microsoft Access window.'

 In Units 39 to 43 you developed some simple macros that could be used with forms and reports. You can use macros to create an application, or custom workspace, and to add features to your application. For example, you can create custom menu bars for forms, assign common actions to menu commands or key combinations, and automate various tasks such as printing daily reports or backing up your database.

Note: We have created the database components first and are now proceeding to integrate them into one application. This is not the way these things should be done! However, it is easier for the beginner to start to understand some of the components before attempting to integrate them. If we were designing a database application for real the same data analysis that led to the table design as shown in FIGURE 8.1 should consider the way in which that data is to be used. This would determine which forms, reports, queries, macros and modules were necessary and the function of each of these.

Task 1: Understanding applications

FIGURE 44.3 shows a menu for adding records to the **Membership** table. Draw on paper a similar menu for adding data to the **Classes** table. Indicate which of the forms and reports that you have already created might be accessed via this menu.

Creating a simple application

The sample application illustrated in the earlier figures in this unit is extremely simplistic. For example, only forms are used for the display of menus; windows, pull-down menus, menu bars and pop-up forms are not used. Yet even these simple menus start to illustrate some important features of good application design.

Screen design in an application is a type of form design, and all of the same design considerations must be taken into account. For example, it is important to choose easily legible fonts and font sizes, and to create an uncluttered screen.

Design must depend upon the application. In particular the sequencing of the screen should make it easy to run through a normal task sequence, and it should be easy to move between related but distinct tasks.

Most systems have three types of users: systems managers (who have responsibility for maintaining the system, managers (seeking management reports and summary data), and operators (who, for example, are on the desk taking bookings, meeting members and answering members' enquiries). These users seek to perform different operations using the system. Menus and menu options must be grouped in such a way that different users find their applications easily accessible. Hence, for example, in FIGURE 44.1, the Main Menu for the Chelmer Database, it is easy to go straight into desk functions such as making a booking, but other functions that might be more useful to managers are 'hidden' under System Maintenance. An additional refinement would be that workstations on the bookings desk did not display the System Maintenance options at all. This would lend greater security on workstations that were in a public access area.

A real system based on multiple tables is very complex to create and would involve much more input than you would probably wish to pursue. Instead, in Task 2 we create a small application based solely on the Membership table, and using some of the forms and reports that we have already created, as well as some special forms which will display the menus.

Task 2: Creating the main or opening menu for the membership table

We wish to create the Main Menu for the Chelmer Leisure and Recreation Centre as in FIGURE 44.1. The process has two stages: the creation of the form, and the creation of and linking of macros to the form. Where possible we use macros that were created in Units 39 to 43.

First to create a form:

1 Open a new form and stretch it.

2 Add a form header and footer.

3 Open the form header and insert the title text in FIGURE 44.1.

4 Open the detail band and insert the buttons as in FIGURE 44.1.

5 Save the form as *Main Menu*.

 6 Next review and create appropriate macros. Macros similar to those required have already been created in Units 39-43. We need:

Button	Macro
Make a booking	Opens a booking form, such as **NewBooking**.
Check a Booking	Opens a booking form at the first record, ready for the user to search using **Edit-Find**.
Add a New Member	Opens a form, such as **Membership**.
System Maintenance	Opens a form, e.g. **System Maintenance Menu**.
Close	Closes the active window.

7 When you have checked that you have all of the above macros, open the form again in design view.

8 Add the macros to the buttons in turn, by clicking on the button and inserting the macro name as the **OnClick** property, on the properties sheet.

Task 3: Creating the system maintenance menu

Using a similar approach to that used in Task 2, create the System Maintenance Menu shown in FIGURE 44.2.

Task 4: Creating the management reports menu

 The Report Menu can be created using similar principles to those outlined in Task 3 Unit 43. Try modifying the menu that you created in that task to look like this.

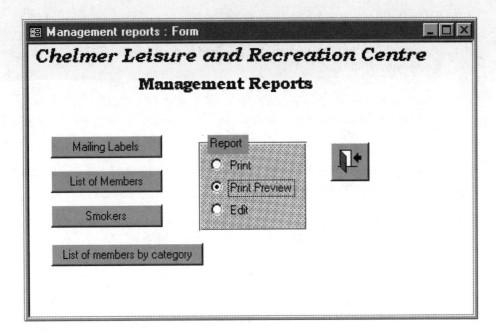

By using conditions in your macro you can perform either print, print preview or edit the report design, depending on the value of the option group control. Set the default of this option group to Print Preview.

Condition	Action	Comment
[Frame0]=2	OpenReport	Open mailing in Print Preview
[Frame0]=1	OpenReport	Print mailing
[Frame0]=3	OpenReport	Open mailing in design view

Integrative tasks

The following tasks call upon application design skills introduced in this unit.

Task 5: Creating the queries menu

Design a Membership Queries Menu which is consistent with the other menus that you have designed, which displays the data below.

Chelmer Leisure and Recreation Centre

Membership Queries Menu

New Query

Existing Query

Task 6: Designing a bookings table main menu

1   Design a Bookings Main Menu for the **Bookings** table which is similar to that for the **Membership** table.

2   What's wrong with this menu for the person on the bookings desk? Think about the functions that this person would need to perform. Think about the questions that customers might ask, for which they would need to provide an answer.

3   Which, if any, of these functions might require the user to have access to data in other tables in the database?

4   Could customers make their own bookings through a system with the main menu in FIGURE 44.1? What additional security might be advisable?

Basic Windows operations

Some readers will not be familiar with Windows and Access may well be one of the first Windows products encountered by them. Any reader who has not previously used Windows is strongly recommended to run through the Windows tutorial which introduces users to mouse techniques and the basic operation of Windows. This tutorial can be found by clicking on **Start**, selecting **Help**, clicking on the **Contents** 'tab', selecting **Introducing Windows**, clicking on **Open** and selecting **Tour: Ten minutes to using Windows**. This appendix briefly summarises some of the key operations and should act as a ready reference to some of the terminology that is used elsewhere in the book.

Mouse pointer shapes

When the mouse is pointed at different parts of the screen, the pointer shape changes allowing you to perform different tasks. Some commands also change the pointer shape.

The table below lists some common pointer shapes as encountered in Access.

Pointer shape	Meaning
I	The pointer over the text area. Click to position an insertion point where text may be typed.
⌖	The pointer appears over menus, non-text areas of windows, inactive windows, scroll bars or toolbars. You can choose a menu and command or click a button. You can use the pointer to drag to make a selection.
⤢	The pointer is over the selection bar, for example, at the edge of a table, or at the left edge of a cell. You can select a cell, a row, or several rows.
⧖	Access is performing a task that will take a few seconds.
‡ ⊹	Appears along the borders between window sections or columns. Drag to resize the section or column.
⥮?	The pointer appears after you press _Shift-F1_. You can point to any item on the screen and click to view specific help.
⬍⬌⬈	The pointer is on a window border. Depending on which, the pointer will assume one of the shapes opposite. Drag to resize the window.

275

This pointer appears when you have selected the **Move** or **Size** command from the **Control** menu. You can move the window to a new position or drag the window border.

 This pointer appears over the grey bar at the top of a column in a table, query or filter. Click to select the column.

 This pointer appears in the record selection bar. Click to select the record.

 This is the drag and drop pointer, which appears when you make a selection, drag the selection to its new location and release the mouse button to drop or insert the selection.

 This is the zoom pointer which appears in print preview.

 The pointer is on a control sizing handle. Depending on which handle the pointer will assume one of the shapes opposite. Drag to resize the control.

 In form or report design this pointer is used to move an individual label or control.

 In form or report design this pointer is used to move a label and control or a selected set of controls.

 This pointer appears with a Toolbox icon and indicates the position of the control on the form or report design. Click to position the control.

Basics of Windows: a quick review

The Windows screen has the following features.

Menu bar

The menu bar shows the titles of the various pull down menus that are available with a given application. To select a menu option, first select the menu by placing the mouse pointer over the name of the menu on the menu bar and click the left mouse button. The menu will appear. Move the mouse pointer to the menu option you require and click the left mouse button again. Note that any menu options displayed in light grey are not currently available. Menus can also be accessed via the keyboard. For example, to select the file menu press *Alt+F* i.e. press *Alt* together with the initial letter of the menu option.

Control menu

The **Control** menu is found on all windows whether they be application windows or document windows. To access the **Control** menu click on the control menu box in the upper left corner of the window, or press *Alt+Spacebar*. The exact contents are different for different windows, but typically basic windows operations such as restore, move, size, minimise, maximise, and close are represented.

Title bar

The title bar tells you which window is displayed. By pointing the mouse at the window's title bar, and then dragging the title bar to a new location the window can be removed.

Task bar

At the bottom of your screen is the task bar. It contains the **Start** button, which you can use to quickly start a program or to find a file. It's also a quick way to get help.

When you start an application, a button appears on the task bar with the name of the application and current document name (if a document is open). You can use this button to switch quickly between the application windows you have open.

Maximize, minimize and restore buttons

Clicking on the **Maximize** button enlarges a window to its maximum size, so that it fills the whole desktop.

Clicking on the **Restore** button will restore a maximised window to its previous size.

Clicking on the **Minimize** button reduces the window to a small icon at the bottom of the screen. When you shrink an application window to an icon, the application is still running in memory, but its window is not taking up space on your desktop.

Clicking on the **Close** button closes the window. ☒

Dialog boxes

Windows uses dialog boxes to request information from you and to provide information to you. Most dialog boxes include options, with each option asking for a different kind of information.

After all the requested information has been supplied you choose a command button to carry out the command. Two that feature on every dialog box are **OK** and **Cancel** . **OK** causes the command to be executed. **Cancel** cancels the operation and removes the dialog box from the screen. These buttons represent the two means of quitting from a dialog box. To choose a command button, click on it, or if the button is currently active, press *Enter*.

There are a number of different kinds of controls found in dialog boxes.

■ **Text boxes** are boxes where you are allowed to type in text, such as a filename. The presence of a flashing vertical bar, or the insertion point, indicates that the text box is active and that you may enter text. If the text box is not active, place the mouse pointer on the box and click. The insertion point will then appear in the box.

277

- **List boxes** show a column of available choices. Items can be selected from a list box by double clicking on the item, or clicking once on the item and then clicking on the **OK** button.

- **Check boxes** offer a list of options that you can switch on and off. You can select as many or as few check box options as are applicable. When an option in a check box is selected it contains a ✓; otherwise the box is empty. To select a check box, click on the empty box.

- **Option buttons** appear as a list of mutually exclusive items. You can select only one option from the list at a time. You can change a selection by selecting a different button. The selected button contains a black dot. To select an option button, click on it.

- **Scroll bars** appear at the side of windows and list boxes. They appear when the information contained in a window cannot be displayed wholly within that window. Both vertical and horizontal scroll bars may be present, depending on whether the database object is too long or too wide to fit on the screen. The small box in the middle of the bar represents the position of the currently displayed screen within the whole object. You can move to a different position in the object by moving this box. You can move this box either by clicking on the scroll bar arrow boxes, clicking on the scroll bar itself, or dragging the box.

Data and data definitions

Membership table data:

Membership no	Category	Lastname	Firstname	Title	Street
1	2	Walker	Andrew J	Mr	16 Dovecot Close
2	1	Cartwright	Denise	Mrs	27 Bowling Green Rd
3	6	Perry	Jason R	Mr	59 Church Street
4	2	Forsythe	Ann M	Miss	2 Ferndale Close
5	1	Jameson	Donna	Mrs	25 Alder Drive
6	3	Robinson	Petra	Miss	16 Lowton Lane
7	5	Harris	David J	Mr	55 Coven Road
8	2	Shangali	Imran	Mr	47 High Street
9	1	Barrett	Martha A	Mrs	7 Oldcott Way
10	1	Weiner	George W F	Mr	6 Church Street
11	6	Ali	David	Mr	33 Meriton Road
12	2	Young	Aileen	Ms	78 Highgate Street
13	5	Gray	Ivor P	Mr	4 The Parade
14	5	Swift	Freda	Miss	23 Ferndale Close
15	1	Davies	Sandra M	Mrs	61 Hallfield Road
16	1	Robinson	Rebecca	Mrs	9 Moss Street
17	2	Everett	Alan	Mr	12 Stanley Street
18	4	Locker	Liam	Mr	2 Beech Close
19	4	Locker	Alison	Miss	2 Beech Close
20	1	Jones	Edward R	Mr	17 Mayfield Avenue

	Town	County	Post code	Telephone no	Occupation	Date of birth
1	Chelmer	Cheshire	CH2 6TR	01777 569236	Builder	12/3/52
2	Meriton	Cheshire	CH9 2EV	01777 552099	Housewife	29/11/60
3	Chelmer	Cheshire	CH1 8YU			3/6/82
4	Chelmer	Cheshire		01777 569945	Receptionist	5/8/73
5	Chelmer	Cheshire	CH2 7FN		Housewife	4/12/70
6	Branford	Staffs	ST10 2DZ	01778 890523		7/7/84
7	Chelmer	Cheshire	CH3 8PS	01777 569311	Retired	22/5/28
8	Chelmer	Cheshire	CH1 7JH	01777 561553	Accountant	15/3/55
9	Meriton	Cheshire	CH9 3DR	01777 557822	Teacher	25/11/60
10	Chelmer	Cheshire	CH1 8YV		Electrician	10/2/58
11	Chelmer	Cheshire	CH4 5KD	01777 569066		14/7/81
12	Branford	Staffs	ST10 4RT	01778 894471	Civil Servant	25/10/51
13	Chelmer	Cheshire	CH1 7ER	01777 565715	Unemployed	12/4/47
14	Chelmer	Cheshire	CH2 8PN	01777 567351	Retired	14/9/27
15	Meriton	Cheshire	CH9 1YJ	01778 891441	Clerk	1/2/65
16	Chelmer	Cheshire	CH2 8SE	01777 568812	Housewife	18/5/68
17	Chelmer	Cheshire	CH3 3CJ		Draughtsperson	30/7/57
18	Chelmer	Cheshire	CH3 8UH			30/12/83
19	Chelmer	Cheshire	CH3 8UH			30/12/83
20	Chelmer	Cheshire	CH2 9OL	01777 567333	Bus Driver	22/12/58

	Date of joining	Date of last renewal	Sporting interests	Smoker	Sex
1	3/2/92	3/2/97	Tennis, squash	Yes	Yes
2	16/7/91	16/7/96	Aerobics, swimming, running, squash	No	No
3	12/12/96	12/12/96	Judo, Karate	No	Yes
4	16/9/91	16/9/96		No	No
5	15/6/92	15/6/96	Aerobics, squash	Yes	No
6	3/1/95	3/1/97	Swimming, Judo	No	No
7	1/2/94	1/2/97	Badminton, cricket	Yes	Yes
8	6/4/92	6/4/96	Weight training, squash	No	Yes
9	4/10/93	4/10/96	Keep fit, swimming	No	No
10	15/7/92	15/7/96	Weight training, squash	No	Yes
11	2/10/94	2/10/96	Judo, swimming, football	No	Yes
12	9/8/92	9/8/96	Keep fit, Aerobics, squash	Yes	No
13	5/1/95	5/1/97		Yes	Yes
14	16/9/93	16/9/96		No	No
15	5/4/92	5/4/97	Aerobics, squash, swimming	Yes	No
16	6/12/91	6/12/96	Tennis, Aerobics	No	No
17	5/11/93	5/11/96	Squash, Fitness training, football	No	Yes
18	13/6/92	13/6/97		No	Yes
19	13/6/92	13/6/97		No	No
20	17/5/91	17/5/96	Weight training	Yes	Yes

Membership category table data

Category no	Category type	Membership fee
1	Senior	£25.00
2	Senior Club	£30.00
3	Junior	£10.00
4	Junior Club	£15.00
5	Concessionary	£18.00
6	Youth Club	£20.00

Classes table data

Class no	Class day	Class time	Class tutor	Class activity	Male/female/ mixed
1	Monday	10:00	Evans	Ladies' Aerobics	Female
2	Monday	11:00	Franks	Weight Training	Male
3	Monday	15:00	Latham	Body Conditioning	Mixed
4	Monday	19:00	Wheildon	Step Aerobics	Mixed
5	Tuesday	10:00	Jackson	Men's Multi-gym	Male
6	Tuesday	14:00	Adams	Ladies' Multi-gym	Female
7	Tuesday	19:00	Jackson	Family Multi-gym	Mixed
8	Wednesday	10:00	Evans	Ladies' Aerobics	Female
9	Wednesday	14:00	Latham	Body Conditioning	Mixed
10	Wednesday	15:00	Franks	Weight training	Female
11	Wednesday	19:00	Franks	Weight training	Mixed
12	Thursday	11:00	Latham	Weight training	Male
13	Thursday	14:00	Wheildon	Step Aerobics	Mixed
14	Thursday	15:00	Adams	Multi-gym	Mixed
15	Thursday	19:00	Latham	Body Conditioning	Mixed
16	Friday	10:00	Latham	Body Conditioning	Female
17	Friday	11:00	Wheildon	Step Aerobics	Mixed
18	Friday	14:00	Jackson	Men's Multi-gym	Male

Bookings table data

Booking no	Room/Hall/Court	Member/ Class	Membership/Class no	Date	Time
1	Fitness Suite	Class	1	13/5/96	10:00
2	Fitness Suite	Class	2	13/5/96	11:00
3	Sports hall 2	Class	3	13/5/96	15:00
4	Sports hall 1	Class	4	13/5/96	19:00
5	Fitness Suite	Class	5	14/5/96	10:00
6	Fitness Suite	Class	6	14/5/96	14:00
7	Fitness Suite	Class	7	14/5/96	19:00
8	Fitness Suite	Class	8	15/5/96	10:00
9	Sports hall 2	Class	9	15/5/96	14:00
10	Sports hall 2	Class	10	15/5/96	15:00
11	Sports hall 2	Class	11	15/5/96	19:00
12	Sports hall 2	Class	12	16/5/96	11:00
13	Sports hall 2	Class	13	16/5/96	14:00
14	Fitness Suite	Class	14	16/5/96	15:00
15	Sports hall 2	Class	15	16/5/96	19:00
16	Sports hall 2	Class	16	17/5/96	10:00
17	Sports hall 2	Class	17	17/5/96	11:00
18	Fitness Suite	Class	18	17/5/96	14:00
19	Court 1	Member	2	13/5/96	18:00
20	Court 2	Member	17	16/5/96	14:00
21	Court 3	Member	15	14/5/96	11:00
22	Court 1	Member	12	15/5/96	19:00

Class list table data

Class No	Membership No
1	2
1	5
1	16
4	4
4	6
5	7
5	10
5	1

Data definitions

Bookings table

Columns

Name		Type	Size
Booking No		AutoNumber	4
	Index: Primary key		
Room/Hall/Court		Text	20
	Required: True		
	Index: Ascending		
Member/Class		Yes/No	1
	Required: True		
Membership No		Number (Long)	4
Class No		Number (Long)	4
Date		Date/Time	8
	Required: True		
	Format: d/m/yy		
	Index: Date+Time		
Time		Date/Time	8
	Required: True		
	Format: hh:mm Short Time		
	Index: Date+Time		

Classes table

Columns

Name		Type	Size
Class No		AutoNumber	4
	Index: Primary key		
Class Day		Text	10
	Required: True		
Class Time		Date/Time	8
	Required: True		
	Format: hh:mm Short time		
Class Tutor		Text	30
	Index: Ascending		
Class Activity		Text	20
	Required: True		
	Index: Ascending		

Name	Type	Size
Male/Female/ Mixed	Text	10

Validation Rule:
"Male" or "Female"
or "Mixed"
Validation Text:
Please enter Male,
Female or Mixed

Membership table

Columns

Name	Type	Size
Membership No	AutoNumber	4

Description: Automatic
membership numbering
Index: Primary key

Category No	Number (Byte)	1

Description: Categories
are 1-Senior, 2-Senior Club,
3-Junior, 4-Junior Club,
5-Concessionary, 6-Youth Club
Validation Rule: <=6
Validation Text: Please
enter a category between
1 and 6
Required: True

Lastname	Text	25

Required: True
Index: Lastname+Firstname

Firstname	Text	30

Index: Lastname+Firstname

Title	Text	10
Street	Text	30

Required: True

Town	Text	25

Default value: Chelmer
Required: True

County	Text	20

Default value: Cheshire
Required: True

Post Code	Text	10

Format:>

Telephone No	Text	12

Name	Type	Size
Occupation	Text	50
Date of Birth	Date/Time	8
Format: Short Date		
Index: Ascending		
Date of Joining	Date/Time	8
Format: Short Date		
Index: Ascending		
Date of Last Renewal	Date/Time	8
Format: Short Date		
Index: Ascending		
Sporting Interests	Memo	0
Smoker	Yes/No	1
Format: ;"Smoker";"Non-Smoker"		
Sex	Yes/No	1
Format: ;"Male";"Female"		

Membership Category table

Columns

Name	Type	Size
Category No	Byte	1
Index: Primary Key		
Category Type	Text	15
Required: True		
Membership Fee	Currency	8
Required: True		

Tutor table

Columns

Name	Type	Size
Lastname	Text	25
Index: Primary Key		
Initials	Text	3
Title	Text	10
Street	Text	30
Required: True		
Town	Text	25
Default: Chelmer		
Required: True		
County	Text	20
Default: Cheshire		
Required: True		
Post Code	Text	10
Format:>		
Telephone No	Text	12
National Insurance No	Text	10
Date of Birth	Date/Time	8
Format: d/m/yy		
Qualifications	Memo	0

Class List table

Columns

Name	Type	Size
Class No	Number (Long)	4
Index: Primary Key		
Membership No	Number (Long)	4
Index: Primary Key		

Access toolbar buttons

Database window

Button	Function
New Database	Creates a new database
Open Database	Opens an existing database
Save	Saves database (inactive)
Print	Print definition of highlighted object
Print Preview	Previews the object definition
Spelling	Runs the spell checker
Cut	Removes selection to the clipboard
Copy	Copies selection to the clipboard
Paste	Pastes the contents of clipboard to current position
Format Painter	Copies formatting (inactive)
Undo	Undoes the last action
OfficeLinks	Export to MS Word mail merge, document or MS Excel
Analyze	Analyse table, analyse performance, documenter
Large Icons	Lists database objects in large icons for the selected object type
Small Icons	Lists database objects in small icons for the selected object type
List	Lists icons alphabetically
Details	Lists icon details, e.g. size and creation date
Code	Displays a Visual Basic module window
Properties	Displays the general properties of the object that is currently selected
Relationships	Displays the Relationships window
New Object	Create a new table, query, form, report, macro, module, or launch Auto Form or Auto Report
Office Assistant	Displays the Office Assistant ready for you to type in a question

Table design view

Button	Function
View	Displays the data in the table in the form of a datasheet
Save	Saves the table
Print	Print (inactive)
Print Preview	Print preview
Spelling	Spell check (inactive)
Cut	Removes selection to the clipboard
Copy	Copies selection to the clipboard
Paste	Pastes the contents of clipboard to current position
Format Painter	Copies formatting
Undo	Undoes the last action
Primary Key	Sets primary key for selected field(s)
Indexes	Displays the Indexes dialog box
Insert Rows	Insert rows
Delete Rows	Delete rows
Properties	Display properties of table
Build	Displays a builder for the selected item or property (only enabled if builder available)
Database Window	Displays the database window
New Object	Create a new table, query, form, report, macro, module, or launch Auto Form or Auto Report
Office Assistant	Displays the Office Assistant ready for you to type in a question

Query design view

Button	Function
View	Displays the data in the query in the form of a datasheet
Save	Saves the query
Print	Print
Print Preview	Print preview
Spelling	Spell check

Button	Function
Cut	Removes selection to the clipboard
Copy	Copies selection to the clipboard
Paste	Pastes the contents of clipboard to current position
Format Painter	Copies formatting
Undo	Undoes the last action
Query Type	Drop down list for choice of Select Query (default type of query), Crosstab query for summarising data, Make Table query, Update query, Append query or Delete query
Run	Runs the query
Show Table	Displays the Show Table dialog box for adding tables
Totals	Displays total row in QBE grid for statistical summary
Top Values	Finds the top values in the active query based on a percentage or number of rows
Properties	Displays the properties of the query
Build	Displays the Expression builder
Database Window	Displays the database window
New Object	Create a new table, query, form, report, macro, module, or launch Auto Form or Auto Report
Office Assistant	Displays the Office Assistant ready for you to type in a question

Datasheet and form view

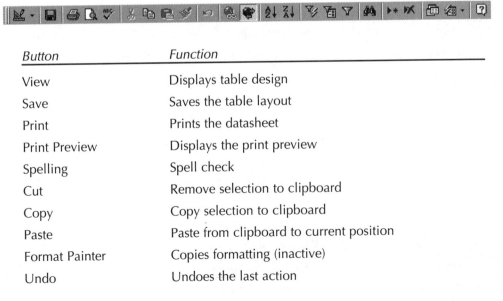

Button	Function
View	Displays table design
Save	Saves the table layout
Print	Prints the datasheet
Print Preview	Displays the print preview
Spelling	Spell check
Cut	Remove selection to clipboard
Copy	Copy selection to clipboard
Paste	Paste from clipboard to current position
Format Painter	Copies formatting (inactive)
Undo	Undoes the last action

Button	Function
Insert Hyperlink	Inserts or modifies a hyperlink address
Web Toolbar	Displays the Web Toolbar
Sort Ascending	Displays records in ascending order of current field
Sort Descending	Displays records in descending order of current field
Filter by Selection	Filters records based on selected data
Filter by Form	Displays a form for the entry of filter criteria
Apply Filter	Displays filtered records
Find	Search for selected data
New Record	Go to new record
Delete Record	Removes record
Database Window	Displays the database window
New Object	Create a new table, query, form, report, macro, module, or launch Auto Form or Auto Report
Office Assistant	Displays the Office Assistant ready for you to type in a question

Form design view

Button	Function
View	Runs the form
Save	Saves the form
Print	Prints the form
Print Preview	Displays the print preview
Spelling	Spell check
Cut	Remove selection to clipboard
Copy	Copy selection to clipboard
Paste	Paste from clipboard to current position
Format Painter	Copies formatting from one control to another; double-click to copy to several controls, *Esc* to finish
Undo	Undoes the last action
Insert Hyperlink	Inserts or modifies a hyperlink address
Web Toolbar	Displays the Web Toolbar
Field List	Displays the field list window
Toolbox	Displays the Toolbox window

Button	Function
AutoFormat	Applies your choice of predefined formats to the form
Code window	Displays an Access Basic form module in the Module
Properties	Displays the properties sheet
Build	Displays a builder for the selected item or property (only enabled if builder available)
Database Window	Displays database window
New Object	Create a new table, query, form, report, macro, module, or launch Auto Form or Auto Report
Office Assistant	Displays the Office Assistant ready for you to type in a question
Object	Select entire form, section of a form or a control
Font	Displays list of font names
Font Size	Displays list of font sizes
Bold	Applies bold typeface
Italic	Applies italic typeface
Underline	Applies underlining
Align Left	Aligns Left contents of label or control
Center	Centres contents of label or control
Align Right	Aligns Right contents of label or control
Fill/Back Color	Drop down background colour selection
Font/Fore Color	Drop down foreground colour selection
Line/Border Color	Drop down border colour selection
Line/Border Width	Drop down border width selection
Special Effect	Drop down special effect (raised, sunken, etc) selection

Report design view

Button	Function
View	Previews report
Save	Saves the report
Print	Prints report
Print Preview	Displays a print preview
Spelling	Spell check

Button	Function
Cut	Remove selection to clipboard
Copy	Copy selection to clipboard
Paste	Paste from clipboard to current position
Format Painter	Copies formatting from one control to another; double-click to copy to several controls, *Esc* to finish
Undo	Undoes the last action
Insert Hyperlink	Inserts or modifies a hyperlink address
Web Toolbar	Displays the Web Toolbar
Field List	Displays the Field list window
Toolbox	Displays the Toolbox window
Sorting and Grouping	Displays the Sorting and Grouping dialog box
AutoFormat	Applies your choice of predefined formats to the report
Code	Displays an Access Basic report module in the Module window
Properties	Displays the properties sheet
Build	Displays a builder for the selected item or property (only enabled if builder available)
Database Window	Displays database window
New Object	Create a new table, query, form, report, macro, module, or launch Auto Form or Auto Report
Office Assistant	Displays the Office Assistant ready for you to type in a question
Object	Select entire report, section of a report or a control
Font Name	Displays list of font names
Font Size	Displays list of font sizes
Bold	Applies bold typeface
Italic	Applies italic typeface
Underline	Applies underlining
Align Left	Aligns Left contents of label or control
Center	Centres contents of label or control
Align Right	Aligns Right contents of label or control
Fill/Back Color	Drop down background colour selection
Font/Fore Color	Drop down foreground colour selection
Line/Border Color	Drop down border colour selection
Line/Border Width	Drop down border width selection
Special Effect	Drop down special effect (raised, sunken, etc) selection

Report and form print preview

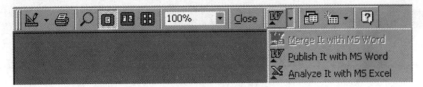

Button	Function
View	Displays report or form design
Print	Prints
Zoom	Toggle to zoom in or out
One Page	Displays print preview one page format
Two Pages	Displays print preview two page format
Multiple pages	Displays print preview multiple page format
Zoom	Controls the amount of magnification
Close	Closes preview and returns to design
Merge It with MS Word	Saves the output of a table, query, form, report or module to a file, and then attaches the file to a message in your electronic mail program
Publish It with MS Word	Saves the output of a table, query, form, report or module to a file in one of the following file formats: Microsoft Excel (.XLS), Rich Text Format (.RTF), or MS-DOS Text (.TXT)
Analyze It with MS Excel	Saves the output of a table, query, form, report or module to a file in one of the following file formats: Microsoft Excel (.XLS), Rich Text Format (.RTF), or MS-DOS Text (.TXT)
Database Window	Displays the database window
New Object	Create a new table, query, form, report, macro, module, or launch Auto Form or Auto Report
Office Assistant	Displays the Office Assistant ready for you to type in a question

Macro design

Button	Function
Save	Saves the macro
Print	Prints the macro
Print Preview	Displays the print preview
Spelling	Spell check
Cut	Remove selection to clipboard
Copy	Copy selection to clipboard
Paste	Paste from clipboard to current position
Format Painter	Copies formatting from one control to another; double-click to copy to several controls, *Esc* to finish
Undo	Undoes the last action
Macro Names	Displays the Macro Name column in the macro window
Conditions	Displays the Condition column in the macro window
Insert Rows	Adds rows to the macro sheet
Delete Rows	Deletes rows from the macro sheet
Run	Runs the active macro
Single Step	Turns single stepping on or off
Build	Displays a builder for the selected item or property (only enabled if builder available)
Database Window	Displays the database window
New Object	Create a new table, query, form, report, macro, module, or launch Auto Form or Auto Report
Office Assistant	Displays the Office Assistant ready for you to type in a question

Module design

Button	Function
Insert module	Inserts a new module into the current database
Save	Saves the module
Print	Prints module
Cut	Remove selection to clipboard
Copy	Copy selection to clipboard
Paste	Paste from clipboard to current position
Find	Search for specified item
Undo	Undoes the last action
Redo	Redoes the last action
Go/Continue	Continues code execution after it has been suspended
End	Terminates code execution
Reset	Stops execution of procedures and reinitialises code variables
Debug Window	Displays a window which can be used to debug code. This window will display values of specified variables
Object browser	Displays all methods and properties in the current, and other available, databases
Quick Watch	Displays the value of a selected expression
Call Stack	Displays the Calls dialog box, in which you can trace all the currently active procedures that your code has called
Compile loaded modules	Compiles all procedures in open modules or modules behind open forms and reports
Toggle Breakpoint	Sets or removes a breakpoint
Step into	Runs one statement at a time, including statements within a called procedure
Step over	Runs one statement at a time, treating a called procedure as one step
Step out	Use to avoid stepping through each line of code in called procedures
Database Window	Displays the database window
Office Assistant	Displays the Office Assistant ready for you to type in a question

Glossary

Access	A relational database product.
Alignment	Whether the characters in a control start at the left side of the control, end at the right side of the control or are centred on the control's position.
Case sensitive	Distinguishing between upper and lower case text.
Alignment	Whether the characters in a control start at the left side of the control, end at the right side of the control or are centred on the control's position.
Check boxes	Boxes offering a list of options which you can switch on or off.
Control	Individual design element.
Control menu	The menu found on all windows accessed by clicking on the Control Menu box in the upper left corner of the window.
Data type	The type of data allowed in a particular field.
Database	A collection of related data.
DataBase Management System (DBMS)	Software used to present data stored in a computer.
Database window	The first window presented after creating or opening a database.
Datasheet view	The view from which you can enter data in tables.
Default value	A value entered in a field automatically by Access.
Design view	The view from which you can design tables, forms, reports and queries.
Detail	The detail of a report, that is, the data from records in a database.
Dialog box	A box used to request information or to provide information.
Dynaset	The result of a query.
Field	A piece of data within a record.
Field description	The description of a field. It may be up to 255 characters long.
Field list	A list of fields that a form was based upon.
Field name	The name of a field. Field names can be up to 64 characters including spaces. Full stops (.), exclamation marks (!) and square brackets ([ ]) are not allowed.
Field properties	Detailed definitions of a data type.
Filter	A means of displaying selected records.
Font	A collection of features that describes how text appears.
Form	An on-screen method of collecting information for a database.
Group footer	Text marking the end of a group in a report.

Group header	Text marking the beginning of a group in a report.
Grouped report	A report with selected fields placed in a row. Records are grouped according to the value of a field in the table or query.
Inner-join	Displays all the records in one table that have corresponding records in another table.
List boxes	Boxes showing a column of available choices.
Macro	Series of keystrokes or steps that you record.
Mailing label reports	Reports for creating mailing labels.
Make table query	Creates one table from another or others.
Maximise button	The button that enlarges a window to its maximum size.
Menu bar	The bar showing titles of various pull down menus that are available in an application.
Minimise button	The button that reduces a window to a small icon at the bottom of the screen.
Module	Programs or sets of instructions designed to perform a specific task or series of tasks.
Null value	An empty field.
One-to-one relationship	Relationship between tables where for a particular field in one table there is only one matching record in the other and vice versa.
One-to-many relationship	Relationship between tables where for one field in one table there are many matching records in the other and vice versa.
Option buttons	A list of mutually exclusive items.
Page footer	Text that appears at the bottom of every page of a report.
Page header	Text which appears at the top of each page of a report such as a running title and page number.
Preview	A miniature version of what is to be printed, displayed on the screen.
Primary key	A field or combination of fields that uniquely identifies a record.
Properties sheet	A list of properties.
Queries	A method of asking questions of a database.
Query By Example (QBE)	A method of querying by which you can describe the characteristics of the data that you are looking for.
Query criteria	The method of framing questions to allow specific records to be retrieved from the database.
Query Design window	The window from which you design a query.
Record	A set of details about an individual item. Each item has a separate record in the table.
Report footer	Information at the end of a report.

Report header	The heading and introductory text at the beginning of a report.
Report	Collection of information suitable for printing.
Restore button	The button that restores a maximised window to its previous size.
Row selector symbols	Symbols at the edge of a table row, which enable you to select a row of information.
Screen forms	The method of customising the way in which the data from records in table or queries are displayed on the screen.
Scroll bars	Bars which appear at the side of windows and list boxes when all the information cannot be displayed within the window. They allow you to scroll through the information.
Single column form	A form which allows the user to input one record at a time.
Single column report	A report with all selected fields in a single column.
String	A collection of characters (letters, numbers, and punctuation marks) that make up the data in a field.
Table Design window	The interface that allows you to define the structure of your table.
Tables	The method by which Access stores data.
Tabular form	A form which displays more than one record on the screen.
Task bar	The bar at the bottom of the screen containing the Start button.
Text boxes	Boxes which allow you to type text.
Title bar	Top section of a window containing the name of the window. Changes colour to indicate whether active or inactive.
Toolbox	A selection of tools by which controls and text may be added to a form.
Unbound form	A blank form which does not have an associated table.
Update query	Updates query in a table.
Validation rules	Tests used to detect mistakes in data entry.
Wizards	Simple methods of creating forms, reports, etc using preset values.
Zero length string	Used to indicate there is no data for the field in that record.

Index